Looking for Rights in All the Wrong Places

PRINCETON STUDIES IN AMERICAN POLITICS
HISTORICAL, INTERNATIONAL, AND COMPARATIVE PERSPECTIVES
Ira Katznelson, Martin Shefter, and Theda Skocpol, Series Editors

A list of titles in this series appears at the back of the book.

Looking for Rights in All the Wrong Places

WHY STATE CONSTITUTIONS CONTAIN AMERICA'S POSITIVE RIGHTS

EMILY ZACKIN

PRINCETON UNIVERSITY PRESS
PRINCETON AND OXFORD

Copyright © 2013 by Princeton University Press

Requests for permission to reproduce material from this work should be
sent to Permissions, Princeton University Press
Published by Princeton University Press, 41 William Street,
Princeton, New Jersey 08540
In the United Kingdom: Princeton University Press, 6 Oxford Street,
Woodstock, Oxfordshire OX20 1TW

press.princeton.edu

All Rights Reserved

Library of Congress Cataloging-in-Publication Data

Zackin, Emily J., 1980-
Looking for rights in all the wrong places : why state constitutions
contain America's positive rights / Emily Zackin.
p. cm. — (Princeton studies in American politics :
historical, international, and comparative perspectives)
Includes bibliographical references and index.
ISBN 978-0-691-15577-7 (hardcover : alk. paper) —
ISBN 978-0-691-15578-4 (pbk. : alk. paper)
1. Civil rights— United States—States. 2. Constitutional law—
United States—States. I. Title.
KF4750.Z95Z33 2013
342.7308'5—dc23
2012041106

British Library Cataloging-in-Publication Data is available

This book has been composed in Sabon

Printed on acid-free paper. ∞

Printed in the United States of America

1 3 5 7 9 10 8 6 4 2

CONTENTS

ACKNOWLEDGMENTS

This book grew out of my dissertation project, and it is a testament to my remarkably good fortune in teachers, friends, and family.

I am deeply indebted to each member of my thesis committee. Its chair, Keith Whittington, was the first to suggest that I read state constitutions, and has since spent countless hours discussing them with me. Keith's assiduity, encyclopedic knowledge, and incisive vision have immeasurably strengthened this work and all of my scholarship. Paul Frymer has consistently steered me toward big and meaningful questions, and served as an endless source of new ideas, support, and advice. I could not have written this without him. While working on her own book about state constitutions, Amy Bridges not only encouraged me to pursue this project, but also shared her exhaustive research, unique expertise, and considerable insights. Over the course of several years and many drafts, and from all the way across the country, Amy has given me invaluable guidance. Last, but certainly not least, I was privileged to have Kim Scheppele serve on my committee. Beginning with my first days of graduate school, Kim has urged me to think across disciplinary boundaries, offered ingenious suggestions about my research, and championed my work with boundless energy. I do not know what I would do without her. Thank you, all.

I've also benefitted from the generosity and counsel of many scholars who, unlike the members of my thesis committee, were under no obligation to read this. Sandy Levinson read several drafts, made crucial interventions, and went out of his way to provide venues in which I could present this research. Richard Bensel volunteered to read an even earlier draft of the entire project, and sent me extraordinarily thoughtful, comprehensive, and useful feedback on each chapter. I will not try to list all of the people who have offered me their help, since that does not seem possible, but Mark Graber, William Forbath, John Dinan, Chuck Epp, Dirk Hartog, Eric Lomazoff, Eileen McDonagh, Ken Kersch, Tali Mendelberg, Jessica Trounstine, Julie Novkov, and Jack Balkin have all played particularly important roles in pushing my thinking forward and encouraging me along the way.

Debbie Becher, my writing buddy, has been intimately involved in my efforts to revise what was a dissertation into a book, and has solved many of the manuscript's most challenging problems. Debbie's willingness to reread and rework each chapter, her keen analysis, and sophisticated thinking have dramatically improved this book. I am not sure it would even exist without her. I am also very grateful to Justin Crowe, Megan Francis, and Melody Crowder-Meyer, who were helpful at every stage of the book-writing process, in every way possible. Few people can boast such brilliant classmates or such generous and devoted friends. Through their endless support, Debbie, Justin, Megan, and Melody ease the difficulties of academic life and amplify its joys.

Princeton librarians David Hollander and Elizabeth Bennett worked with me to uncover obscure primary sources and state court opinions. I depended on them completely, and on the heroic efforts of the staff at the interlibrary loan office. Amanda Irwin Wilkins, who directs the Princeton Writing Center, taught me how to work productively, how to teach writing, and how to believe that I really might finish my dissertation. I still miss our afternoon chats.

I am also indebted to Chuck Myers at Princeton University Press for his interest in my project, and for shepherding it (and me) through the publication process. I appreciate the work and time of the anonymous reviewers, whose criticism enhanced the argument here, as well as the careful attention of copyeditor Karen Verde. My new colleagues at Hunter College have been universally welcoming and helpful as I finished this manuscript and began teaching, and Aaron Greller provided truly excellent research assistance.

I developed many of the ideas in this book during my year as a fellow at the University of Virginia's Miller Center for Public Affairs, where Sid Milkis and Brian Balogh were extraordinarily helpful and kind. I continue to appreciate their generosity and guidance and to emulate their scholarship. My class of Miller Center fellows was also quite stimulating, and Tom Burke, my Miller Center "dream mentor," deserves the title. The opportunity to participate in the Fellowship of Woodrow Wilson Scholars at Princeton, and to present this work to the other fellows under the warm and rigorous leadership of John Darley, helped me to refine and improve my argument.

My undergraduate professors at Swarthmore College have nurtured and challenged me from my very first forays into academic thinking. Scott Gilbert, Carol Nackenoff, Ken Sharpe, and Rick Valelly remain cherished mentors. I am also indebted to the friends I've known since long before I started this project. Their contributions to my life extend well beyond this book, but Paul Asman, Parag Butala, Judy Chen, Rachel Fershleiser, Marta Johnson, Gil Jones, Kwindla Kramer, Nina Kurvilla, Katie Tunning, Tiffany Lennon, Jill Lenoble, Nisha Mehta, Matthew Oransky, Amanda Schneider, and Renee Witlen all helped me through the challenges of writing it.

My parents and sister have expressed their unqualified belief in my abilities for as long as I can remember. Their commitment to learning and their enjoyment of ideas have shaped me and inspired my scholarship. I am often reluctant to show them my work, but I always strive to write for an audience possessed of their clarity of thought and soundness of judgment.

For the past ten years, Roban Kramer has been my partner in all things, including this project. I rely on his loving care and supreme competence, and aspire to his kindness, intellectual curiosity, and wisdom. It is my profound pleasure to go through life with him, and to share that life with the many others who helped me write this.

Looking for Rights in All the Wrong Places

CHAPTER 1

Looking for Rights in All the Wrong Places

❖

On January 15, 1870, Illinois's third constitutional convention had been under way for just over a year, and an experienced coal miner named George Snowden wrote a letter to one of its delegates. In it, he explained that his poor health had prevented him from writing sooner, but that in reading a newspaper account of the constitutional convention, he was moved to communicate with its members. He wrote, "as a miner, I thought it but proper that the miner's interest ought to be considered in that convention. I do not know that it is right in a legal sense, but I know it will do no harm for you to consider what the miners ought to have as their rights— either in the convention or in the legislature."[1] He went on to detail the protections that the miners "ought to have as their rights," listing specific regulations like requirements for ventilation and escapement shafts in coal mines, the mandatory presence of mining inspectors, and laws compelling mine owners to pay damages to injured miners.

Snowden might well have been pleased by the outcome.[2] The new state constitution established the duty of the state legislature to enact several of the safety regulations he listed, and thereby obligated government to protect the state's miners from the dangerous conditions in which they were forced to work.[3] Illinois's miners had, in fact, been organized to demand this kind of protection for some time, but had not been able to secure the protective regulations they sought from the state's legislature. After a decade of trying, they turned to the state's constitutional convention, where they successfully

[1] Illinois Constitutional Convention, Debates and Proceedings of the Constitutional Convention of the State of Illinois: Convened at the City of Springfield, Tuesday, December 13, 1869 (Springfield: E. L. Merritt & Bro., printers to the Convention, 1870), 270.

[2] In fact, the *Workingman's Advocate*, the official newspaper of the National Labor Union, responded to the new constitutional provision with "jubilation." See Amy Zahl Gottlieb, "The Influence of British Trade Unionists on the Regulation of the Mining Industry in Illinois, 1872," *Labor History* 19, no. 3 (1978): 404.

[3] The final article stated, "it shall be the duty of the general assembly to pass such laws as may be necessary for the protection of operative miners, by providing for ventilation, when the same may be required, and the construction of escapement shafts, or such other appliances as may secure safety in all coal mines, and to provide for the enforcement of said laws by such penalties and punishment as may be deemed proper."

secured this constitutional right to governmental protection from the particularly dangerous features of work in the mines.

Of course, when most people think about America's constitutional rights, they do not think about miners or about Illinois law. Instead, they think about the U.S. Constitution, its Bill of Rights, and the Supreme Court opinions that have shaped its meaning. Studies of the federal Constitution and the changes in its meaning have dominated discussions about American constitutional law. As a result, most accounts of American constitutional rights describe these rights as limitations on the scope of government. American rights, we are often told, protect their bearers from tyrannical government by forcing government to restrain itself from intervening in social and economic life. They do not mandate more government or offer protection from threats that do not stem directly from government itself. While other nations have constitutional rights to an active, welfarist state, often known as positive rights, constitutional rights in the United States are often thought to protect people from government alone, not to mandate that government protect them from other sorts of dangers. In other words, America is widely believed to be exceptional in its lack of positive constitutional rights and its exclusive devotion to negative ones. But how accurate is this conception?

As I will demonstrate, the conventional wisdom about the nature of America's constitutional rights is incomplete, and therefore incorrect. The problem is not that scholars have misinterpreted the federal Constitution or its history, but that most observers have taken the history of the federal Constitution and the federal Supreme Court to be the only one, or the only one worth considering. They have leapt effortlessly, and indeed unconsciously, from the assertion that the federal Constitution lacks positive rights to the claim that *America* lacks positive rights, at least at the constitutional level. It is this error that I endeavor to correct.[4]

The texts of state constitutions force us to question the ubiquitous assertions that America lacks positive constitutional rights. Illinois was not alone in creating constitutional rights to interventionist and protective government, nor was this provision for miners the only positive right it created.[5] Throughout the nineteenth and twentieth centuries and across the United States, activists, interest groups, and social movements championed positive

[4] For other scholarly work noting the existence of positive rights at the state level and the significance of this difference between state and federal constitutional law, see John J. Dinan, *The American State Constitutional Tradition* (Lawrence: University Press of Kansas, 2006). See also H. Hershkoff, "Positive Rights and State Constitutions: The Limits of Federal Rationality Review," *Harvard Law Review* 112, no. 6 (1999); and Hershkoff, "State Courts and the 'Passive Virtues' Rethinking the Judicial Function," *Harvard Law Review* 114, no. 7 (2001).

[5] For instance, Illinois's farmers were successful in their movement to convince the state's constitutional convention to create mandates requiring the legislature to regulate railroad and warehouse prices in order to protect farmers from discriminatory rates. Gretchen Ritter, *Goldbugs and Greenbacks: The Antimonopoly Tradition and the Politics of Finance, 1865–1896* (New York: Cambridge University Press, 1997), 129–30.

rights, and built support for their inclusion in state constitutions. As a result of these political campaigns, state constitutions have long mandated active government intervention in social and economic life, and have delineated a wide array of situations in which government is not only authorized, but actually obligated to intervene. State constitutions contain many different kinds of mandates for interventionist and protective government, not only with respect to laborers, but also with respect to government's obligations to care for the poor, aged, and mentally ill, preserve the natural environment, provide free education, and protect debtors' homes and dignity.

This book focuses on three political movements to add these kinds of positive rights to state constitutions. In particular, it examines the campaign for education rights, which spanned the nineteenth and twentieth centuries, the movement for positive labor rights, which occurred during the Gilded Age and Progressive Era, and the push to add environmental bills of rights to state constitutions during the 1960s and 1970s. Together, these cases serve to highlight not only the historically and geographically contingent variations in the form and function of America's positive rights tradition, but also its extraordinary length. The arguments and political calculations of the three rights movements I examine displayed remarkable continuity across diverse issue areas, vast geographic distances, and entire centuries. It is in this recurrent recourse to constitutional politics, along with the textual provisions in state constitutions, that I identify a sustained positive-rights tradition.

State level organizations' own descriptions of their views and goals provide compelling evidence for the existence of a coherent rights tradition. The leaders of each constitutional movement maintained that government's obligation to protect its people was too important to remain optional, and the protections they sought were too critical to leave at the mercy of legislative discretion. They insisted that the most salient threat to society was not too much government, but too little, and that constitutional law ought not only restrain government, but also force it to provide substantive protections. Many of the organizations that championed positive constitutional rights explained their understanding of the provisions they sought and of their political context through newspapers, newsletters, and internal memos. Their champions also made stirring arguments on behalf of these rights on the floor of states' constitutional conventions and in academic journals. Yet because they exist at the state level, these sustained and often-successful campaigns for positive constitutional rights have been widely overlooked.

This study also sheds new light on the origins of constitutional rights. Most accounts of rights' creation, both within and outside the United States, hold that dominant political coalitions write new rights into constitutions when (and precisely because) they are worried about losing their dominant positions. On this account, movements for new rights are fundamentally conservative projects, intended to maintain the status quo. However, the origins of the positive rights in state constitutions are quite different. Like the Illinois miners who campaigned for constitutional protections, many positive-rights' advocates did not intend to crystallize existing political arrangements. Instead, these activists hoped to rewrite the rules of politics and transform their societies. In the chapters that follow, I demonstrate that rights movements in the United States have used state constitutions for reasons that theories of constitutional politics have tended to miss. I also argue that constitutional theorists have largely overlooked the positive rights that these movements created.

American Constitutional Exceptionalism

American constitutional law is often said to be exceptional in its lack of rights to governmental protection from social and economic privation. While many other nations' constitutions enshrine positive rights, which obligate the state to intervene in order to protect citizens from nongovernmental dangers, American rights are often thought to be negative rights, protecting citizens only from intrusive government by prohibiting governmental intervention. In other words, the U.S. Constitution appears to be dedicated exclusively to limiting the scope of government and to keeping government out of the lives of its citizens. Thus, assertions about America's exceptional constitutional rights are still very much the norm.

America's political development was once thought to be similarly unusual. When compared with Europe, the industrializing United States appeared exceptional in its lack of protective social and economic regulations, and its citizens seemed to evince a strong and unusual aversion to government. Thanks in large part to historical studies of state and local governance, this story about American political development has been dramatically revised and this version of American exceptionalism widely rejected. Few scholars would still endorse the idea that America's political development was exceptional in its lack of governance. The resemblance between the outdated theory of American exceptionalism and the current theory of American *constitutional* exceptionalism should give us pause, and should prompt us to ask whether the standard view of America's constitutional tradition may also require revision.

Of course, the idea that America's constitutional tradition is exceptional is grounded in considerable empirical analysis. There is indeed strong evidence that the American constitutional tradition is exceptionally hostile to positive rights. While many prominent political figures, including several U.S. presidents, have argued on behalf of positive rights, few (and arguably no) positive-rights claims have ever changed either the U.S. Constitution's text or the Supreme Court's interpretation of it. Thus, America's welfare state is widely believed to consist of statutory law alone, and is generally understood as a matter of legislative and majoritarian choice, rather than constitutional obligation.

Even the dramatic expansion of the United States' social safety net during the New Deal seems to confirm the assessment. In the wake of the Great Depression, Franklin Roosevelt explained, government must take active steps to protect citizens from economic and physical risk in order for them to take advantage of America's traditional political liberties. He argued the Constitution's negative liberties were only meaningful under conditions of economic security, and listed the social and economic safeguards that must undergird the political liberties contained in the Bill of Rights. This list, which Roosevelt named the "Second Bill of Rights," included rights to housing and medical care and protection from unemployment and hunger.[6] However, to the degree that these governmental commitments to social welfare became a part of federal policy, it was through statutory programs, like Social Security and Medicare. To be sure, many of these protective policies have engendered enduring political support, and as a matter of practical politics, the statutes that embody them may be quite difficult to repeal. However, the positive-rights claims underlying New Deal policy were never constitutionalized through a formal amendment to the text of the Constitution or through changes in Supreme Court doctrine. Absent a constitutional mandate, Congress remains free to scale back or eliminate any statutory entitlement program that becomes unpopular, as it did with Aid to Families with Dependent Children (AFDC) in 1996.

Hoping to find a constitutional mandate for a more robust welfare state than the one that is already embodied in statutory law, several litigation movements have looked to the Fourteenth Amendment. Yet these movements have met with extremely limited success, and the Supreme Court has generally declined to read either the Equal Protection or Due Process clause as a mandate for active government intervention.[7] To be sure, several landmark cases seem to imply or contain a positive-rights reading of the Fourteenth Amendment, but these decisions have not served as the foundation for any more extensive positive-rights jurisprudence, and the Court has ex-

----

[6] Cass R. Sunstein, *The Second Bill of Rights: FDR's Unfinished Revolution and Why We Need It More Than Ever* (New York: Basic Books, 2004).

[7] Furthermore, the phrasing of the Fourteenth Amendment makes it a problematic vehicle for the pursuit of interventionist government action because even this positive-seeming provision is worded as a restraint on state governments, rather than a call to action. Thus, even the Due Process and Equal Protection clauses may be read simply as an extension of the negative liberties in the Bill of Rights to the states. Burt Neuborne explains it this way: "Like so many provisions of the Bill of Rights, from which it was copied, the due process clause is phrased as a prohibition, not an affirmative command: 'nor shall any state' is the equivalent of 'a state shall not.' Moreover, what the states are forbidden to do is to 'deprive; people of certain things'." Burt Neuborne, "State Constitutions and the Evolution of Positive Rights," *Rutgers Law Journal* 20, no. 4 (1989): 865.

plicitly rejected the positive-rights reading in its subsequent cases.[8] Instead, the Court has consistently ruled that protective and redistributive policies are questions of majoritarian choice, not matters of constitutional duty. Government may well choose to protect citizens from the threats that do not stem directly from government. However, the Court has been quite explicit in its repeated determination that the U.S. Constitution imposes no obligation for it to do so. Thus, most observers agree that even if the U.S. Constitution ought to be read differently or might have been interpreted in another way, it is not currently understood to contain positive rights. Indeed, campaigns on behalf of positive constitutional rights seem to have fizzled without ever gaining significant traction in either a court of public opinion or law.[9] Even one of the nation's most prominent welfare-rights advocates,

[8] For instance, the majority opinion in *Brown*, 347 U.S. 483 (1954), did declare: "Today, education is perhaps the most important function of state and local governments," and "such an opportunity, where the state has undertaken to provide it, is a right which must be made available to all on equal terms." This statement might well suggest that government has a responsibility to educate its citizens. However, the Court stopped short of declaring education to be a fundamental, constitutional right, and did not rule that any government was obligated to provide it. In fact, only twenty years after it decided *Brown*, in *San Antonio School District v. Rodriguez* 411 U.S. 1 (1973), the Court explicitly denied the existence of positive education rights in the federal Constitution. Another promising decision from the perspective of positive rights' advocates was the case of *Goldberg v. Kelly*. In *Goldberg*, the Court ruled that New York State's practice of terminating AFDC benefits without first providing recipients with a hearing violated the Fourteenth Amendment by depriving AFDC recipients of their property without due process of law. This decision was initially considered a great victory for the larger project of forcing the government to actively protect its poorest citizens. However, the Court based its ruling on the idea that government must provide welfare benefits in particular cases only because the termination of someone's benefits without a hearing violated a constitutional restriction on the state, not because it violated a positive constitutional mandate. Even according to the ruling in *Goldberg*, the state's welfare termination constituted an unlawful action not because the Constitution required that the government actively provide aid, but because welfare benefits were deemed a form of property. This ruling forbid the state to deprive people of their property, but never obligated government to provide any. Yet, even this apparent victory for constitutional welfare rights, therefore, was rooted in a logic of negative rights and limited government. The Court roundly rejected welfare-rights lawyers' subsequent attempts to locate further welfare rights in the Fourteenth Amendment. R. Shep Melnick, *Between the Lines: Interpreting Welfare Rights* (Washington, DC: Brookings Institution, 1994).

[9] Other examples of positive-rights movements that have arguably fizzled include the efforts of the early civil liberties movement, which emphasized citizens' social and economic rights as central to true freedom of expression, and argued that these rights were already protected by existing constitutional provisions. It abandoned this focus by the 1930s in favor of a negative, autonomy-based conception of liberty. Laura Weinrib, "From Public Interest to Private Rights: Free Speech, Liberal Individualism, and the Making of Modern Tort Law," *Law and Social Inquiry—Journal of the American Bar Foundation* 34, no. 1 (2009). In addition, Akhil Amar has argued that the drafters of the Thirteenth Amendment, which outlaws slavery, envisioned this constitutional provision as a guarantee of a minimum standard of economic security Akhil Reed Amar, "Republicanism and Minimal Entitlements: Of Safety Valves and the Safety Net," *George Mason University Law Review* 11, no. 2 (1988): 49–51. This interpretation was also never widely accepted.

who, in the 1960s, pioneered the case that the Constitution contained justiciable welfare rights, has begun to argue that the U.S. Constitution may actually lack these rights.[10] This view of American constitutionalism has, quite understandably, given rise to the argument that America's constitutional tradition is distinct from those of other industrialized nations.

Assertions about America's constitutional exceptionalism are commonplace.[11] For instance, noted law professor Cass Sunstein has declared that "the constitutions of most nations create social and economic rights, whether or not they are enforceable. But the American Constitution does nothing of the kind." He goes on to ask, "Why is this? What makes the American Constitution so distinctive in this regard?"[12] Many scholars have answered this question with classically exceptionalist tropes, particularly with reference to America's unique political culture.[13] For instance, prominent constitutional scholar Frederick Schauer writes, "American distrust of government is a contributing factor to a strongly libertarian approach to constitutional rights. The Constitution of the United States is a strongly negative constitution, and viewing a constitution as the vehicle for ensuring social rights, community rights, or positive citizen entitlements of any kind is . . . highly disfavored."[14] Other theorists have followed suit, opining that "the constitutionalization of positive rights will not occur absent a shift in America's classically liberal political culture."[15] Andrew Moravcsik has written that, while he doubts that such abstract cultural differences can, on their own, explain divergent policy outcomes, "Americans [do] tend to shy away

[10] Frank I. Michelman, "The Supreme Court, 1968 Term," *Harvard Law Review* 83, no. 1 (1969); Michelman, "Socioeconomic Rights in Constitutional Law: Explaining America Away," *International Journal of Constitutional Law* 6, no. 3–4 (2008).

[11] For instance, one constitutional scholar has opined that "by limiting political authority and the very scope of politics itself, the American system aims to allow maximum opportunity for individual flourishing . . . fairness rather than justice is the hallmark of our legal aspirations and our cherished rights." David Abraham, "Liberty without Equality: The Property-Rights Connection in a 'Negative Citizenship' Regime," *Law and Social Inquiry—Journal of the American Bar Foundation* 21, no. 1 (1996): 3. Another scholar described the scholarly consensus this way: "One common and influential view of the [U.S.] Constitution suggests that it creates, almost exclusively, negative obligations of government and negative rights." David A. Sklansky, "Quasi-Affirmative Rights in Constitutional Criminal Procedure," *Virginia Law Review* 88, no. 6 (2002): 1233.

[12] Cass R. Sunstein, "Why Does the American Constitution Lack Social and Economic Guarantees?" *Syracuse Law Review* 56, no. 1 (2005): 4.

[13] Sunstein himself does not believe this cultural explanation is correct, and argues instead that America's lack of positive constitutional rights is the result of historical contingency. He attributes America's lack of postive rights to Nixon's (narrow) electoral win and to his conservative Supreme Court appointments.

[14] Frederick Schauer, "The Exceptional First Amendment," in *American Exceptionalism and Human Rights*, ed. Michael Ignatieff (Princeton, NJ: Princeton University Press, 2005), 46.

[15] Curt Bentley, "Constrained by the Liberal Tradition: Why the Supreme Court Has Not Found Positive Rights in the American Constitution," *Brigham Young University Law Review* 2007, no. 6 (2007): 1723.

from state intervention to redress social inequality—now established in most advanced industrial democracies as the primary fiscal task of the state. The aversion to state intervention is a distinctively American trait as compared to the political cultures of other advanced industrial democracies."[16]

Other explanations for America's divergent constitutional development not only hold its distinct constitutional culture responsible, but explain that cultural difference with reference to America's unusual history. For instance, Dieter Grimm, a law professor and former Justice on the Federal Constitutional Court of Germany, has argued that the different nature of America's revolution accounts for the difference in its constitutional rights. He explains, "The American colonists lived under the English legal order, yet without the remnants of the feudal and the canon law still alive in their motherland . . . Colonists referred to natural law as the true source of fundamental rights in order to justify the break with the motherland . . . To fulfill this function negative rights were sufficient."[17] Americans' lack of experience with feudalism endowed them with a distinct political and legal culture. Thus, Grimm argues that negative rights continue to characterize the American tradition, while Europe has taken a very different course, and concludes that "the contrast seems deeply rooted in different historical experiences; different perceptions of dangers; different trusts in the state on the one hand, the market on the other; different ideas about the role of political and legal institutions; a different balance between individual freedom and communal interest."[18] In other words, individual freedom from governmental control, the desire to keep government at arm's length, to protect people and particularly their property and economic arrangements from state power distinguish America's constitutional tradition from Europe's.[19]

NOT SO EXCEPTIONAL AFTER ALL

Arguments about America's exceptional rights tradition will be immediately recognizable to those familiar with the broader theory of American exceptionalism. Scholars of American politics were once widely agreed that American political development was notably aberrant. While European

---

[16] Andrew Moravcsik, "The Paradox of U.S. Human Rights Policy," in *American Exceptionalism and Human Rights*, ed. Michael Ignatieff (Princeton, NJ: Princeton University Press, 2005).

[17] Dieter Grimm, "The Protective Function of the State," in *European and US Constitutionalism*, ed. Georg Nolte (New York: Cambridge University Press, 2005), 140.

[18] Ibid., 154.

[19] Progressive Era historian Charles Beard is widely credited with generating the theory that American rights originated with a desire to preserve private property and are, consequently, devoted to circumscribing the government's authority. Charles Austin Beard, *An Economic Interpretation of the Constitution of the United States* (New York,: Macmillan Co., 1913). As we see from Grimm's analysis, this view has remained influential, despite its age.

countries developed strong, centralized welfare states as they industrialized, nineteenth-century America appeared virtually stateless and notably lacking in welfarist bureaucracies. Americans' deep suspicion of government and their single-minded devotion to the protection of private property were often used to explain America's divergent political path.[20] As we have seen, the conventional wisdom about America's constitutional tradition still echoes with these exceptionalist tropes about Americans' unusual history, their resulting fear of government, and their conspicuous difference from the rest of the world.

It is important to note the close resemblance between the classic description of American exceptionalism and the commonplace assertions of American *constitutional* exceptionalism because scholars currently consider the broader theory of American exceptionalism to be largely incorrect. New waves of research have demonstrated that Americans have long embraced government and that American political culture cannot be described as simply anti-statist or exclusively liberal.[21] As historian Daniel Rodgers explains, "Arguments based on assumptions of timeless, holistic, homogenously structured national values still exist, of course. But it is safe to say that fewer and fewer historians subscribe to them."[22] The development of the American state no longer appears to be defined by an exceptional commitment to

[20] Most famously, Louis Hartz argued that Lockean liberal ideology exerted a hegemonic influence on American politics. It was Americans' preoccupation with laissez-faire capitalism and a lack of experience with feudalism, Hartz explained, that explains why Americans never built a European-style welfare state. Louis Hartz, *The Liberal Tradition in America; an Interpretation of American Political Thought since the Revolution*, 1st ed. (New York: Harcourt, 1955). America's different history, others elaborated, endowed it with a different political culture, and this cultural difference served as a boundary condition, preventing European-style socialism from flourishing in the United States. Bernard Bailyn, *The Ideological Origins of the American Revolution* (Cambridge, MA: Belknap Press of Harvard University Press, 1967).

[21] Some scholars, of course, have questioned the degree of liberal hegemony in American political thought, and have demonstrated the existence and political influence of other, often conflicting, intellectual traditions. In particular, it is now widely agreed that republicanism and racist thinking have also powerfully influenced American ideas about politics. See Rogers M. Smith, *Civic Ideals: Conflicting Visions of Citizenship in U.S. History*, The Yale ISPS Series (New Haven: Yale University Press, 1997). In addition, scholars of labor history have demonstrated that the American labor movement was not merely duped into acquiescence by liberal rhetoric, but that American laborers found themselves in a different institutional context than their European counterparts, and responded with a different set of political strategies. See Amy Bridges, "Becoming American, the Working Classes of the United States before the Civil War," in *Working Class Formation: Patterns in Nineteenth Century United States and Europe*, ed. Aristide Zolberg and Ira Katznelson (Princeton, NJ: Princeton University Press, 1986); Victoria Charlotte Hattam, *Labor Visions and State Power : The Origins of Business Unionism in the United States*, Princeton Studies in American Politics (Princeton, NJ: Princeton University Press, 1993); William E. Forbath, *Law and the Shaping of the American Labor Movement* (Cambridge, MA: Harvard University Press, 1991). Thus, the lack of a viable socialist party in America is not the result of a cultural deficit among American laborers, but of the institutional constraints they faced.

[22] Daniel T. Rodgers, "American Exceptionalism Revisited," *Raritan* 24, no. 2 (2004): 43.

laissez-faire capitalism or an extraordinary suspicion of government intervention.

Studies of state and local politics have played a key role in undermining the notion of American exceptionalism. When we expand our examination of American governance beyond the federal level, even nineteenth-century America no longer appears to lack regulatory, protective government. On the contrary, it is quite clear that state governments regulated social life in a variety of arenas, and established interventionist policies to promote social welfare well before the New Deal.[23] Historian William Novak has been particularly influential in establishing that, even during the supposedly stateless nineteenth century, governmental regulation was a pervasive feature of American politics. Americans' everyday lives, Novak demonstrates, were permeated by the assumption that government's proper function was to continually intervene, regulate, and perfect community life. It was simply state and local governments that played this interventionist role.[24] Even the federal government itself now appears to have been far more interventionist during the nineteenth century than was once believed. Building on existing norms of state and local governance, the federal government of the nineteenth century worked in partnership with state, local, and private intermediaries to meet social and economic needs.[25] As a result of this research, few would continue to defend assertions of American exceptionalism, especially in their strongest form. However, many continue to describe America's constitutional tradition as exceptional. Constitutional exceptionalism has thus outlived the dogma from which it was derived.

It is high time that we applied our knowledge of American political development to our assessment of America's constitutional rights. We should ask, in other words, whether American constitutionalism would continue to look exceptional if we broadened our view of governance to include states. I will argue that the answer is a resounding no. Just as it is mistaken to take the measure of the American state by looking only at the federal government, it is misleading to assess America's rights tradition exclusively with reference to the United States Constitution. The study of state and local governance has discredited claims about America's exceptional political development. Similarly, this study of state constitutions challenges assertions about the exceptional nature of America's constitutional rights.

---

[23] See for example Gwendolyn Mink, *The Wages of Motherhood : Inequality in the Welfare State, 1917–1942* (Ithaca, NY: Cornell University Press, 1995).

[24] William J. Novak, *The People's Welfare: Law and Regulation in Nineteenth-Century America*, Studies in Legal History (Chapel Hill: University of North Carolina Press, 1996), 42.

[25] Brian Balogh, *A Government out of Sight: The Mystery of National Authority in Nineteenth-Century America* (Cambridge: Cambridge University Press, 2009); Kimberley S. Johnson, *Governing the American State: Congress and the New Federalism, 1877–1929*, Princeton Studies in American Politics (Princeton, NJ: Princeton University Press, 2007).

First Central Argument: America Has
Positive Rights

This book's first central argument is that Americans have a long tradition of enshrining positive rights in constitutions, but that we must look at state constitutional politics to find them. State constitutions contain a plethora of positive-rights provisions that cover a wide range of topics. In fact, these constitutional provisions closely resemble the positive rights in constitutions all over the world. For instance, Article Twenty-four of the Belgian constitution of 1970 states, "Everyone has the right to education . . . Access to education is free until the end of mandatory schooling," while the Missouri constitution of 1865 declared, "The general assembly shall establish and maintain free schools for the gratuitous instruction of all persons . . . between the ages of five and twenty-one years." Article twenty-four of the 1993 Peruvian constitution states that "The worker is entitled to a fair and adequate remuneration enabling him to provide for himself and his family . . . ," and the Wyoming constitution of 1889 says, "The rights of labor shall have just protection through laws calculated to secure to the laborer proper rewards for his service." These U.S. constitutional mandates, created in the nineteenth century, are still in place today. While the kinds of socioeconomic protections in the Peruvian and Belgian constitutions are often thought to be missing from American constitutional law, the texts of America's state constitutions have contained *at least comparable* guarantees for well over a century.

Not only do the texts of state constitutions contain mandates for interventionist and protective government, but the politics surrounding the creation of these provisions reveal that many of their champions argued for their inclusion in constitutions using the very logic that defines positive rights. The advocates of protective constitutional provisions consistently argued that, for a certain segment of the population, intrusive government and the risks such government posed to private property and individual liberty were not the most salient or urgent threats to the well-being of every citizen. For at least certain groups of people, restrictions on government and protections for private property would mean little unless government also provided protection from other, even more immediate dangers—like poverty, dangerous working conditions, and environmental catastrophe. Furthermore, the advocates of positive constitutional rights insisted that protections against these nongovernmental threats were too fundamental to be left in the hands of legislatures. In other words, the movements on behalf of positive rights at the state level sought to weave a social safety net of heartier stuff than mere statutes. Statutory law would certainly compose much of the protection they sought, but they insisted that it must be reinforced by constitutional mandates. These crucial safeguards could not be a matter of legislative choice, these movements declared, but must instead be secured as obligations on the state, and must therefore be placed in the state's highest law. Different political movements, over different centuries, and across many states made this argument, and many of them succeeded in having protective guarantees added to state constitutions.

It may seem difficult to believe that highly salient commitments on issues of national importance could be reflected only in state constitutions, while omitted from the federal document. However, the federal government played a far smaller role than state and local governments in crafting social policy throughout much of American history. This is arguably the case even today, but it is entirely clear in the case of pre–New Deal politics. Before the 1930s, state governments were primarily responsible for regulating working conditions and employment relationships, for establishing public education, protecting the public health, supervising the management of natural resources like land and water, and caring for the aged, indigent, and insane. In fact, under the dominant interpretation of the Constitution's Commerce Clause, Congress wasn't even thought to possess the authority to regulate in many of these areas. This is not to say that the federal government had no role in shaping America's social policies. However, states were primarily responsible for enacting the laws that governed these realms of social and economic life. Since states were the primary sources of law in most areas of social policy, their fundamental laws were the natural targets for activist groups seeking a more interventionist and protective state. Throughout the nineteenth and early twentieth centuries, Americans understood themselves to be living simultaneously under (at least) two governments of consequence (their state and federal governments), and under two meaningful constitutions (their state and federal constitutions). As we will see, even well into the twentieth century, the policies of state governments were significant enough that some organizations continued to devote resources to shaping America's state constitutions.

One final reason that we might expect to find positive rights in state constitutions, even if they are absent from the Bill of Rights, is that the Bill of Rights was added to the federal Constitution in order to satisfy Anti-Federalists that the new national government would not impinge too dramatically on the sovereignty of the existing state governments. The Bill of Rights was not written to apply to state governments, but was created primarily to ensure that the new national government would not replicate the recent, unwanted intrusions of the British colonial system. It is no wonder, then, that the federal Constitution's Bill of Rights seems (at least at first blush) to devote itself almost entirely to limiting government. Thus, while the Bill of Rights may reflect a suspicion of the federal government, we cannot infer from this document that even its drafters were suspicious of all government.

SECOND CENTRAL ARGUMENT:
RIGHTS MOVEMENTS CAN BE AIMED AT CHANGE

The book's second central argument is that when we look at the movements to create the positive rights in state constitutions, we gain new insights into why people engage in constitutional politics, and why they try to create new constitutional rights. This argument begins with a well-known puzzle about the origins of constitutional rights. Rights tell government what it must do and thereby limit government's choices. It seems strange, therefore, that any actors powerful enough to shape a polity's highest law would include binding restraints on their own discretion. Surely, those empowered to write a constitution would prefer to leave their options open and their discretion complete. How, then, can we explain the emergence of constitutions, and especially of constitutional rights?

The most famous solutions to the puzzle of how we get constitutional rights hold that the people powerful enough to shape a constitution's content realize that their political influence may not always loom so large. Therefore, in the interests of preserving their grip on the state well beyond their tenure in office, ruling coalitions enshrine their favorite policies in the form of constitutional rights. Constitutional courts will then be able to enforce these rights and uphold the policies they reflect even against the will of future ruling coalitions and/or democratic majorities. This story about the origins of rights explains that constitutions are not designed to bind their authors in the present, but are created to bind their authors' counterparts in the future.

To be sure, many American social movements comprised of relative outsiders have mobilized around the claim that their constitutional rights were being violated and that the Constitution demanded a transformed political order. The Civil Rights movement is one well-known example of this phenomenon, and at least since the Civil Rights movement, scholars of rights have described the central role of rights consciousness in Americans' efforts to organize for political change, and have described the symbolic power of rights rhetoric in these struggles for political legitimation and recognition.[26] They have documented many examples of relative outsiders attempting to make (or at least realize) new political meanings from existing constitutional texts, and of reformers who have demanded political change by insisting that the country has forsaken the central values already embodied in its Constitution.[27] However, scholars who have asked about the origins of constitutions, rather than struggles over the meaning of existing texts, have

[26] For example, see Stuart A. Scheingold, *The Politics of Rights: Lawyers, Public Policy, and Political Change* (New Haven: Yale University Press, 1974).

[27] See, for example, Bruce A. Ackerman, *We the People: Transformations* (Cambridge, MA: Belknap Press of Harvard University Press, 1998).

tended to conclude that new constitutional texts, and even new bills of rights, are drafted by political insiders seeking to forestall change and entrench their influence. While it is well-understood that movements may use the rhetoric of rights to seek political change, the conventional wisdom about the origins of constitutional documents still holds that new textual rights are born of elite and conservative projects.

Studies of constitution writing (as opposed to examinations of evolving constitutional meanings) have described textual rights provisions as products of elite entrenchment projects. This reigning theory about the origins of new textual rights has the three central components: (1) that rights are created by dominant regimes, (2) in an attempt to maintain the status quo, (3) by ushering the judiciary into politics. I argue that, while these factors explain the emergence of constitutional rights under some conditions, none of these elements is necessary for the creation of new constitutional rights.

When we examine the origins of America's positive rights, it quickly becomes apparent that the proponents of new constitutional rights need not hold positions of legislative dominance, are not always seeking to preserve the status quo, nor are they consistently hoping to usher the judiciary into politics. As we will see, the positive rights in state constitutions were often created by different kinds of political actors, and for very different reasons. These movements were not ruling elites or dominant legislative coalitions, but were composed of relative outsiders who were frequently frustrated with the legislative process. When they could not get the policy changes they wanted through the legislature, the advocates of positive rights were sometimes able to add the rights they championed to state constitutions. It was possible for such legislative outsiders to use state constitutions in this way because state constitutional conventions allowed activists and social movements to sidestep legislatures, changing constitutions even where legislative change was challenging or impossible. Some states permitted constitutional amendment through the initiative and referendum process, allowing activists to circumvent legislative coalitions even in the absence of constitutional conventions. These motives for the creation of new rights point to a kind of constitutional politics that is not oriented around long-term stability or entrenchment, but around the achievement of immediate change.

Since so much constitutional theory assumes that constitutions are geared toward permanence and defined in large part by their rigidity, this focus on short-term political change offers a new way of thinking about the distinguishing features of constitutional law and the origins of constitutional rights. In fact, a focus on short-term, political change is such an unfamiliar way of thinking about constitutional politics that many have argued that state constitutions and their authors have been woefully misguided. The framers of state constitutions have drafted not only the broad and seemingly timeless principles that we typically associate with constitutional law, but have also filled state constitutions with detailed policy instructions that require frequent revision. This malleability and specificity render state constitutions so different from our standard image of constitutions that these characteristics have led many to dismiss state constitutions as failures of higher lawmaking. If state constitutions are really unworthy of their titles, we can hardly revise our view of American rights and their origins based solely on the study of their drafting. But, as this book will show, state constitutions are more than pale imitations of their federal counterpart. They are the products of debates about fundamental political values and sites of thoughtful and serious lawmaking. Indeed, principled movements for government protection have rendered these constitutions rich repositories of the rights that seem absent from the federal Constitution.

THE REST OF THE BOOK

Chapter 2 addresses why state constitutions have been so widely derided and consistently excluded from descriptions of America's constitutional tradition. In particular, it examines the impression that these documents are too detailed to serve as repositories of national political commitments, or even any kind of principled commitment. As a result of their details, state constitutions appear to reflect idiosyncratic anxieties rather than national concerns, to be products of pluralistic competition rather than deliberate judgment, and to enshrine trivial policies rather than fundamental promises. I argue however, that all of these critiques stem from a misreading of state constitutions. Placed in their proper historical and political context, state constitutions are quite clearly reflections of national affairs, careful thought, and weighty values. Having demonstrated that state constitutions are recognizably constitutional, I then address the book's two central arguments.

The first central argument is that America has positive constitutional rights. In order to make this claim, chapter 3 provides a definition of rights, and describes the distinction between the categories of positive and negative rights. It then defends the distinction between positive and negative rights against some of its most prominent critics. I argue that, while constitutional theorists have questioned whether it is possible to distinguish positive and negative rights at very high levels of abstraction, the leaders of the rights movements described in this book argued that, at the level of their lived experience, there was a very real difference between rights that protected them only from the state, by forcing the state to restrain itself, and rights that forced the state to intervene in order to protect them.

The book's second central argument is that rights movements invest in constitutional change not only because they want constitutions to bind future elites, but also because they want to overcome immediate political obstacles that they cannot surmount through statutory law alone. In addition, it is not only hegemons or elites who champion new textual rights. Indeed, many of the positive rights in state constitutions were not crafted by ruling coalitions, but were championed by relative outsiders, hoping to change rather than preserve the status quo. In chapter 4, I detail the variety of political calculations that drove activists, organizations, and social movements to pursue the creation of positive constitutional rights. I also demonstrate that the motives of these rights advocates are quite different from those described by existing theories about who writes new rights and why they do it.

The next three chapters are case studies of particular positive-rights movements. Each case study provides evidence for both of the book's central arguments. Chapter 5, a study of constitutional education rights, focuses on the common school movement, which originated in the Jacksonian period and continued through the Reconstruction era. The common school movement successfully established the states' constitutional duty to provide education, and its leaders argued that government had a moral duty to expand opportunities for children whose parents could not otherwise afford to educate them, and insisted that state legislatures should be legally obligated to fulfill it. This movement was quite clear that the value of constitutional rights lay in their potential to promote policy changes by forcing legislatures to pass the kinds of redistributive policies they generally avoided. This chapter provides what may be the strongest evidence for an American positive-rights tradition that exists primarily at the state level. Throughout American history and even in the face of federal involvement, state and local governments have been responsible for establishing and maintaining public school systems. Furthermore, every state constitution currently includes a provision about public education, and many state supreme courts have explicitly declared these provisions to be educational rights.

Chapter 6, a study of labor rights, addresses an area in which active state intervention has been far more controversial, and in which constitutional rights are typically thought to have restrained the American state, not expanded its responsibilities. In fact, the quintessential arguments about America's exceptional anti-statism have focused on the labor movement. This chapter demonstrates that the American labor movement pursued the creation of constitutional rights even during the Gilded Age and Progressive Era, when courts were at their busiest enforcing constitutional rights to the liberty of contract and nullifying protective labor regulations in their name. At the same time, the proponents of protective governance also created new constitutional rights (at the state level) to legitimize, and indeed to mandate, governmental protection for laborers. Thus, this chapter demonstrates that, even in the area of labor regulation, Americans have successfully pursued the creation of positive constitutional rights. It also establishes that rights are not always designed to judicialize controversies, but are also created to exclude the judiciary from policymaking.

Chapter 7 examines the campaigns for constitutional rights to environmental protection. This case is particularly interesting not simply because it challenges the assertion that America lacks positive rights, but also because of its timing. In the 1960s and 1970s, when Congress was passing landmark environmental regulations and an entire executive agency had been developed to address the subject, environmental activists still staged state-level campaigns to add new positive rights to their constitutions. Thus, this case study allows us to investigate the value of state constitutional rights in an era of expanding federal responsibility. It also demonstrates that, like the education and labor rights before them, these environmental-rights provisions were intended to mandate active and protective government at the state level. They were also designed to enable political change and to facilitate the construction of a political movement, not to entrench the status quo.

This study examines both the nature and political origins of America's positive constitutional rights, and its arguments raise a number of questions that I hope future research will pursue. One such question is the extent to which these positive rights worked or mattered. While I describe instances of their successful enforcement and the political value of particular positive rights in particular cases, I do not advance a general argument about the efficacy of either positive rights or state constitutions. In other words, this book focuses on the causes, rather than the consequences, of the provisions it highlights.

Finally, this study is an empirical look at rights movements and their aims; I do not develop an argument about the normative desirability of positive rights or of the politics that surrounds them. My case studies of positive-rights movements do tend to emphasize their redistributive and progressive features. Yet it is just as important to recognize that these rights movements were often committed to the proposition that only members of their own race or religion should benefit from the state's intervention and protection, and they maintained this position to the detriment of some of the most vulnerable residents of their states. The constitutional tradition I document here is, like most of American politics, appealing in some respects and abhorrent in others. Therefore, I conclude the book with a discussion of the exclusionary and racist side of the movements that championed positive rights. Whatever we ultimately conclude about their normative value, however, these movements for positive rights have clearly shaped America's constitutional law.

CHAPTER 2

Of Ski Trails and State Constitutions
SILLY DETAILS OR SERIOUS PRINCIPLES?

W hen you read state constitutions, it can sometimes seem that the people who wrote them must have failed to grasp the purpose and the
nature of constitutional law. State constitutions do contain declarations of
guiding principles and outline the basic structures of state government, but
in most cases, these recognizably constitutional features are surrounded,
even engulfed, by hundreds of mundane administrative details.As the *New
York Times* put it, for example, the "great phrases [of New York's constitu-
tion] all but drown in the fine print." For example, the article pointed out,
the state constitution even concerns itself with the construction of ski trails.[1]
In fact, New York's "ski trails" provision has become emblematic of the
outlandish level of detail in most state constitutions.[2]

The fact that so many state constitutions contain provisions about policy
choices as detailed as the construction of ski trails has cast doubt on whether
these constitutions are really constitutional at all. James Gardner, for example, argues that provisions like this one discredit the entire enterprise of
state constitution writing. "What can one say about the character of a people who enshrine these types of provisions in their constitutions," he asks.
"Can one say of New Yorkers . . . that they are a people who cherish their
liberty to ski?"[3] Because the sovereign body that drafted the state constitu-

[1] John P. MacKenzie, "New York's Old, and Fat, Constitution," *New York Times*, New
York, April 20, 1987, A18.

[2] Douglas S. Reed, *On Equal Terms: The Constitutional Politics of Educational Opportu-
nity* (Princeton, NJ: Princeton University Press, 2001), 89; G. Alan Tarr, *Understanding State
Constitutions* (Princeton, NJ: Princeton University Press, 1998), 2; John Clarke Adams, *The
Quest for Democratic Law: The Role of Parliament in the Legislative Process* (New York:
Crowell, 1970), 73; Malcolm Edwin Jewell and Samuel Charles Patterson, *The Legislative
Process in the United States* (New York: Random House, 1966), 138; Michael A. Bamberger,
Reckless Legislation: How Lawmakers Ignore the Constitution (New Brunswick, NJ: Rutgers
University Press, 2000), 17; Gerald Benjamin and Henrik N. Dullea, *Decision 1997: Constitu-
tional Change in New York* (Albany, NY: Rockefeller Institute Press, 1997), 16; Robert A.
Schapiro, "Identity and Interpretation in State Constitutional Law," *Virginia Law Review* 84,
no. 3 (1998): 391.

[3] James A. Gardner, "The Failed Discourse of State Constitutionalism," *Michigan Law Review* 90, no. 4 (1992): 819.

tion was petty enough to enshrine details like the width of ski trails in its fundamental law, Gardner tells us, he finds it difficult to credit that body with a comprehensive vision or "a meaningful history of purposeful debate."[4] If the framers of New York's constitution could not be bothered to take seriously their own fundamental law, surely it would seem that *we* should not waste our time in the attempt.

Before we accept state constitutions as a meaningful component of the American political tradition, then, it seems we must first address this nagging "ski-trails" problem. In other words, we must consider whether these odd-looking documents are a legitimate element of the American constitutional tradition, and whether we should really revise our conception of American constitutional rights based solely on their (highly detailed) contents. In order to answer these questions, it is necessary to explore why the detailed nature of state constitutions strikes so many observers as so problematic.

I believe that state constitutional details seem disturbingly unconstitutional for four, related reasons. First, these details can appear idiosyncratic and parochial. Thus, they seem to reflect unique local anxieties and interests rather than national political concerns. Second, these details appear to be an extension of politics as usual, rather than a product of detached, disinterested, and visionary planning. Third, state constitutions' details appear to focus on mundane and trivial policy decisions, instead of enshrining weighty commitments or fundamental guarantees. Finally, detailed state constitutional provisions have been accused of hobbling the states they created, rather than facilitating their fruitful development. At the heart of each of these concerns over detail lies the conviction that state constitution-making is not appropriately or sufficiently principled to create true constitutions. As a result, the critics of state constitutions sometimes argue and regularly imply that these documents (and particularly their details) can lay only dubious claim to the title of "constitution."

After exploring each of these critiques of state constitutionalism, I argue that state constitutions, even their very detailed provisions, can and do reflect nationwide, principled commitments. Not only do these details often address issues of national salience, but their origins, while in some ways different from those of the federal Constitution, are not inherently less elevated. Indeed, the origins of these provisions highlight the ways in which state constitutions reflect their champions' principled (and quite familiar) use of constitutions and constitutional politics. As we will see, even the notorious ski trails provision reflects quintessentially constitutional aims. To recognize the principled nature of state constitutionalism, however, we must reconsider the ubiquitous assumptions about "higher lawmaking" and states' idiosyncrasies that have animated its critics.

[4] Ibid., 820.

Do State Constitutions Reflect Idiosyncratic
Anxieties or National Concerns?

If we take the U.S. Constitution as a model, it can be quite jarring to learn that Florida's current constitution bans the use of a particular kind of fishing net, or that Oklahoma's constitution currently includes a provision relating to the operation of grain elevators.[5] If one hears only these examples or reads only a single constitution that contains them, one might well conclude that state constitutions reflect narrow, local concerns and particularistic interests as much as, or more than, they reflect any kind of nationwide commitments. It would seem that such documents could hardly serve as an adequate foundation for any argument about the character of American constitutional law or its national rights tradition.

However, when one examines contemporaneous constitutions together, the regional and national problems and controversies that shaped them become wholly unmistakable. In fact, scholars of state constitutionalism are generally quick to note that these detailed provisions reflect larger trends in constitution writing.[6] The "particularistic" interests that seem to have shaped state constitutions were rarely unique to their own states, and the study of state constitutions at higher levels of aggregation quickly brings their commonalities into focus. Although state governments are often described as isolated "laboratories" in which new policies can be tested without danger to the nation as a whole,[7] it is a mistake to imagine states as a disorganized array of isolated decision makers. While it is certainly possible to find idiosyncratic provisions in more than one state constitution, most address a similar set of policy problems. What may appear as an odd and misplaced detail in a single state constitution is therefore very likely to appear in many other contemporaneous constitutions as well.

This coordination among state constitutions is, in part, a result of the efforts of their framers to study the latest state constitutional practices, and to apply the lessons that other states offered as they designed their own fundamental laws. Throughout the nineteenth and twentieth centuries, constitutional conventions and advisory commissions on constitutional revision have engaged in broad comparative studies of constitutional law, and bor-

[5] See Florida Constitution of 1968, Article 10, Section 16; and Oklahoma Constitution of 1907, Article 9, Section 33.

[6] Tarr, *Understanding State Constitutions*; Dinan, *The American State Constitutional Tradition*; Robert F. Williams, *The Law of American State Constitutions* (Oxford, New York: Oxford University Press, 2009).

[7] This metaphor is often attributed to Justice Brandeis. In a dissenting opinion, Brandeis wrote, "It is one of the happy incidents of the federal system that a single courageous state may, if its citizens choose, serve as a laboratory; and try novel social and economic experiments without risk to the rest of the country." *New State Ice Co. v. Liebmann*, 285 U.S. 262 (1932), 311.

rowed heavily from one another. Constitutional conventions' delegates not only discussed the situations and constitutions of neighboring states, but also conducted comparative surveys that were national in scope. As Christian Fritz has demonstrated, the delegates to nineteenth-century state constitutional conventions regularly consulted compilations of America's state constitutions, many of which were even published in pocket-sized editions for easy reference.[8] They also discussed the social problems that other states faced, as well as the success or failure of their constitutional solutions. Delegates often defended the provisions they supported with reference to the other states that had adopted similar constitutional mechanisms.[9]

Constitutional similarities were not only the product of their framers' studies, but also the products of the coordinated efforts of national social movements, working through states. Well before constitutional conventions' first meetings, the leaders of these movements typically attempted to ensure that the convention would consider their demands. Thus, the similarities among state constitutions can be explained in large part by the work of nationwide interest groups, like farmers' organizations, labor unions, and women's groups, which promoted their agendas through and across individual states.[10]

As early as the first decades of the nineteenth century, state-level organizations within the same broad movement communicated and coordinated across vast geographic distances, reporting on both legislative and constitutional developments in other states, and sharing experiences about the most successful tactics. As we will see, publications like labor newspapers, teachers' journals, and environmental magazines all informed their readers about constitutional developments of even far-flung states, and urged their readers to fight for similar provisions in their own state constitutions. In the run-up to New Mexico's constitutional convention, for example, the *New Mexico Journal of Education* asked existing state superintendents of education to recommend the most desirable constitutional provisions. It then printed the advice for the benefit of the state's own constitutional convention. Similarly, in her work on behalf of protective labor legislation, Florence Kelley (Illinois's first state factory inspector) published a book reviewing the status of maximum hours laws in states across the country and recommending that

[8] Christian G. Fritz, "The American Constitutional Tradition Revisited: Preliminary Observations on State Constitution-Making in the Nineteenth Century West," *Rutgers Law Journal* 25, no. 4 (1994): 976.

[9] In 1921, the National Municipal League even began publishing a "model state constitution" with the hope of further standardizing these documents through the provision of a template. W. Brooke Graves, "Fourth Edition of the Model State Constitution," *American Political Science Review* 35, no. 5 (1941).

[10] Elisabeth Stephanie Clemens, *The People's Lobby: Organizational Innovation and the Rise of Interest Group Politics in the United States, 1890–1925* (Chicago: University of Chicago Press, 1997).

proponents of labor regulation follow Utah's example in pursuing the constitutional right to an eight-hour day, especially for those laboring under particularly dangerous conditions.[11] Twentieth-century environmental activists also shared ideas for common constitutional rights. In 1968, for example, *Audubon* magazine published the text of New York's "environmental bill of rights," recommending that its readers consider supporting the inclusion of a similar provision in their own state constitutions. Indeed, nationwide efforts to influence the development of state constitutions have been so vigorous and long-lived that the study of changing details in state constitutions is, to a large extent, also the study of American social movements.

The phenomenon of active, popular, and nationwide engagement in state constitutional meaning is particularly visible today in the twenty-first-century struggle over gay marriage. As chapter 5 demonstrates, the advocates of public schooling were attempting to shape national education policy through state constitutions as early as the second half of the nineteenth century. Without the proper context, individual state constitutions can sometimes read like an eclectic laundry list of unique and narrow concerns. However, many of the details that seem so idiosyncratic in isolation were actually common constitutional responses to salient national controversies and widespread political movements.

ARE STATE CONSTITUTIONS PRODUCTS OF PLURALISTIC COMPETITION OR DISINTERESTED JUDGMENT?

Of course, it is entirely possible to recognize national trends in constitution writing, but still view state constitutions (in all their trendy detail) as anathema to the legitimate constitutional endeavor. Thus, many who have noted that state constitutions include a predictable set of detailed policies still see those details as extremely troubling. Their objection is premised, in part, on the idea that proper constitutional drafting is not conducted through competition between interest groups, but through detached and reasoned judgments. Thus, the framers of the U.S. Constitution are regularly described as disinterested political theorists of the highest order. By contrast, state constitutions appear to be bloated with the demands of many narrow interest groups and polluted by the bargains they have struck.[12]

The details in state constitutions appear to be evidence that these documents reflect pluralistic competition, rather than principled judgments about

[11] Florence Kelley, *Some Ethical Gains through Legislation* (New York: The Macmillan Company, 1905).

[12] Lawrence Meir Friedman, *A History of American Law*, 3rd ed. (New York: Simon & Schuster, 2005), 74–5.

how to frame a government.[13] After all, state constitutions often specify particular projects to which the state's monetary resources must be committed, and many even include details about how this money should be raised and distributed. In other words, since state constitutions appear to enshrine the detailed outcomes of petty bargains, they appear to lack sufficiently lofty origins. Thus, like many others, James Gardner has explained that upon examination, "we find state constitutions wanting. . . . The stories to which they lend themselves are not stories of principle and integrity, but stories of expediency and compromise at best, foolishness and inconstancy at worst."[14]

It is true that state constitutions are so detailed in large part because these documents provide so many points of entry for the direct participation of citizens and citizen groups. Unlike the amendment procedures specified in the federal Constitution, the amendment procedures for state constitutions promote broad popular involvement in their development. For instance, while the federal Constitution may be revised through convention, Congress must establish such a convention, and a two-thirds majority of the states' legislatures is required to force Congress into convening one. This is a rigorous amendment procedure, and the federal Constitution has never been amended through this process. At the state level, constitutional conventions can typically be convened through either a majoritarian or supermajoritarian vote of the legislature and approved directly by voters. Fourteen states even allow citizens to vote at regular intervals on whether to call a convention without a prior legislative proposal. As a result, the "persistent demands of reform-oriented interest groups" have frequently been sufficient to bring state constitutional conventions into being.[15] Once a convention is called, its delegates are generally elected through a direct vote of the citizenry, and these elections offer further opportunities for citizen participation and for the influence of organized groups. Furthermore, amendments to the federal Constitution (introduced through a supermajoritarian vote of both houses of Congress) must be ratified by three-quarters of the states, typically through state legislatures. By contrast, state constitutional amendments (while frequently introduced through supermajoritarian legislative procedures) are generally ratified through a direct vote of the state's electorate. These statewide plebiscites offer yet another opportunity for direct popular participation in state constitutional change. Of course, the initiative and referendum procedure for amending state constitutions (introduced in Ore-

[13] Alan Tarr describes this view of state constitutions this way: "Given this understanding of state constitution-making, one would not expect the products of this process to embody a coherent design or overarching perspective on politics any more than one would expect it of a collection of state statutes." Tarr, *Understanding State Constitutions*, 58.

[14] Gardner, "The Failed Discourse of State Constitutionalism," 822.

[15] Elmer E. Cornwell, Jr. , Jay S. Goodman, and Wayne R. Swanson, "State Constitutional Conventions: Delegates, Roll Calls, and Issues," *Midwest Journal of Political Science* 14, no. 1 (1970): 107.

gon in 1902 and since adopted by seventeen other states) is particularly remarkable in this respect, enabling citizens to amend state constitutions through petitions and popular votes alone. As of 2005, there had been 233 state constitutional conventions and only one federal convention.[16] Furthermore, as of 1996, an average of 120 amendments per state had been added to state constitutions, while the federal constitution has only been amended twenty-seven times.[17]

Because the U.S. Constitution is so hard to amend formally, its meaning has, for the most part, evolved through changes in judicial doctrine.[18] While popular movements have clearly influenced the federal Constitution's meaning, therefore, they have generally pursued constitutional change through litigation. As a result, the short and ambiguous provisions of the federal Constitution have remained largely unchanged at the level of their text, lending the Constitution an air of stability and changelessness. In addition, even for those who recognize that the meaning of the Constitution has changed through litigation, this particular mode of change appears to lift constitutional questions above the competition and bargaining that characterize other forms of political decision making, and to replace it with a principled and reasoned method of resolving disputes.

Whereas the text of the federal Constitution is quite difficult to revise, it is relatively easy to change the text of state constitutions through popular pressure. Consequently, activists seeking to influence the meaning of state constitutions have often engaged in a form of politics closely associated with electoral and legislative competition.[19] For instance, interest groups often sought to ensure that candidates for membership in constitutional conventions vowed to promote the agenda of their organization. Montana's League of Conservation Voters even circulated a questionnaire to all of the candidates in elections for the state's 1971 constitutional convention, asking about their position on environmental rights in the constitution.[20] Labor unions used similar tactics, extracting promises of cooperation from candidates in exchange for their electoral support. Several labor groups even decided to try to staff constitutional conventions with their own members.[21]

---

[16] Williams, *The Law of American State Constitutions*, 95.

[17] Tarr, *Understanding State Constitutions*, 24.

[18] Stephen M. Griffin, *American Constitutionalism: From Theory to Politics* (Princeton, NJ: Princeton University Press, 1996).

[19] Of course, the meaning of state constitutions can and does change through informal mechanisms as well. See, for example, Michael Besso, "Constitutional Amendment Procedures and the Informal Political Construction of Constitutions," *Journal of Politics* 67, no. 1 (2005).

[20] Montana Constitutional Convention of 1971–2 (Helena: Montana Legislature in cooperation with the Montana Legislative Council and the Constitutional Convention Editing and Publishing Committee, 1982), 1229.

[21] See, for example, "Labor Unionists Have Put Candidates in the Field," *Michigan Union Advocate*, Detroit, July 19, 1907, 1. See also "Workingmen and the Convention," *New York Times*, New York, October 24, 1893, 4.

The advocates of state constitutional change also published pamphlets, staged rallies, organized speaking tours, and campaigned in elections and statewide referenda. They circulated proposed articles for inclusion in the constitution and hired lobbyists to attend constitutional conventions in order to promote those articles. These tactics are neither separate from nor elevated above popular pressure and electoral competition in the way that the judicial process often appears to be. As a result, the provisions they generated have often been characterized as catalogues of interest groups' contests and bargains over state resources, rather than the products of disinterested and far-sighted deliberation.

It is a mistake to dismiss state constitutional politics as mere horse-trading simply because its form appears to differ from the federal model of detached and principled judging. First of all, this charge fails to distinguish the tactics of constitutional movements from the content of their demands. Pluralistic politics may center on groups' bids for a bigger piece of some pie, but pluralistic competition may also focus on the pursuit of fundamental values. Thus, sustained public interest in the content of state constitutions and democratic competition to shape their meaning should hardly be deemed unprincipled on its face. Furthermore, the allocation of a polity's resources is a decision in which fundamental values are often (perhaps always) implicated. Although the distribution of the state's resources was often at stake in state constitutional controversies, popular constitutional activism was hardly confined to petty squabbling. As we will see, many of the popular movements to influence state constitutions invoked broad principles as they engaged in a competition for voters' support and delegates' obedience.

Not only did popular movements outline broad principles of governance in their efforts to shape state constitutions, but the politics surrounding the federal Constitution are not as different from the state model as state constitutions' critics would have us believe. For example, both bargaining and elections played a significant role in shaping the federal Constitution, not just those of the states. In fact, several provisions of the U.S. Constitution were famously the result of bargains between particular interests, including America's bicameral legislature and its notorious three-fifths clause. In addition, the meaning of the federal Constitution is, like that of state constitutions, shaped through electoral competition. Although the federal Constitution is interpreted by Supreme Court justices with life tenure, rather than revised by popular amendments, Supreme Court justices are nonetheless selected and confirmed by elected officials. While the Supreme Court may lag behind public opinion, therefore, it is by no means severed from it.[22] The Court is also discouraged from rendering widely unpopular decisions by the fact that it lacks the budgetary and police powers to enforce its own deci-

[22] Robert Dahl, "Decision-Making in a Democracy: The Supreme Court as a National Policy-Maker," *Journal of Public Law* 6, no. 2 (1957): 284–91.

sions, and must rely on elected officials for this function. It is further constrained by the fact that Congress may attempt to curb judicial power in the face of unpopular decisions, and in the hope of reaping electoral gains.[23] Consequently, the federal Constitution's meaning has changed dramatically over time as political winds shifted and new policy preferences have come to dominate the political landscape.[24]

In what has become an extremely influential argument, Bruce Ackerman posits the existence of rare historical moments in which the views of the entire electorate foment and then legitimate changes in the meaning of the Constitution. These "constitutional moments" are so rare, Ackerman tells us, because, most of the time, most of the people are largely indifferent to debates about constitutional meaning. Once in a great while, however, disagreements about the Constitution create such a political crisis that the entire citizenry is forced to pay attention and voice an opinion. At such moments, Ackerman argues that the citizenry has effectively amended the Constitution by deciding on new constitutional meanings, which the Supreme Court will then enforce.[25] Like state constitutions, the U.S. Constitution is neither above nor immune from popular pressure. However, popular pressure at the federal level is typically seen to have legitimated shifts in the Constitution's meaning. At the state level, where we witness the existence of sustained constitutional movements, rather than ephemeral constitutional moments, this popular involvement is widely viewed with suspicion.

If democratic constitutions must mediate the tension between the competing goals of minority rights and majority rule,[26] then we might say that state constitutions have simply struck a more majoritarian balance than their federal counterpart.[27] Indeed, the impressive degree of popular involvement in shaping state constitutions might well convince us to take state constitutions more, not less, seriously as a mirror of Americans' political commitments.[28] In any case, we should not mistake constitutional provisions shaped through grass-roots organizing and electoral competition as inherently unprincipled. To be sure, responsiveness to popular pressure is not an unmitigated virtue. A constitutional system capable of resisting popular pressure may also be

---

[23] Tom S. Clark, *The Limits of Judicial Independence, Political Economy of Institutions and Decisions* (New York: Cambridge University Press, 2010).

[24] Kenneth Ira Kersch, *Constructing Civil Liberties: Discontinuities in the Development of American Constitutional Law* (Cambridge: Cambridge University Press, 2004).

[25] Ackerman, *We the People: Transformations*.

[26] Christopher L. Eisgruber, *Constitutional Self-Government* (Cambridge, MA: Harvard University Press, 2001).

[27] As John Dinan has demonstrated, the drafters of many state constitutions designed flexible constitutions precisely so that ordinary citizens might wrest control of the state from entrenched economic elites. John J. Dinan, "'The Earth Belongs Always to the Living Generation': The Development of State Constitutional Amendment and Revision Procedures," *Review of Politics* 62, no. 4 (2000).

[28] Dinan, *The American State Constitutional Tradition*.

more capable of protecting important principles in the face of public outrage than one that cannot.[29] However, it is important to remember that popular pressure and pluralistic competition may arise from principled commitments, and we cannot infer a lack of principle simply because state constitutions were shaped through pluralistic competition.

ARE STATE CONSTITUTIONS TRIVIAL OR WEIGHTY?

Of course, most critiques of state constitutions not only cite concerns about the political tactics through which their detailed provisions were added, but also chafe at their seemingly trivial content. Despite its different emphasis, this objection also stems from the conviction that real constitutions are defined, at least in part, by their elevated, higher-lawmaking origins. Proper constitution-making, we are told, must transcend not only the competition that characterizes ordinary politics, but also the mundane particulars with which ordinary politics is occupied. In other words, constitutional lawmaking ought to address only the framework and principles of good government, not muck about in the minutia of everyday policies. Here again, we learn that state constitutions should look more like the U.S. Constitution, which establishes governing institutions, endows them with broad powers, and then places principled limits on their purview and discretion.

Like its fellows, this critique of state constitutionalism trades on an idealized and largely inaccurate picture of the federal constitutional endeavor. After all, the practical meaning of the federal Constitution's majestic statements of principle has been worked out in the context of specific policy battles.[30] Thus, while the Constitution's text may be less detailed than those of the states, its law and meaning are equally bound up in detail. Furthermore, as Richard Primus has demonstrated, even the rights originally chosen for inclusion in the federal Constitution were not (or at least not only) statements of timeless and universal values, but reflections of very timely and specific dissatisfactions with the British colonial system.[31] The Third Amendment's prohibition on quartering soldiers in any house without the consent of its owner during peacetime, for instance, can hardly escape characterization as a detailed policy provision.

---

[29] Indeed, litigation is often celebrated as a mode of constitutional change precisely because it allows Supreme Court justices to consider principled arguments and protect unpopular minorities, rather than bending to popular whims. John Hart Ely, *Democracy and Distrust: A Theory of Judicial Review* (Cambridge, MA: Harvard University Press, 1980).

[30] Keith E. Whittington, *Constitutional Construction: Divided Powers and Constitutional Meaning* (Cambridge, MA: Harvard University Press, 1999).

[31] Richard A. Primus, *The American Language of Rights, Ideas in Context* (Cambridge: Cambridge University Press, 1999).

The critique of state constitutional detail as embarrassingly trivial has an even larger problem than its idealized view of the federal Constitution. The standard critique assumes a clear distinction between specific policy details (which belong only in statutes) and statements of fundamental values or frameworks for government (which belong in constitutions). However, these two categories are not necessarily distinct, and certainly not mutually exclusive. Many, if not all, of the details in state constitutions simultaneously describe highly specific policies and reflect the important principles of governance that these policies were created to advance. In fact, even the infamous ski trails provision exhibits this dual character. It is both a highly detailed policy mandate and the recognition of a fundamental value.

Since the ski trails provision is such a ubiquitous emblem of state constitutional failure, it may be instructive to inquire about its real origins. When we do so, it is immediately obvious that the drafters of the ski trails provision were neither overwhelmed by their devotion to snow sports nor confused about the difference between constitutions and statutes. Instead, they promoted the amendment only so that the state legislature could construct ski trails in an area designated as protected wilderness. In 1941, when the ski trails provision was created, this construction project was widely understood to require special authorization in the constitution itself because another, older provision mandated that the state's forest preserve be "forever kept as wild forest land," and further specified that no timber could ever be removed from the protected area. Since the construction of ski trails required the removal of timber, the state could not build them without first revising the constitution. Thus, the advocates of the ski trails provision were attempting to create a narrow exception to a countervailing constitutional mandate.

It is not immediately clear, however, that this history helps to defend state constitutional detail against the charge of triviality. Indeed, detractors of state constitution-writing note that high levels of detail have, over time, given rise to even higher levels of minutia.[32] Though less detailed than the ski-related amendment, the "Forever Wild" provision exemplifies the complications associated with "freezing" specific policy details in a constitution. Once a specific rule about the disposition of forestland was inscribed and rigidified in the constitution, even a trivial change to that rule necessitated the creation of an equally trivial constitutional amendment. Again, therefore, it seems that those who drafted New York's constitution must simply have lacked the foresight to do it properly. By placing this detailed

---

[32] For instance, legal historian James Willard Hurst has written: "Not only did the practice [of adding details to a constitution] depart from the general notion of the dignity of constitutions; it also violated the proved practical wisdom of not freezing detailed policy into a form hard to change." James Willard Hurst, *The Growth of American Law: The Law Makers* (Boston: Little Brown, 1950), 203.

policy in their constitution, they invited even further cluttering of their fundamental law.

We cannot ask the nineteenth-century framers of the Forever Wild provision whether, in hindsight, they wish they had omitted this detailed policy mandate.[33] However, we do know that, placed in the same position, and with time on their side, their successors celebrated this constitutional provision, despite the even more detailed amendments that had been required to modify it. At New York's constitutional convention of 1967, for instance, convention delegates supported the Forever Wild provision in force. Notwithstanding the thirteen amendments (including the ski trails amendment) that had been passed to carve out narrow exceptions to the Forever Wild provision, they praised it lavishly.[34] The president of the constitutional convention even declared, "I believe that the 1967 Constitutional Convention should not go down in history as the one which abridged the right of the people of the State to the protection of one of the State's greatest natural resources."[35] This description of the Forever Wild provision, as a right of the people to the protection of the state's resources, echoed the arguments of its earliest champions.

The framers of the original Forever Wild provision included details about the management of the state forest in order to establish and safeguard the state's natural environment and the people who depended on it. By the 1890s, it was clear that irresponsible logging practices could denude forests, and many worried that if the forest were destroyed, its streams would cease to flow, and that this outcome would threaten the viability of commercial waterways like the Hudson River and Erie Canal.[36] The state legislature had, by this time, created several different commissions to oversee and protect the state's forest. However, in the years leading up to the state's constitutional convention of 1894, widespread concern emerged about whether the forest commission could or would provide adequate protection for the state's wilderness. One installment of the *New York Times'* eleven-part series on the continued irresponsibility of logging in the protected forestland announced, "Shameful Work going on in Adirondacks—Everything Being Ruined by the Rapacious Lumberman—State Employees Engaged in the

[33] The Forever Wild Provision was created as part of the 1894 state constitution.

[34] One delegate to the convention argued that the Forever Wild provision allowed the state to address its changing needs without placing the forest at too great a risk. He explained, "the power and speed with which men and machines can radically change the face of the Forest Preserve has multiplied a 'hundredfold' since 1894." In the face of increasingly powerful and efficient means of deforestation and development, he argued, "the constitutional amendment procedure [had] worked to permit slow, conservative change." New York State Office of Legislative Research, *Constitutional Protection of the Forest Preserve* (Albany, 1967), 25.

[35] Ibid., 20.

[36] Frank Graham and Ada Graham, *The Adirondack Park: A Political History*, 1st ed. (New York: Knopf, distributed by Random House, 1978), 99.

Business."[37] To make matters worse, the appointed chair of the forest committee, Theodore Basselin, was actually a lumber baron.[38]

Not only did the forest commission seem untrustworthy, but even the legislature itself appeared to be unduly sympathetic to lumbering interests. Only a year before the constitutional convention was scheduled to begin, the legislature passed a "cutting bill," authorizing the forest commission to sell timber from any part of the forest preserve to private logging interests.[39] In his subsequent report to the state land office, the state engineer and surveyor predicted that lumbering under this law would seriously damage the Adirondack forest.[40] At this same time, the northern part of the state was suffering from a drought, and forest fires were raging throughout the Adirondacks.[41] In the midst of these fires, the popular press raised the specter of the forest's total destruction at the hands of loggers.[42] Several decades after the constitutional convention, one scholar described the situation this way: "There was unhampered legislative control . . . that played for the most part into the greedy hands of the lumber interests. The net result was to convince all true friends of the forests, and a majority of the voters, that the guarding of the woods could not safely be left to a free-handed legislature."[43]

To many who worried about the health of the forest preserve, the competence of the forest commission, and the character of the legislature, the constitutional convention of 1894 seemed to offer a solution. Since the legislature (and its forest commission) could not be trusted to make decisions about the use or health of the state's wilderness, they hoped that protection for the state's forests could be secured directly through constitutional amendment. In order to ensure that the legislature and the forest commission would be unable to make irresponsible decisions about the use of the state forest, the convention adopted a constitutional provision that deprived the commission and even the legislature of discretion over the management of this land. The provision not only mandated that the area in question be "forever kept as wild forest land," but also permanently forbade the removal of any timber.[44]

---

[37] Cited in Philip Terrie, "The Adirondack Forest Preserve: The Irony of Forever Wild," *New York History* 62, no. 3 (1981): 227.

[38] The *New York Herald* quipped that the forest commission ought to change its motto from "protect the forests" to "protect the forests from Basselin." Graham and Graham, *The Adirondack Park: A Political History*, 123.

[39] Ibid., 124.

[40] Terrie, "The Adirondack Forest Preserve: The Irony of Forever Wild," 283.

[41] Ibid., 284.

[42] Ibid.

[43] Alfred L. Donaldson, *A History of the Adirondacks* (New York: Century Co., 1921), 167–8.

[44] The specific terms and wording of this provision were actually drafted by the New York Board of Trade and Transportation, which was concerned about the viability of the state's waterways. Graham and Graham, *The Adirondack Park: A Political History*, 127.

The Forever Wild provision is, like its ski trails amendment, highly detailed. After all, it specifies that no timber can be removed from a particular part of the state. However, as the history and legacy of this provision illustrate, it is not only a meticulous set of instructions about the precise policy the legislature had to adopt, but also a constitutional commitment to the broad principle of responsible treatment of the environment. The reason that it attempted to realize this broad principle by constitutionalizing a detailed policy is that the constitutional convention did not trust the legislature or its forest commission to implement ambiguous instructions about political values. In order to keep the legislature in check, to ensure that it would govern in accordance with their broad values, they drafted exhaustive policy instructions.

In the years after the adoption of the Forever Wild provision, a preservationist organization, known as the Association for Protection of the Adirondacks, litigated under the Forever Wild provision when it perceived encroachment on the wilderness. Even when the state legislature authorized the Forest Commission to build a bobsled track for the 1932 Olympics (to be held in Lake Placid), the Association sued the conservation commissioner, arguing that the construction of a bobsled track would violate the Forever Wild provision of the state constitution by requiring the removal of timber. Two courts agreed,[45] and the Court of Appeals explained: "However tempting it may be to yield to the seductive influences of outdoor sports and international contests, we must not overlook the fact that constitutional provisions cannot always adjust themselves to the nice relationships of life." The decision then described the framers' intention to protect the state's wilderness from any possible abuses, and continued, "this plea in behalf of sport is a plea for an open door through which abuses as well as benefits may pass. The Constitution intends to take no more chances with abuses, and, therefore, says the door must be kept shut."[46] Eleven years after the bobsled case, when the forest commission wanted to build ski trails in the forest preserve, it was widely understood that a constitutional amendment would be necessary to authorize their construction.

The history of New York's ski trails amendment demonstrates that the seemingly mundane details in state constitutions do not reflect the lack of principle in state constitutional politics. Out of context, it may seem obvious that ski trails (or bobsled tracks) are an appropriate topic for statutory law alone, and that they are not deserving of constitutional treatment. However, it should now be clear how fundamental values were centrally implicated in the issue of ski trails. The value of wilderness as well as the significant chal-

[45] See *Association For the Protection of the Adirondacks v. Alexander MacDonald*, 288 A. D. 73 (1930), and *Association for the Protection of the Adirondacks. v. Alexander MacDonald*, 253 N.Y. 234 (1930).

[46] *The Association for the Protection of the Adirondacks et al. v. Alexander MacDonald, Conservation Commissioner of the State of New York, et al.*, 253 N.Y. 234, 242 (1930).

lenges in preserving it help to explain why reasonable and serious people felt the need to address ski trails in their constitutions. Gardner is correct that New Yorkers did not value ski trails so highly that they felt the "need to place them beyond the reach of temporary majorities and transient passions, and to permit their alteration only by future direct action of the people themselves."[47] However, the ski trails amendment is, nevertheless, the direct result of New Yorkers' attempts to protect the state's wilderness in just that way.[48] The state constitution includes details about the management of the state forest precisely because it embodies such a firm commitment to the broad principle of environmental preservation.

The ski trails provision is an emblem of the supposedly inappropriate detail and the apparently petty concerns that have debased state constitutions. Yet, upon closer inspection, even this provision appears purposeful, sensible, and principled. It is not alone. State constitutions do contain many detailed policies, but these policy instructions do not necessarily represent a departure from recognizable constitutional practices. On the contrary, many reflect a familiar use of constitutional politics. Like the ski trails provision, these state constitutional details typically circumscribe governmental discretion, offering a solution when the governing institutions they established could not be trusted to handle a particular kind of policy. State constitutions' specificity, therefore, is not an indication of their triviality, but a mechanism through which their framers hoped to limit government's choices in order to ensure that its officials would act in accordance with principled commitments. We will see this dynamic repeated in each of this book's case studies of positive-rights movements. The detailed provisions that these movements championed were not products of their petty squabbles and narrow visions, but of their practical concerns about legislative compliance. Properly understood, as a check on the discretion of the state and its officers, these detailed provisions and the movements to create them are recognizable as quintessentially constitutional in nature. They limit the discretion of particular branches of government over particular types of policies, and thus fulfill one of the central and most recognizable roles of constitutional law.

[47] Gardner, "The Failed Discourse of State Constitutionalism," 819.

[48] In 1877, for example, one plea for the state to preserve the Adirondack forests read, "Nature herself has here formed a park that only needs preserving . . . Let the state preserve that which Nature has so kindly bestowed with a lavish hand." Cited in Charles R. Simpson, "The Wilderness in American Capitalism: The Sacralization of Nature," *International Journal of Politics, Culture, and Society* 5, no. 4 (1992): 570. When the constitutional convention of 1915 reexamined the wisdom of the forest provision, many delegates expressed a similar sentiment. One declared: "There is twenty million dollars' worth of timber [in the forest preserve], but the question for you to decide is, what are we to do with that timber? Shall we treat it as we should if it belonged to you and me as a purely commercial proposition, or shall we handle and keep it for the other greater reasons that outweigh a hundred times the commercial side." Cited in Philip Terrie, "Forever Wild Forever: The Forest Preserve Debate at the New York State Constitutional Convention of 1915," *New York History* 70, no. 3 (1989): 269–70.

Limiting Government's Discretion
without Limiting Its Scope

The detailed provisions in state constitutions, like the Forever Wild provision, were often crafted as checks on legislative discretion, and this history has engendered one further critique. The details in state constitutions have been accused of hobbling the very governments they establish. For instance, Kermit Hall has argued that, as state constitutions grew more detailed, they "became antigovernment, stripping from political officials the legal authority they needed to govern." According to Hall, the framers of state constitutions hampered their governments on purpose, because they were fearful that government would become too effective and expansive. Thus, Hall tells us, "The assumptions underlying state constitutions were not just laissez-faire; they were positively hostile, save in a few limited areas, to the exercise of government power." He continues, "state constitutions since the mid-nineteenth century have reflected the .persistent localism and anti-governmentalism that underlie much of American political culture . . ."[49] The detailed provisions in state constitutions are often interpreted in this way, as anti-statist measures and reflections of Americans' deep suspicion of government power.

It is certainly the case that misgivings about state legislatures have driven constitutional conventions to place limits on legislatures. This practice is particularly conspicuous in nineteenth-century constitutions, many of which placed restrictions on the gifts and benefits that legislators could receive from corporations, established relatively low caps on state indebtedness, and forbade the state from financing internal improvement projects.[50] These measures were responses to a disastrous history of states' efforts to attract industry and promote economic development, efforts which bankrupted or nearly bankrupted many state governments. During the national economic boom of the 1830s, states participated in what one historian has described as a "headlong venture in deficit spending."[51] State legislatures issued bonds to finance the creation of canals, railroads, and banks, often dispensing significant benefits to these enterprises, including the grant of monopoly charters.[52] Following the economic collapse of 1839, these policies plunged state governments into crisis, causing many to question their legislatures' competence. Constitutional conventions, which were often called in direct response to the states' economic crises, moved quickly and decisively to place limits

---

[49] Kermit L. Hall, "Mostly Anchor and Little Sail: The Evolution of American State Constitutions," in *Toward a Usable Past: Liberty under State Constitutions*, ed. Paul Finkelman and Stephen E. Gottlieb (Athens: University of Georgia Press, 1991).

[50] Tarr, *Understanding State Constitutions*, 112–16.

[51] Marvin Meyers, *The Jacksonian Persuasion Politics and Belief* (Stanford: Stanford University Press, 1957), 85.

[52] Ibid.; Tarr, *Understanding State Constitutions*, 110.

on legislatures in the hopes that these restrictions would prevent them from being drawn back into risky speculation, or worse yet, corrupted by wealthy corporate interests.[53] Many of the provisions that resulted, like anti-corruption measures and limits on state indebtedness, were indeed designed to prevent government from intervening in the ways that it had before. However, other limits on legislative discretion had an entirely different purpose.

It is easy to assume that any restriction on the legislature must be a move toward smaller, more limited government. However, we should not confuse the desire to limit legislative choices with the goal of limiting the role of government. Similarly, we should not conflate the curtailment of the state's discretion with the reduction of its scope. Constitutional provisions may limit legislative discretion not only by restraining the state, but also by telling government that it must actively intervene in the state's social and economic life. Many of the provisions in state constitutions were not only aimed at telling state legislatures what they could no longer do, but also telling them what they had to do. In other words, state constitutions not only contain prohibitions on particular types of legislative activity, but also include mandates for legislative action.

While certain kinds of legislative participation in economic activities were understood by many nineteenth-century constitution-makers to be risky and undesirable, a total lack of legislative involvement in markets was also seen to pose unacceptable risks. Thus, constitutional drafters not only required legislatures to refrain from speculative participation in the market, they also required legislatures to intervene in the state's economic life in order to mitigate some of the undesirable effects of the capitalist system. For example, the widespread anger at the "wildcat" banks and monopolistic railroads of the 1830s resulted in many constitutional mandates that the state create particular banking regulations and engage in legislative action to protect the railroads' employees and customers.[54] Several constitutions even included protections for debtors, requiring legislatures to ensure that homesteads under a certain value would be protected from forced sale to meet the demands of creditors.[55] One delegate to the Michigan constitutional convention of 1850 explained that the purpose of these constitutional provisions was to "throw around every homestead, every fireside, every hearth-stone, the shield of its protection—to stay the proud waves of wealth, capital, and usury, from carrying over the homes of suffering, crushed, bleeding humanity."[56] As this explanation attests, nineteenth-century move-

[53] Tarr, *Understanding State Constitutions*, 112.

[54] Ibid., 115.

[55] Between 1845 and 1860, Texas, Wisconsin, California, Michigan, Indiana, Maryland, and Minnesota all added homestead exemptions to their constitutions. Lena London, "Homestead Exemption in the Wisconsin Constitution," *Wisconsin Magazine of History* 32, no. 2 (1948): 176.

[56] Cited in Martin Hershock, "To Shield a Bleeding Humanity: Conflict and Consensus in Mid-Nineteenth Century Michigan Political Culture," *Mid-America An Historical Review* 77, no. 1 (1995): 47.

ments for greater state intervention and protection used state constitutions in their attempts to establish social safety nets. The detailed provisions they drafted were not intended only to restrain the state, but also to force their legislatures into an expanded and protective role.

The creation of detailed constitutional mandates for an interventionist welfare state was not limited to the nineteenth century. As we will see, in the face of ongoing resistance to public schooling and redistributive taxation to fund it, education activists throughout the nineteenth and twentieth centuries have resorted to the creation of detailed constitutional instructions. Similarly, labor activists of the Gilded Age and Progressive Era wanted constitutions to mandate that government protect them from corporations' use of blacklists and private, strike-breaking armies, using constitutional provisions to establish the regulatory programs that legislatures had been reluctant to establish and courts reluctant to endorse. Environmental activists have continued this tradition even into the late twentieth century, using state constitutions to place clean-up funds beyond the use of legislatures and to ban specific practices that threatened the natural environment. All of these provisions are detailed, but they are not idiosyncratic, petty, or trivial. On the contrary, they reflect considered and widespread attempts to realize important principles in the face of recalcitrant legislatures and/or hostile courts. Having addressed the concern that state constitutions are not genuinely constitutional, we must now consider whether their detailed mandates for protective government can really be characterized as positive rights.

Defining Positive Rights

Environmental activists of the 1960s and '70s routinely insisted that constitutional law ought to do more than simply restrain the state. They wanted government to protect people from corporations that were polluting the air and water, threatening their health, and impeding their ability to enjoy the natural world. They warned that if government did not actively intervene to prevent the degradation of the natural environment, there would be no open spaces, no clean air or water left, and that people would sicken and die. Government, they explained, should be forced into action to protect Americans from this calamity.

Almost a century earlier, labor activists had just begun to make very similar arguments. They too were certainly opposed to unchecked government power, but they insisted that government ought to protect laborers from the large corporations that employed them. Railroad companies, mining enterprises, and factory owners, for instance, forced their employees to work extremely long hours, under dangerous conditions, for very little pay. They hired strike-breaking armies and circulated blacklists to punish the employees who pursued reform. Governments, labor activists insisted, should intervene; state legislatures should be required to address these serious and immediate threats to laborers' lives.

Decades before that, education activists made comparable claims, this time on behalf of poor children. Without active government help, they explained, children born to parents who could not educate them were doomed to a life of ignorance and poverty. They argued that states must be compelled to intercede, establishing free schools of sufficiently high quality that they could protect unlucky children from the consequences of their birth.

The education, labor, and environmental movements that I examine here were quite different from one another. They occurred at different times, and had different leader, members, tactics, and concerns. Their differences, however, render their similarities all the more striking. Each of these groups declared a need for interventionist, welfarist government and contrasted such protection with the restrained and indifferent government they encountered. To varying degrees, they all reported a direct conflict between the principles of limited, laissez-faire government and the sorts of policies they were working to enact. At the level of lived experience, therefore, the leaders and spokesmen of these movements described a dramatic difference between a government bound to intervene on their behalf and one that would promise only to restrain itself.

Faced with significant resistance to the types of governmental intervention that they championed, these groups attempted to mandate those interventions by inserting new provisions into their state constitutions. Whether they promoted the inclusion of detailed policy instructions or broad declarations of governments' duties, the movements on behalf of constitutional labor protections, public schools, and environmental safeguards all argued that state constitutions should mandate particular kinds of government action to ensure that the state was legally obligated to protect people from dangerous economic circumstances and powerful private entities.

In the chapter that follows, I argue that we should understand the constitutional mandates these groups championed as positive rights. I begin with a general definition of rights (as the bases for justified demands), and then argue that positive rights are those that require government intervention in order to protect people from threats that are not directly or solely governmental. Negative rights, by contrast, require government to restrain itself in order to protect people from threats that stem directly from an overbearing and intrusive state.[1] Next, I address the scholarly controversy over this distinction, concluding that at the level of lived experience, it is both possible and useful to distinguish between these different kinds of protections. Indeed, the value of this distinction is evidenced by the variety of terms scholars use to describe the kind of right that this book highlights (social rights, economic rights, and second-generation rights are some of the most common). This book uses the term "positive rights," and this chapter focuses on defining them. Whatever we decide to call these rights, however, the rest of this book argues that we should recognize them as a consistent feature of America's constitutional tradition.

Mandatory Constitutional Provisions as Rights

One very general definition of a right is "the basis for a justified demand," and many of the activists who shaped state constitutions clearly hoped to craft the kinds of constitutional provisions that would justify their demands on government.[2] In other words, rights entitle citizens not simply to request

[1] This distinction is different from the one Isaiah Berlin famously drew. Berlin did use the term negative liberty to describe a lack of coercion. However, he used the term positive liberty to describe the freedom to choose one's government. The term "positive rights" is (in general and in this book) used to describe a different set of guarantees. See Isaiah Berlin, "Two Concepts of Liberty," in *Four Essays on Liberty*, ed. Isaiah Berlin (Oxford: Oxford University Press, 1969); essay originally published in 1958.

[2] This definition is modified from Henry Shue's explanation of rights. See Henry Shue, *Basic Rights: Subsistence, Affluence, and U.S. Foreign Policy* (Princeton, NJ: Princeton University Press, 1980).

particular policies from their government, but also to demand that government enact those policies as a matter of obligation. As we will see, the common school, labor, and environmental movements crafted constitutional language designed to limit governments' discretion, requiring their states to enact specific policies and forbidding them to adopt others. Education, labor, and environmental activists all intended to create this kind of obligation through their pursuit of constitutional politics. Thus, I classify their campaigns to create these obligations as rights movements. For purposes of this study, I understand people to have created constitutional rights through the writing and ratification of mandatory constitutional provisions, and I use the term "right" to refer to the provisions themselves. To be sure, many advocates of constitutional change argued that higher truths necessitated the creation of the provisions they championed. However, I use the term "right" simply to describe the mandates included in constitutional law, rather than the existence of any normative principle or moral duty. In other words, I am concerned with rights as a form of positive, rather than natural, law.[3]

In addition to the constitutional provisions that use the term "rights," several other types of provisions in state constitutions appear to justify demands on the state by telling the government what it must do (and/or cannot do). These mandatory provisions include those that explicitly establish a state duty (e.g., "it is the duty of the general assembly to establish an eight-hour day"), those that declare the legislature "shall" or "must" take a particular kind of action (like "the legislature shall enact legislation establishing an eight-hour day"), and those that establish such policies directly (for example, "eight hours and no more shall constitute a lawful day's work"). On the basis of their text alone, then, one might well conclude that these textual provisions are, indeed, rights.[4]

---

[3] Carl Wellman defines legal rights this way: "Any assertion that a legal right exists, rests on the reason or reasons that support it. Primarily, these are reasons found in judicial reasoning, the legal norms and factual statements from which a court could validly conclude that some right exists. Derivatively, they are the reasons to which a lawyer or legal scientist could validly appeal to establish the truth of the statement that some right exists in a legal system." Carl Wellman, *Real Rights* (Oxford: Oxford University Press, 1995), 13. Demands made on the basis of moral rights, by contrast, are entirely justified by moral truths and require no legal or institutional grounding. Although there are many different theories of moral rights, they all describe rights as inalienable, inherent in the human condition, and inextricably linked to human flourishing. One version of this argument states that rights are justified by "important human interests, like autonomy and well-being." Cécile Fabre, *Social Rights under the Constitution: Government and the Decent Life* (Oxford: Oxford University Press, 2000), 15–16. Natural rights theories and assertions of human rights are subsets of this category of moral rights.

[4] Of course, the federal Constitution also contains textual provisions that create mandates on government. For instance, the First Amendment requires Congress to refrain from passing certain kinds of laws. This kind of obligation, the obligation to refrain, is a paradigmatic form of constitutional rights, and many rights movements have developed to demand that government honor these requirements to refrain from particular forms of action. The federal Constitu-

Of course, it is famously possible for a single constitutional text to gener-ate a wide variety of interpretations, and it is consequently unwise to clas-sify particular provisions as rights based on their text alone. As we saw in the previous chapter, it can be quite misleading to read a constitutional pro-vision without any reference to its social context or the actors whose subse-quent interpretations and agendas have endowed it with political meaning. In addition to their text, therefore, I examined the publications and speeches of the reformers that designed and promoted these provisions in order to demonstrate that these textual provisions were crafted and widely under-stood to be mandatory. It is important to note that I do not investigate the movements that championed positive rights because I believe their authors' understandings have, or ought to have, a uniquely authoritative status. In-stead, I examine both the texts of state constitutions and the politics sur-rounding them to make an argument about their meaning at the time of their creation. I am not arguing that judges should interpret state constitu-tions according to the intent of their framers. (In fact, I do not advance any theory about how or whether judges ought to read and enforce state consti-tutions.) Instead, my goal is to demonstrate that Americans have staged many successful campaigns to include mandates for protective, interven-tionist government in their constitutions.

By focusing on popular campaigns for constitutional changes, I highlight a politics of rights that resides largely (though not entirely) outside of the constitutional interpretations handed down by courts. While I do note in-stances in which courts have interpreted and enforced these provisions, I classify these provisions as rights based not on judges' interpretations of these provisions, but on the understandings, claims, and plans of the move-ments that championed them and used them to justify their demands. It is in these popular movements for protective government, their recurrent re-course to constitutional politics, and their success in shaping state constitu-tions, that I identify a previously overlooked rights tradition.

DEFINING POSITIVE AND NEGATIVE RIGHTS

America is not supposed to have constitutional rights to an active, welfarist government, let alone a robust and enduring tradition of successful move-ments on their behalf. In fact, constitutional scholars have widely asserted

---

tion also contains other kinds of requirements. For instance, the president must report on the state of the union, and tax bills must originate in the House of Representatives. Historically, these mandates have not served as the bases for either popular or elite demands on government, and thus we do not typically think of them as constitutional rights. Yet, in a world where the federal government did not seem to be honoring these requirements, we might well imagine the emergence of a movement based on these mandates. Thus, while we do not typically classify these mandates as rights, they certainly fit the definition of rights that I adopt in this book.

that American constitutional rights are negative rights, and that while other nations have included positive rights in their constitutional law, the United States has not. Many have explained that Americans are simply far too suspicious of government to have enshrined positive rights in their constitutional law. Indeed, the conventional wisdom holds that American rights focus almost exclusively on keeping government out of people's lives, that movements for other kinds of rights have generally failed to alter the country's constitutional commitments, and as a consequence, that positive rights remain foreign to America's constitutional tradition (see chapter 1).

But what does it really mean to claim that America has positive constitutional rights or, for that matter, that America is missing them? What features define positive rights as positive and distinguish them from negative ones? A great deal of ink has been spilled answering these questions, and different scholars have emphasized different distinguishing features. In order to rebut the charge that America lacks positive rights, I have attempted to synthesize the variety of definitions at play in the current use and understanding of these terms. Instead of endorsing a single theorist's view on this subject, I have tried to capture the widely shared understanding of what these terms mean.

Many different theorists have described the division between positive and negative rights in many different ways. However, I believe the division between these categories is generally composed of two separate distinctions. One distinction between positive and negative rights (pictured on the horizontal axis of figure 3.1) hinges on the kind of protection that the right provides. Negative rights protect their bearers from threats that stem solely from the state itself. Positive rights, on the other hand, protect their bearers from threats that are not solely the result of a state's existence or activities. For example, Frank Cross's test to distinguish a positive from a negative right involves imagining the total abolition of government.[5] Under these conditions, negative rights would be secured because government could no longer pose a threat. Rights not automatically secured in such a scenario must be positive. For instance, a governmental obligation to provide housing to those who cannot afford it would be classified as a positive right if it required active government to protect the rights-bearer from homelessness. The requirement that government refrain from punishing citizens' speech, on the other hand, is a negative right, because it protects citizens from the state's capacity to silence them. This framework captures an important component of the way these terms are widely understood, but it is not the only one.

A second distinction between positive and negative rights hinges on the kind of demand for which that right serves as a basis. Positive rights against the state require government to do or provide something, while negative

[5] F. B. Cross, "The Error of Positive Rights," *UCLA Law Review* 48, no. 4 (2001): 866.

rights require only that government refrain from doing something. In his explanation of the difference between positive and negative rights, Charles Fried employs this second distinction. He explains, "A positive right is a claim to something—a share of material goods, or some particular good like the attention of a lawyer or doctor, or perhaps the claim to a result like health or enlightenment—while a negative right is a right that something not be done to one, that some particular imposition be withheld."[6] The vertical axis of figure 3.1 describes the degree of intervention or restraint that the rights-bearer can demand. Negative rights are the bases of demands for restraint by the government, while positive rights are the bases of demands for intervention.[7] Here again, it is useful to think about the difference between a right to housing and a right to free speech. A right that requires government to intervene by providing the homeless with shelter is a positive right, while a right that requires government to refrain from silencing speech is a negative right.

The primary differences between positive and negative rights can be visualized along two separate axes. The resulting idea-space is pictured in the schematic shown in figure 3.1.

In describing rights against the government, the two distinguishing features of negative rights resolve into a single, coherent concept: a negative right protects its bearers from governmental threats by serving as the basis for a demand that government restrain itself. Similarly, a positive right protects its bearers even from non-governmental threats by serving as the basis for a demand that government intervene to protect and/or aid the threatened rights-bearer. It is possible for rights to require an enormous amount of governmental intervention, a very modest degree of intervention, or something in between. Similarly, it is possible for government to play a larger or smaller role in creating the threat from which a particular right offers protection. Positive and negative rights, in other words, are ideal types, rather

---

[6] Charles Fried, *Right and Wrong* (Cambridge, MA: Harvard University Press, 1978), 110.

[7] Wesley Hohfeld pioneered and popularized this way of distinguishing between different sorts of rights. He was distressed that legal scholars and judges were using the term rights to mean many different and often incompatible things. Hohfeld aimed to demonstrate that the term "rights" was actually used to describe two very different relationships. Some rights implied the existence of a duty on the part of another to do or provide a particular thing. Other rights, which Hohfeld called liberties, implied the existence of a duty on the part of another to refrain from interfering. A claim-right, Hohfeld explains, describes a relationship in which one person or organization owes something to the rights-bearer. Thus, one person's claim-right to something announces the other's correlative duty to do or provide that thing. By contrast, a liberty describes a relationship in which one person or organization cannot interfere with an activity of the rights-bearer. For every liberty, then, there exists a correlative non-right to interfere with the content of that liberty. This distinction between claims and liberties is the second way that modern scholars think about the difference between positive and negative rights. Wesley Newcomb Hohfeld, "Some Fundamental Legal Conceptions as Applied in Judicial Reasoning," *Yale Law Journal* 23, no. 1 (1913).

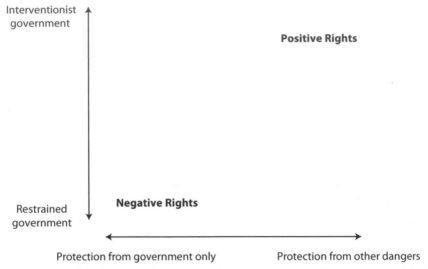

Figure 3.1: Two dimensions of positive and negative rights

than well-bounded categories. I have, therefore, placed these terms in a continuous idea space, rather than describing them in a two-by-two table.[8]

The Controversy Surrounding the Positive-Negative Distinction

Libertarian theorists have often embraced the distinction between positive and negative rights in order to deny the existence of positive rights and discredit the project of constitutionalizing them. Such scholars argue not only that positive and negative rights are distinct from one another, but also that negative rights are either the only real rights, or the only rights that make

---

[8] This two-dimensional understanding of positive and negative rights can help us to understand and classify rights that previously seemed to occupy a confusing netherworld between the two categories. For instance, criminal process rights (such as those contained in the Fourth, Fifth, Sixth, and Eighth Amendments of the U.S. Constitution) have occasionally been classified as "quasi-affirmative," and some have argued that they occupy a middle ground between positive and negative rights. Sklansky, "Quasi-Affirmative Rights in Constitutional Criminal Procedure." The mandate that government actively provide criminal defendants with an attorney places criminal process rights high on the dimension of government intervention, and causes them to resemble positive rights along this dimension. However, criminal process rights are intended to protect against a purely governmental threat. After all, government provision of a defense attorney is intended to protect a criminal defendant from the ongoing threat that the state poses to his life and livelihood. Ibid., 1234. Therefore, these rights fall in the top-left quadrant of this idea space. They do not occupy a middle ground between positive and negative rights, but are identical to each kind of right along only one dimension.

sense to include in constitutions.[9] I use the terms "positive" and "negative rights" for an entirely different purpose. I do not characterize particular rights as positive in order to dismiss them or suggest their inferiority. On the contrary, I argue that state constitutions and the politics that have surrounded them demonstrate that positive rights are an important and enduring feature of the U.S. constitutional tradition. However, there remains a strong association between scholarship that defends the distinction between positive and negative rights and the insistence that positive rights are illegitimate or secondary.

In response to claims that positive rights are inappropriate fodder for constitutional law, many of those who believe that government should intervene in social and economic life have objected to the existence of any real difference between positive and negative rights. These scholars have problematized the distinction between positive and negative rights as a matter of political theory, generating important questions about whether this terminology has any conceptual value. For example, Henry Shue has objected to the distinction between positive and negative rights in response to those who defend rights to personal security as legitimate (because such rights are negative), while denying the existence of rights to subsistence (because these rights are positive). Shue demonstrates that, in order to guarantee that people are able to realize even the so-called negative right to personal security, members of society are required to restrain themselves in certain ways, and to actively intervene in others. For instance, society must refrain from depriving others of liberty, and also intervene in order to ensure that no one else deprives others of liberty, and to aid those who have already been deprived.[10] Shue then argues that positive and negative rights are indistinguishable because, like security rights, all rights require both restraint and active intervention if they are to be fully realized.[11]

Shue's critique of the distinction between positive and negative rights is certainly compelling, but it loses a great deal of its power in the context of the American constitutional tradition. In fact, it entirely ceases to apply to narrower constitutional rights, like the right to refuse to quarter troops in one's home.[12] Indeed many of the parts of the Bill of Rights are neither phrased nor widely understood to imply positive duties to protect or aid the

[9] For an example of the argument that positive and negative rights are basically indistinguishable, see R. L. Lippke, "The Elusive Distinction between Negative and Positive Rights," *Southern Journal of Philosophy* 33, no. 3 (1995). For an example of the claim that positive rights do not belong in constitutions, see, Cross, "The Error of Positive Rights."

[10] Shue, *Basic Rights: Subsistence, Affluence, and U.S. Foreign Policy*, 53.

[11] Shue's insight here is that security rights do not impose a single correlative duty, but multiple obligations—some of which require intervention and some of which require restraint. The right to personal security is only meaningful, he argues, if it imposes the duty to refrain from depriving people of their security, the duty to protect people from the deprivation of their security, and the duty to aid those deprived of security.

[12] Fabre, *Social Rights under the Constitution: Government and the Decent Life*, 53.

deprived. On the contrary, federal constitutional rights are often phrased and interpreted as explicit instructions to the government only to refrain from particular actions. Thus, even granting Shue's objection in the context of broad, general, or abstract statements of rights, it nonetheless remains possible to distinguish between the federal Constitution's prohibitions on government action and state constitutional mandates for government intervention. However, Shue's objection to the distinction between positive and negative rights is only one of many.

For those whose work has demonstrated that poverty and its attendant dangers are ultimately products of governmental policy, it has seemed particularly counterproductive to distinguish between governmental activity and restraint, or to claim that there are any social dangers in which government is not implicated. The Critical Legal Studies (CLS) movement has developed the foundation for this critique. While CLS scholars, themselves, have devoted little attention to the terms "positive" and "negative rights," those working within their tradition have argued that government restraint is always an illusion and that all of the economic and social threats that citizens face ultimately stem from government itself. Even when government appears to be restraining itself, for instance allowing the parties in a dispute to bargain freely, government structures are continually biasing the process and outcomes of those negotiations. Indeed, in the area in which American government is said to be most restrained, that of private economic bargaining and contracting, government is always active and influential, through the laws and institutions it establishes. Because these ubiquitous structures operate in the background, they are often invisible. However, one of the major insights of the CLS movement was that when we learn to see government operating in the background, the distinction between public and private law, and public and private relationships, appears largely fictitious.[13] If there is no way to distinguish a public sphere from a private one, then surely there is no way to distinguish government activity from government restraint.[14] Because government is always operating, any notions of governmental restraint must be merely a legal fiction.

---

[13] Duncan Kennedy, *Sexy Dressing, Etc.* (Cambridge, MA: Harvard University Press, 1993).

[14] Stephen Holmes and Cass Sunstein have developed a similar critique. They argue that, since the state must be active in enforcing even negative rights, all rights are effectively positive. Rights of any kind, they point out, require government expenditure. Therefore, if we want any rights at all, we must want an active state. See Stephen Holmes and Cass R. Sunstein, *The Cost of Rights: Why Liberty Depends on Taxes* (New York: Norton, 2000). As Alan Gewirth has pointed out, however, it is entirely possible to separate the costs associated with the enforcement of any right from the costs associated with the content of the right itself. Thus, while all rights may require government to establish a court system, some require not only the creation of an enforcement mechanism, but the creation of additional institutions (like public schools or public housing) to fulfill their promises of protection. Surely, then, it remains possible to distinguish between the content of positive and negative rights, notwithstanding the enforcement costs associated with all rights. See Alan Gewirth, "Are All Rights Positive?" *Philosophy and Public Affairs* 30, no. 3 (2001): 330.

One implication of the CLS rejection of the public/private distinction is that the distribution of society's resources and the resulting social inequalities must stem not only from private decisions and power relations, but also from government itself. Because government rules structure the distribution of resources, it makes little sense to distinguish governmental from extra-governmental threats. For instance, if we recognize hunger or homelessness as the product (at least in part) of governmental rules and structures, hunger and homelessness appear just as governmental a threat as the danger that government will take one's property directly. If we cannot distinguish threats posed by government from the threats that are not posed by government, it is doubly impossible to distinguish positive from negative rights.

Notwithstanding the important insights of the CLS movement, at the level of their lived experiences, the activists who shaped state constitutions perceived an important difference between governmental action and restraint. They also distinguished between threats posed directly by government itself and dangers that stemmed from other sources. These two dichotomies may crumble if we recognize the many ways that government is implicated in shaping all realms of society. However, the movements I describe here were focused on the proximate, rather than ultimate, causes of the problems they sought to mitigate, and saw interventionist government as a possible solution to those problems. For instance, common school activists argued that a government that established redistributive taxation to create free and high-quality schools could protect poor children from a life of irremediable poverty, while a government that refused to intervene in this way could not. Similarly, labor activists saw unsafe conditions, long hours, and low wages, corporations' blacklists, and their strikebreaking armies as dangers from which they required protection. A government that only restrained itself could not offer them any protection from the labor market or their employers. A government that extended itself by establishing and enforcing labor regulations, on the other hand, could protect them. Likewise, environmental activists believed that environmentally destructive industrial practices were a serious threat to the nation's supply of clean air and water, and as a significant hazard to people's health. A government that refused to intervene could do little to address these dangers, but one that established and enforced rules against environmentally destructive practices, or better yet used state resources to remedy existing damage, could offer people valuable protection. Leaders in all these movements expressed outrage that government could look on passively while private actors and/or economic circumstances posed serious threats to people's well-being. Each of the movements I studied, especially the labor movement, recognized that government might well intervene in ways that would harm as well as help them. Thus, these groups certainly wanted government to restrain itself from engaging in certain kinds of intervention. However, they believed that constitutions ought to establish rights not only as a means of protection from tyrannical government, but also as a means of ensuring that government would protect people from the dangers that economic circumstances and private actors posed. Although few of these activists used the terms "positive" and "negative" rights, their pleas for new constitutional protections certainly distinguished between these categories.

Even in academic circles, skepticism about the terminology of "positive and negative rights" has failed to erode the widespread conviction that there are different kinds of rights, and that the differences between them are worth talking about. Among critics of the positive-negative distinction, themselves, for example, it is still quite common to differentiate between constitutional rights that seem to mandate that the state protect its less powerful members and those that limit the state in order to protect citizens from a tyrannical, overbearing government. This practice is particularly common among scholars of international human rights law, who often convey their sense that there are different sorts of rights with terms "first- and second-generation rights." First-generation rights refer to provisions that secure civil and political liberties, much like negative rights, while second-generation rights are concerned with the promotion of social and economic equality, much like positive rights.[15] Another widely used term, which conveys a very similar idea, is "social rights," or "social and economic rights." These terms are generally used to describe rights like the right to a decent standard of living, the right to education, food, clothing, and housing. While the categories may not overlap perfectly, "these social and economic rights" do seem to exhibit significant overlap with positive rights, and second-generation rights. Indeed, those who shy away from the term "positive rights" frequently use the term "social and/or economic rights" in its stead. Even Cass Sunstein, who has famously argued that "all rights are positive,"[16] has asked why the U.S. Constitution lacks social and economic rights.[17] Whether one ultimately adopts or rejects the terminology "positive and negative rights," these categories, along with very similar distinctions, have clearly remained both useful and ubiquitous.

We can use many different names to describe the kind of rights that this book highlights. Even within the same movement for constitutional change, different writers, speakers, and constitutional delegates adopted different terms for these constitutional mandates. Many did not name or categorize these provisions at all, simply describing their content and purpose. I have been calling them "positive rights," and distinguishing them from "negative rights," but my argument might easily be rephrased to read that America has

---

[15] Ishay also defines "third-generation rights" as rights that protect their bearers' abilities to maintain their ethnic, national, or linguistic identities. Micheline Ishay, *The History of Human Rights: From Ancient Times to the Globalization Era* (Berkeley: University of California Press, 2004).

[16] Holmes and Sunstein, *The Cost of Rights: Why Liberty Depends on Taxes.*

[17] Sunstein, "Why Does the American Constitution Lack Social and Economic Guarantees?"

"second-generation rights" or "social and economic rights" guaranteed in its constitutional law. However, even if we accept the conventional distinction between positive and negative rights, we can still recognize both kinds of constitutional rights in the United States.[18]

As we will see in greater detail through the book's case studies, leaders from each movement maintained that the constitutional protections they championed were just as crucial in securing citizens the opportunity to flourish as any of Americans' most familiar and cherished constitutional rights. In their campaigns to add education, labor, and environmental rights to state constitutions, activists argued that the protections they sought were simply too fundamental and important to remain optional and insecure. Their insistence on the necessity of these rights and their success in creating them belies the claim that Americans are too suspicious of government to mandate state intervention on behalf of those in need. Mandates for protective, interventionist governance are not outside America's constitutional tradition, but are very much a part of it.

---

[18] I have adopted this language in part because it is still used to claim that American constitutional rights are concerned only with limitations on the state. I have also adopted this terminology because the distinction between positive and negative rights is relatively clear and precise, allowing me to pinpoint just what it is that the American constitutional tradition is supposed to lack. While I recognize the danger of reproducing problematic conceptual distinctions, other scholars have problematized this distinction in part to make the same kinds of arguments that I am making through the use of these terms. In addition, the distinction between positive and negative rights successfully captures the analyses of the activists and movements that I studied as well as their own descriptions of their needs.

Why Write New Rights?

UNDERSTANDING CONSTITUTIONAL DEVELOPMENT
APART FROM ENTRENCHMENT

In the previous chapters, I argued that state constitutions embody popular commitments to an active, interventionist, and protective state. Thus, the study of these constitutions helps us to make better inferences from American rights to American ideals. To read constitutions only as mirrors of norms and values, however, is to miss the way in which constitutions are also political documents, crafted in the midst of ongoing battles for control of government policies, and modified by groups of people hoping to gain an advantage in those struggles. Because the conflicts that shape constitutions are often about fundamental political commitments, these documents reflect both moral principles and messy power struggles. As a result, when we examine the origins of positive rights, we learn not only about the principled commitments that those rights embody, but also the political functions that those rights were designed to carry out. The champions of positive rights wanted to enshrine their commitments in constitutions not only as a means of expressing devotion to particular values, but also because they were engaged in fierce battles over the direction of state policy. By learning why their leaders pursued state constitutional change, we can better understand the strategic, political calculations that give rise to new rights. Those calculations are the focus of this chapter.

We might well imagine that activists seeking a protective and interventionist state could simply forgo constitutional politics altogether. After all, the common school movement wanted state legislatures to establish common schools, the labor movement wanted legislatures to enact protective labor policies, and the environmental movement wanted state legislatures to regulate industrial practices. In each case, these activists were ultimately seeking new legislation. Why, then, did they devote any resources to constitutional change? Why did they not simply take their case to their legislatures?

The answer is that constitutions can do different kinds of political work than legislation. Unlike statutory law, for instance, constitutions place specific policy issues on the agendas of particular branches of government while simultaneously removing those issues from the purview of others. Consequently, constitutions allowed political movements to place mandates on legislatures that had previously been reluctant to respond to their demands. At the same time, constitutional provisions allowed these activists to overturn or preempt state high court decisions that threatened their legislative progress, excluding courts from particular policy struggles. Constitutions can also enable litigation, thereby overturning legislative decisions. Finally, constitutional provisions serve as highly visible banners around which these groups can rally their members. These accounts of the reasons that political actors create constitutional rights paint a different picture from the one offered by existing explanations for constitutional development.

Most of the literature on constitutional development explains constitutional drafting and change as the result of regimes' attempts to entrench their favorite policies by enabling judicial review. These traditional explanations focus on the enforcement capacity of constitutional courts and on the long-term consequences of constitutions. They emphasize that constitutions are distinguished from statutory law by their unique ability to preserve an existing policy, through judge-made law, even after it has ceased to appeal to electoral majorities. The reigning theories of constitutional development, therefore, hold that legislative majorities or dominant political parties write constitutional provisions to entrench their established policies, especially when they sense that their own political influence is waning.

In this book, I offer additional accounts of constitutional development, and in so doing I identify several unique features of constitutional law, other than its (widely recognized) capacity to entrench established policies by allowing courts to protect them. For instance, political actors may concentrate on the immediate political advantages that constitutions can confer instead of constitutions' longer-term capacities. Furthermore, many of the organizations chronicled here identified enforcement strategies for these constitutional provisions that did not depend on courts. In fact, constitutional changes may be motivated by the desire to keep courts out of particular policy struggles. I argue, therefore, that it is a mistake to elide the concepts of entrenchment, judicialization, and constitutional development. The study of state constitutions allows us to distinguish among these processes, enhancing our view of the forces that shape constitutional development and expanding existing theories to account for differences in constitutional structure. In order to appreciate the conventional entrenchment story, as well as the additional accounts of constitutional development, however, it is first necessary to understand the classic idea of constitutions as constraints.

CONSTITUTIONS AS CONSTRAINTS

Many of the central questions in constitutional theory stem from the view that constitutions are, at their core, constraints on the exercise of political power. By outlining the rules through which government operates, for instance, and by establishing the limits of legitimate political conduct, constitutions render the mechanisms of government more rigid. Constitutional rights then proscribe particular policy choices, further limiting the discretion of lawmakers. Viewed in this way, as devices that bind a polity and limit political options, the appeal of constitution-writing is somewhat mysterious. Why would a government or polity trade its unfettered potential for a set of binding restrictions?

One answer is that restrictions are good for us. For instance, Jon Elster has famously compared the project of constitution-writing to that of Ulysses, when he ordered his sailors to bind him to the mast of his ship to protect him from dangerous temptation.[1] Constitutions, Elster explained, play the same role, constraining a society's choices in order to shield it from pursuing temptations that might threaten its survival. Such temptations include the pursuit of policies that, while potentially popular, might ultimately undermine the functioning of the democratic system by denying access to minorities, or the censorship that results from officeholders' impulse to outlaw the criticism of their own regime.[2] Like Ulysses, members of a polity recognize that these options are likely to appeal to democratic majorities and/or political officeholders, but believe that yielding to such temptations will ultimately prove fatal to the political system. To ensure the polity's continued survival, therefore, its members bind themselves through constitutional law.

For all its evocative power, the Ulysses metaphor raises questions about timing. After all, Ulysses' sailors eventually untied him. Constitutions, on the other hand, seem to bind societies over time and across generations, limiting not only the choices of their authors, but the choices of their heirs as well. As Andrei Marmor has explained, a constitution is "not like Ulysses who ties *himself* to the mast, but rather like a Ulysses who ties *others* to the mast with him."[3] This feature of constitutional law, its ability to entrench particular constraints over long time horizons, has been the focus of an enormous body of constitutional theory.

Normative theorists, for instance, have been unable to agree about whether the ability to bind polities over time is constitutionalism's highest virtue or its greatest vice.[4] This disagreement about the normative legitimacy

---

[1] Jon Elster, *Ulysses and the Sirens: Studies in Rationality and Irrationality* (New York: Cambridge University Press, 1979).

[2] Ely, *Democracy and Distrust: A Theory of Judicial Review*.

[3] Andrei Marmor, *Interpretation and Legal Theory*, rev. 2nd ed. (Oxford: Hart, 2005), 145. In more recent work, Elster himself has expressed doubts about the Ulysses metaphor for constitutionalism because he too has become convinced that constitutions are as often used to bind others as they are to bind one's self. Jon Elster, *Ulysses Unbound: Studies in Rationality, Precommitment, and Constraints* (New York: Cambridge University Press, 2000).

[4] Jed Rubenfeld articulated the conventional sentiment that the great virtue of constitutions is their ability to bind societies over time: "Written constitutionalism can only be properly understood, it can only claim legitimate authority, as an effort by a nation to achieve self-government over time, where self-government over time refers not to an ideal of governance at each successive moment . . . but rather to the nation's struggle to lay down temporally extended

of intergenerational binding has shaped theories about how judges ought to interpret constitutions over time, and even about the normative legitimacy of judicial review.[5] Judges' ability to enforce intergenerational commitments has rendered the practice of judicial review appealing to some, while convincing others of its moral illegitimacy.[6] Regardless of one's position on any of these questions, it is clear that all of these prominent debates within the field of normative political theory find the long-term consequences of constitutions to be their most salient feature.

The empirical literature on constitutionalism has, in many ways, mirrored the normative literature, identifying the important elements of constitutional politics as those that create enduring fetters, and singling out judicial review as the central institution that maintains those restrictions over time. However, while the normative literature has tended to focus on whether polities *ought* to bind themselves and their heirs through constitutions, the empirical literature has asked why those in power actually agree to it. Why would any regime with enough political power to shape a constitution ever want to impose constitutional limitations on the exercise of that power?

Much of the empirical literature has converged on a single answer to these questions: entrenchment. Broadly speaking, the core of the entrenchment thesis is that political actors pursue constitution-writing in order to fortify and ingrain their preferred policies against a downturn in their

---

commitments and to honor those commitments over time . . . It was and is America's most innovative, most radical, and most influential contribution to the theory and practice of self-government." Jed Rubenfeld, "Moment and the Millennium," *George Washingtom Law Review* 66, no. 5/6 (1998): 1105. Others have expressed the opposite conviction. Most famously, perhaps, Thomas Jefferson believed that one generation had no moral right to bind the next. For example, he wrote: " . . . it may be proved that no society can make a perpetual constitution, or even a perpetual law. The earth belongs always to the living generation. They may manage it then, and what proceeds from it, as they please, during their usufruct. They are masters too of their own persons, and consequently may govern them as they please. But persons and property make the sum of the objects of government. The constitution and the laws of their predecessors extinguished them, in their natural course, with those whose will gave them being. This could preserve that being till it ceased to be itself, and no longer. Every constitution, then, and every law, naturally expires at the end of 19 years. If it be enforced longer, it is an act of force and not of right." Letter from Thomas Jefferson to James Madison, Sept. 6, 1789, Paul Leicester Ford, ed., *The Works of Thomas Jefferson*, vol. 6 (New York, London: G. P. Putnam's Sons, 1904).

[5] Joseph Raz, "Intension in Interpretation," in *The Autonomy of Law: Essays on Legal Positivism*, ed. Robert P. George (Oxford: Oxford University Press, 1996); Randy Barnett, "An Originalism for Nonoriginalists," *Loyola Law Review* 45, no. 4 (1999); R. M. Dworkin, *Taking Rights Seriously* (Cambridge, MA: Harvard University Press, 1977); Keith E. Whittington, *Constitutional Interpretation: Textual Meaning, Original Intent, and Judicial Review* (Lawrence: University Press of Kansas, 1999).

[6] Russell Hardin, *Liberalism, Constitutionalism, and Democracy* (Oxford: Oxford University Press, 1999). Jeremy Waldron, *Law and Disagreement* (Oxford: Oxford University Press, 2001), 122–3.

political fortunes. Entrenchment has now become so closely associated with the idea of constitutionalism that some scholars have even begun to assert that all entrenched policies, even those without obvious ties to any constitutional document or doctrine, attain constitutional or "near-constitutional" status by virtue of their entrenchment alone.[7] These kinds of assertions illustrate how tightly entwined scholarly ideas about constitutionalism and entrenchment have become.

The Central Insights of Entrenchment Theories

There are several different versions of entrenchment theory, but all of them explain what ruling elites hope to gain by creating constitutions. One version of the entrenchment story is that regimes agree to adopt constitutional restraints when members of their own coalition force them to do it, in order to entrench the terms of a political bargain between them. England's Glorious Revolution has become the classic example of this phenomenon.[8] Before the Glorious Revolution, the monarchy financed its government in part through "forced loans" from its nobles. Unsurprisingly, this was not a popular system among the nobles, particularly because monarchs repaid their loans only sporadically, often altering the terms of their original agreements. Even less popular was the Crown's custom of simply seizing the goods it required. These practices (among others) provoked a revolution, which resulted in the overthrow of James II. The monarchy was subsequently reestablished, but only on the condition that it did not resort to its previous system of raising revenue. The monarchy was left with little choice but to accept these limitations on its power, and this bargain between the nobles and the Crown was effectively constitutionalized when it became an enduring and fundamental principle of British law.[9] Thus, one solution to the puzzle of why those in power would bind themselves through a constitution is simply that their continued rule depends upon it.

The presence of independent courts that could prevent the government from reneging on its agreements conferred further credibility on the Crown's promises. By enshrining their bargain in a constitution, Douglass North and Barry Weingast have argued that the triggers for defection from the ruling coalition were rendered explicit, and the sovereign's incentives to honor its commitments were consequently rendered more credible, especially in the presence of an independent judiciary capable of enforcing them. Thus, this

[7] William Eskridge and John Ferejohn, "Super-Statutes," *Duke Law Journal* 50, no. 5 (2001).

[8] Douglass C. North and Barry R. Weingast, "Constitutions and Commitment: The Evolution of Institutional Governing Public Choice in Seventeenth-Century England," *Journal of Economic History* 49, no. 4 (1989).

[9] Ibid.

constitution's function was to entrench a policy bargain in order to maintain a ruling coalition. This example demonstrates the broader principle that constitutional entrenchment, facilitated by courts, allows ruling regimes to maintain the coalitions that keep them in power.

A second answer to the question of why ruling regimes agree to adopt constitutional restraints is that they adopt constitutions because they believe they are unlikely to remain in power. While they are not hoping to entrench themselves, these regimes nonetheless use constitutions to entrench their preferences. In this scenario, ruling elites establish constitutions in attempts to safeguard the policies they have already established against the threat of a new elite's ascendance. The logic of this strategy is that policies embedded in the constitution can be defended by courts even after the law-makers who wrote them are no longer in power. Ran Hirschl's work on the development of four different national constitutions demonstrates that the adoption of constitutional rights in these countries has been motivated by elites' desires to shift particular political conflicts into the judiciary, with the hope that the judiciary will insulate their political preferences against those of changing electoral majorities. In Hirschl's view, legal and political elites cooperate in their construction of rights to maintain their hegemony by hindering new legislative majorities in their attempts to reverse existing policies.[10] Here again, constitutional development is explained with reference to constitutions' capacity to entrench policies through judicial enforcement.

Given the entrenchment strategy outlined above, it is not terribly surprising that ruling coalitions not only create constitutions that will allow sympathetic courts to defend their favorite policies, but also strive to leave courts even more sympathetic than when they found them. Conveniently, regimes can render courts more sympathetic to their policies simply by appointing like-minded justices. In the United States, for example, political parties have routinely used the Supreme Court appointments process to safeguard their preferred policies by attempting to appoint ideologically friendly justices. Parties hope that their appointees will shape constitutional doctrine in ways that will protect the policies they favor from legislative tinkering, and that justices will continue to defend policies in this way, even when their appointing party no longer controls the legislature. This explanation for constitutional development is often described as "partisan entrenchment."[11]

Clearly, only a court that is relatively independent of the other political branches will be able to defend the policies of a defunct regime from the

---

[10] Ran Hirschl, *Towards Juristocracy: The Origins and Consequences of the New Constitutionalism* (Cambridge, MA: Harvard University Press, 2004).

[11] Howard Gillman, "How Political Parties Can Use the Courts to Advance Their Agendas: Federal Courts in the United States, 1875–1891," *American Political Science Review* 96, no. 3 (2002); Jack Balkin and Sanford Levinson, "Understanding the Constitutional Revolution," *Virginia Law Review* 87, no. 6 (2001).

policymaking efforts of a new one. Consequently, studies of entrenchment have become closely entwined with research about the creation of strong constitutional courts. Much of the recent work on constitutional emergence and change has begun to focus primarily on explaining the development of strong, independent judiciaries, capable of exercising judicial review.[12] Thus, recent versions of entrenchment theory have converged on the view that constitutions, and the rights they contain, are legislative (and executive) creations, targeted at limiting the policy choices of subsequent partisan regimes by enhancing the power of courts to intervene in particular areas of policymaking. Entrenchment and judicialization have become so closely associated with one another that little of the recent literature bothers to distinguish between them.

As we have seen, then, the empirical literature on constitutional development currently offers two answers to the question of why those in power would agree to bind themselves through a constitution:

1. Existing regimes (at the behest of coalition members) establish constitutions or seek constitutional change in order to demonstrate the credibility of their own commitments through a written (and judicially enforceable) agreement.
2. Legislatures (perhaps united with the executive branch) establish constitutions or seek constitutional change to enable the judiciary to hamper future regimes' efforts to reverse existing policies.

Both explanations describe constitutional development as the result of a dominant regime's willingness or desire to entrench existing policy, and both emphasize the role of judicial enforcement in carrying out this entrenchment project.

Existing entrenchment theories emerged from studies of national constitutions. However, several of their insights also help to explain instances of development of the United States' state constitutions. As we will see, environmental and educational activists in the late twentieth century drafted and lobbied for constitutional provisions precisely in order to judicialize these policy areas, hoping that litigation would protect and even extend their preferred policies. In addition, legislative majorities sometimes drafted constitutions explicitly out of concern that they might be replaced. One paradigmatic example of a legislative majority seeking constitutional change in order to guard its preferred policies from future majorities is the drafting of Reconstruction constitutions of the former Confederate states. When

[12] Kevin J. McMahon, *Reconsidering Roosevelt on Race: How the Presidency Paved the Road to Brown* (Chicago: University of Chicago Press, 2004); Tom Ginsburg, *Judicial Review in New Democracies: Constitutional Courts in Asian Cases* (Cambridge: Cambridge University Press, 2003); Keith E. Whittington, *Political Foundations of Judicial Supremacy: The Presidency, the Supreme Court, and Constitutional Leadership in U.S. History*, Princeton Studies in American Politics (Princeton, NJ: Princeton University Press, 2007).

Unionists were able to take power in these states, one of the many policy changes they effected was to establish education rights for black citizens. These constitution writers knew that if their opponents were able to regain power, those policies would be one of their earliest targets. Francis Cardozo, a black educator and delegate at the South Carolina constitutional convention of 1868, actually articulated the express belief that the convention should use the constitution for entrenchment, arguing for a constitutional provision this way: "I do desire we shall use the opportunities we now have to our best advantage, as we may never have a more propitious time . . . We know that when the old aristocracy and ruling power of this state get into power, as they undoubtedly will, they will never pass such a law as this."[13] This explicit statement of a constitution drafter's desire to entrench particular policies against the efforts of incoming regimes illustrates the major claim of partisan entrenchment theories. Congress too used its power over territories applying for statehood to entrench its preferred policies through state constitutional guarantees. However, the study of state constitutional development not only confirms the value of entrenchment theories, it also demonstrates that entrenchment theories alone do not do an adequate job of explaining all instances of and motivations for constitutional drafting and revision.

ADDITIONAL EXPLANATIONS FOR CONSTITUTIONAL DEVELOPMENT

Despite their considerable value, the existing accounts of the motivations for constitutional development are incomplete. They explain constitutional changes with reference to ruling coalitions' desire to forestall political change, and their attempts to involve the judiciary in policymaking. But what about the nineteenth-century common school activists who couldn't get the state legislature to levy taxes for the support of public schools, or the twentieth-century environmental activists who wanted the state to do a better job of fighting pollution? These groups were deeply troubled by the status quo, and were devoted to changing rather than entrenching it. Furthermore, labor organizations of the Gilded Age and Progressive Era had nothing but trouble with courts, and were vehement that judges should do less, not more, policymaking. It would seem that existing theories of constitutional development are unable to explain why any of these groups would pursue the creation of new constitutional rights, and yet we know that they did. By studying their motives, we can develop new accounts of the actors who write constitutions and the reasons that they do it.

[13] Quoted in David B. Tyack, Thomas James, and Aaron Benavot, *Law and the Shaping of Public Education, 1785–1954* (Madison: University of Wisconsin Press, 1987), 133.

Through this study of the origins of positive rights in state constitutions, I offer three additional explanations for the creation of new constitutional provisions. They are:

1. Legislatures (or those that support their policies) alter constitutions to exclude hostile courts from particular policy battles.
2. Interest groups (within or outside the legislature) pursue constitutional change as a tool of political organizing.
3. Interest groups outside the legislature pursue constitutional change in order to motivate legislatures to pass their preferred policies.

I describe each of these scenarios in further detail below.

First, constitutions have been shaped by legislative majorities' attempts to limit the influence of courts over particular policy issues. At the beginning of the twentieth century, for instance, New York's highest court determined that legislation creating an eight-hour workday was unconstitutional, and labor organizations responded by placing the right to an eight-hour day directly in the state constitution. In some cases, legislatures amended constitutions even before establishing controversial policies in order to ensure that courts would not invalidate the legislation they were about to pass. During the Progressive Era, the Vermont legislature, for example, was so concerned about whether the judiciary would declare a proposed workmen's compensation law unconstitutional, that it sought a constitutional amendment on the subject before even passing the law. These instances of constitutional change stemmed from the desire of legislative majorities to ensure that courts would be unable to undo the work of legislatures, and that legislatures would remain in control of policymaking.

Second, activists and interest groups also sought constitutional change in order to enhance the credibility of their movements and to facilitate their efforts at political organizing. Michael McCann has termed this phenomenon "movement building." In his study of the way that rights claims empower their bearers, McCann notes that rights may facilitate the process of "raising citizen expectations regarding political change, activating potential constituents, building group alliances, and organizing resources for tactical action."[14] After positive rights were placed in constitutions, the groups that added them often claimed these constitutional provisions as huge victories, publicizing them to their own members and crediting their own activism. The organizations that pursued constitutional changes often characterized these changes as evidence that the citizens of the state had finally accepted the truth of their message and/or employed new constitutional provisions as banners around which to organize a new surge of legislative lobbying. When Maryland held a constitutional convention in 1967, for example, environ-

---

[14] Michael W. McCann, *Rights at Work : Pay Equity Reform and the Politics of Legal Mobilization, Language and Legal Discourse* (Chicago: University of Chicago Press, 1994), 11.

mental organizations requested a constitutional provision in part to "stimulate and help integrate their efforts."[15] And when Massachusetts ratified an environmental provision in its constitution, it claimed the provision as its own victory, declaring that "After a long and involved fight led by the Massachusetts Forest and Park Association, legislative arm of the conservation movement, the voters of the commonwealth [had] won the right to have a say on their right to clean air and water."[16]

Third, not only were these constitutional provisions passed for purposes of organizing within political movements, they were also passed with the hope that they would actually motivate legislatures to heed the movements' demands. Thus, many of the positive rights in state constitutions were not created by legislatures with the hope of controlling lawmakers of the future. Instead, these constitutional provisions were promoted by legislative outsiders, and aimed at motivating the existing legislature. Proponents of active state intervention or regulation often attempted to realize their policy visions by extracting appropriate statutes from legislatures. When this failed, they turned to constitutions to mandate legislative action through higher law. In Ohio, for example, the state's public school advocates were so frustrated with the state legislature's history of inaction by the middle of the nineteenth century that they decided to use the state's constitutional convention of 1850 to mandate the creation of a statewide public school system.[17] Similarly, in states drafting their first constitutions, interest groups used constitutions to direct the legislatures' initial policy steps in the hope that it would see its legislative agenda adopted promptly upon the attainment of statehood. Some new constitutions even directed the legislature to take certain steps within its first legislative session, or within a particular number of years after the constitution's adoption. For instance, the North Dakota Constitution of 1889 §148 read, "The legislative assembly shall provide at their first session after the adoption of this constitution, for a uniform system for free public schools throughout the state."

These additional accounts of constitutional change differ from existing entrenchment theories in several important and overlapping ways. First, they do not explain constitutional development primarily as the consequence of someone's effort to render a policy more stable over time. Second, they allow for the possibility that constitutional change may originate outside the legislature. Third, they suggest that constitutional change is not always intended to usher the judiciary into policymaking.

---

[15] Maryland Constitutional Convention of 1967, *Proceedings and Debates of the 1967 Constitutional Convention*, vol. 104, Archives of Maryland (Maryland State Archives, 2000), 759.

[16] " Bill of Rights on 1972 Ballot: Citizens to Vote on Clean Air and Water," *Forest & Park News* 25, no. 2, Boston (Spring 1971): 1.

[17] Molly O'Brien and Amanda Woodrum, "The Constitutional Common School," *Cleveland State Law Review* 51, no. 3 & 4 (2004): 612.

These additional accounts of constitutional development also augment entrenchment theory by demonstrating that constitutional changes are not always motivated by a desire to maintain the status quo. Entrenchment theories (particularly Hirschl's) characterize rights as inherently conservative and predict that new rights are likely to emerge only at the tail end of a political shift or conflict. By attending to the origins of positive rights in state constitutions, we learn that reformers targeted state constitutions because of their potential to force legislatures to establish new state policies, not simply to entrench existing ones. Because state constitutional changes could, and often did, emerge from institutions other than legislatures, many of these changes were targeted not at future legislators, who might strive to depart from the status quo, but at existing ones, who refused to. Thus, these instances of constitutional change were not attempts at hegemonic preservation, but often reflected the efforts of relative outsiders to demand immediate change from their legislatures.

Of course, it is important to note that many relative outsiders have made arguments about constitutional rights as a way to demand political change. These movements to shape the evolving political meaning of the federal constitutional rights have received a great deal of scholarly attention, as has the power of constitutional discourse and rights rhetoric to legitimate political movements' demands for change.[18] Throughout American history, reformers and subjugated groups have famously, and sometimes very successfully, described their goal as the vindication of the Constitution's true meaning. Both inside and outside of courts, reform movements have employed a rhetoric of constitutional rights to demand inclusion, drawing together phrases from the Declaration of Independence, the Bill of Rights, and the Reconstruction Amendments of the Federal Constitution in order to legitimate their claims to equal membership in a free, capable, and empowered citizenry. Dirk Hartog has termed this reading and use of the Constitution "the constitution of aspiration and struggle," and has noted that these aspirational rights movements have drawn from diverse sources beyond the American legal tradition in order to imbue the existing document with new meanings.[19]

What is so interesting about the rights movements this book describes is not simply that they were characterized by aspiration and struggle, but that they were working for the adoption of new constitutional texts, rather than the reinterpretation of existing ones. They were not (or not only) employing the rhetoric or idea of rights to argue for new understandings of the government's obligations, but actually writing new textual mandates into constitu-

---

[18] Charles R. Epp, *The Rights Revolution: Lawyers, Activists, and Supreme Courts in Comparative Perspective* (Chicago: University of Chicago Press, 1998); Scheingold, *The Politics of Rights: Lawyers, Public Policy, and Political Change.*

[19] Hendrik Hartog, "The Constitution of Aspiration and 'the Rights That Belong to Us All'," *Journal of American History* 74 (1987).

tions. As we have seen, the creation of new, binding constraints on government (particularly new textual provisions) is typically understood as a bulwark against reform. State-level movements to adopt new constitutional provisions demonstrate that this is not always the case.

INSTITUTIONAL STRUCTURES AND CONSTITUTIONAL CHANGE

The non-entrenchment explanations for constitutional development presented here have not emerged from studies of the federal Constitution. They originate from this examination of state constitutions because state constitutions have been revised through different mechanisms than their federal counterpart, and this different institutional structure has given rise to different kinds of rights politics. As we have seen, state constitutions are often easier to amend than the U.S. Constitution, and many can be altered directly through popular referendum. Therefore, the revision procedures in state constitutions made it possible for frustrated outsiders, not only dominant legislative coalitions, to influence the content of constitutions. Yet this assertion about the power of outsiders to influence state constitutions raises several questions. First, how was it possible for citizen groups to influence the text of state constitutions when they were unable to make even legislative change?

Constitutional change was possible under these circumstances because the mechanisms of state constitutional change were often different from those of statutory change. One mechanism that allowed activist groups to direct lawmakers through constitutional changes was the constitutional convention. These conventions were almost always elected separately from legislatures, and were consequently often characterized by different membership.[20] Another clear example is the initiative and referendum process, which allowed activist groups to circumvent the legislature by seeking only popular support for a particular constitutional provision. In the face of recalcitrant legislatures, this mechanism of constitutional change made it possible to establish policy mandates for lawmakers without needing to win their consent. As chapter 6 demonstrates, this feature was particularly important to labor organizations of the Gilded Age and Progressive Era, who believed that state legislatures had been corrupted by corporate influence, and would therefore never legislate in the interests of labor. Thus, along with

[20] The constitutional conventions held in Southern states during Reconstruction provide the most vivid example of this phenomenon. These conventions were often composed of Northern reformers as well as freed slaves, and they produced constitutions with elaborate provisions about state-financed schooling, where education had previously been treated as a private responsibility. David B. Tyack and Robert Lowe, "The Constitutional Moment: Reconstruction and Black Education in the South," *American Journal of Education* 94, no. 2 (1986).

their substantive demands for positive rights, labor organizations often lobbied to add this means of circumventing the legislature directly to their constitutions.[21]

The fact that activist groups used constitutions to demand action from legislatures highlights a second, important difference between the processes of state and federal constitutional change and raises a second question about the reasons relative outsiders to the legislative process sought constitutional change. Before the second half of the twentieth century, the activists and constitutional convention delegates this book describes placed little emphasis on whether their rights provisions would be enforced by the judiciary. Until the late twentieth century, most proponents of positive constitutional rights gave very little thought to the possibility of enforcing these rights through litigation. Of course this assertion must prompt us to ask how, in the absence of judicial enforcement, any political actors could have seriously believed that legislatures would heed the constitutional mandates they put in place. The answer is that, instead of relying on judges, many activist groups planned to enforce their newly adopted constitutional mandates themselves. Because these constitutional provisions were ratified through statewide elections, and particularly when they passed by large margins, activists could point to constitutional provisions as evidence of electoral support for particular policies in order to motivate legislatures to act. Recalling the plebiscites that had just occurred, positive rights' advocates admonished legislators that, not only were they legally obligated to take particular kinds of action, but that their electoral fortunes very likely depended on it.[22] In this way, the institutional structure of state constitutional change enabled activist groups to render constitutional rights politically effective, even in the absence of litigation.

A second strategy for enhancing the efficacy of positive constitutional mandates was to craft extremely detailed provisions, mandating that legislatures enact specific policies. Such provisions were intended to be so clear and directive that they would be embarrassing for legislatures to ignore. Many included precise policy prescriptions, including things like the number of hours in a legal workday or the tax structure through which public schools would be financed. Constitutional conventions' debates and activists' publications are replete with declarations that legislators must swear to uphold the constitution, and would therefore be forced to carry out the

---

[21] Delos F. Wilcox, *Government by All the People; or, the Initiative, the Referendum, and the Recall as Instruments of Democracy* (New York: The Macmillan Company, 1912).

[22] This mode of enforcing rights may be particularly applicable to positive rights, which require the legislature to pass laws and establish new institutions. It may be more important to have judicial help enforcing limitations on government's scope (i.e., negative rights) through the nullification of laws. What is clear, however, is that proponents of positive constitutional rights believed that these provisions would facilitate their quest for active, interventionist legislation, even in the absence of judicial enforcement.

unambiguous instructions now embedded within it.[23] Since it is unlikely that so detailed a policy will remain optimal for very long periods, it only makes sense to include such details in a constitution if it is possible to change the constitution fairly frequently. Thus, the relative ease of amending state constitutions and the norms that allowed for frequent amendments made this enforcement strategy (and path to constitutional development) more viable at the state than the federal level.

MUST CONSTITUTIONS BE STABLE OVER TIME?

So far, I have described constitutions that are both highly responsive to public pressures and exceedingly detailed. Both features reflect the fact that state constitutions are fairly malleable, especially compared with the federal document. This trait will, of course, remind many that state constitutions do not seem to be sufficiently constitutional. In chapter 2, I argued that their detail created this impression, but state constitutions are also widely disparaged because of how frequently they change. This objection stems, in part, from the now-familiar view that the true (or perhaps primary) purpose of constitutions is to entrench particular policies over long time horizons. Yet, I suggest that we should view state constitutions' responsiveness to social change as a feature that allows us to expand the existing understanding of constitutional development.

The story of state constitutional rights demonstrates that people pursue constitutional change for purposes other than the long-term entrenchment of their favorite policies. In fact, activists hoped that constitutions would enable them to do political work that would have been impossible through statutory law. For instance, only constitutional changes can legally reverse the rulings of high courts when they have nullified statutes on constitutional grounds. Statutes are largely powerless to combat high court rulings, and even if constitutions change very frequently, they can still serve this purpose. Unlike statutes, constitutions govern all of the political branches simultaneously, determining which institutions can influence particular areas of policymaking. While the entrenchment literature has focused on constitutions' ability to judicialize conflicts, state constitutional development demonstrates that constitutions have also been used to un-judicialize them, and to seat control over particular policy areas firmly in the legislature. Similarly, even

[23] For instance, an education advocate in Indiana explained: "The Constitutional injunction is direct, positive, immediate, and coming with the authority and sanction of an immense majority of the people." Thus, he concluded that "The question of free schools is no longer a question in Indiana . . . It is the sworn duty of the Legislature to carry out this great provision in the Constitution." Daniel Read, *Address on the Means of Promoting Common School Education: Delivered in the Hall of the House of Representatives, at Indianapolis, on the Evening of Dec. 30, 1851* (Indianapolis: The House of Representatives. J.P. Chapman, State Printer, 1852), 7.

highly changeable constitutions can mandate that legislatures pass statutes, and can thereby help lobbyists to make their demands more powerful. Because statutes must come from within legislatures, statutory law cannot be used to direct legislatures in the way that constitutional law can. Finally, constitutions have greater symbolic value than statutes, and political organizers strove to translate that symbolic value into larger, more influential, and more energized movements. The fact that state constitutions changed frequently did not stop activists from announcing that the positive-rights provisions for which they had worked amounted to major political victories and represented the true voice of the people. All of these political roles are uniquely constitutional. Despite their changeable nature, then, it is clear that state constitutions are not simply glorified statutes. They perform several political functions of which statutes are simply not capable.

One might be willing to concede that state constitutions are genuine constitutions but nonetheless remain tempted to conclude that, because of their changeable nature, state constitutions are still less constitutional than the federal version. Yet this conclusion is premised on the highly problematic assumption that the federal Constitution is, itself, stable over time. While the text of the Constitution has changed little, its agreed-upon meaning (at least as it relates to specific conceptions of which practices it allows and disallows) has changed dramatically over time.[24] Some may argue that such change is normatively illegitimate. However, few would object to the empirical claim that the federal Constitution is now widely understood to mean very different things than it once did.

The federal Constitution is vulnerable to change in a number of ways. First, political actors can and have constructed the meaning of formerly vague or indeterminate pieces of the Constitution, creating constitutional meaning where none existed before.[25] Not only do formerly un-interpreted pieces of constitution take on meaning in the context of political conflict, but agreed-upon meanings also change in the face of new controversies. For instance, the political projects of Progressives, New Dealers, and Civil Rights leaders rendered the meaning of the Bill of Rights almost unrecognizably different from previous understandings.[26] What's more, as any student of case law can attest, constitutional changes are not all, or even primarily, about broad sweeping statements of fundamental values, but instead are brought into being through the explication of specific pieces of text as they relate to the mundane details of particular cases. Thus, the existence of ongoing and detailed constitutional change is widely recognized at the federal level.

[24] Griffin, *American Constitutionalism: From Theory to Politics*.

[25] Whittington, *Constitutional Construction: Divided Powers and Constitutional Meaning*.

[26] On the point see: Akhil Reed Amar, *The Bill of Rights: Creation and Reconstruction* (New Haven: Yale University Press, 1998); Ackerman, *We the People: Transformations*; Kersch, *Constructing Civil Liberties: Discontinuities in the Development of American Constitutional Law*.

Whether we focus on changes in political doctrine or on politics beyond the bench, it is quite clear that the U.S. Constitution is not said to entrench because it is unchangeable, but because it is harder to change than statutory law. Stability seems like an important feature of constitutionalism not because the federal Constitution never changes, but because it is more difficult to change than are federal statutes. Yet, state constitutions are also harder to change than state statutes. While the procedures for constitutional change have varied over time and across states, almost all states require that a statewide plebiscite ratify a new constitution or new constitutional provision. Statutes, by contrast, are passed simply by a majority vote of the legislature. Many states also require that two successive legislatures pass a constitutional amendment before a statewide referendum can be called, and some states require passage of constitutional amendments by a legislative supermajority. While their extensive detail may appear to make state constitutional provisions just as changeable as statutes, the procedures necessary to make formal changes are, in general, patently more demanding.

Furthermore, it is only when we compare the number of textual changes to the federal and state constitutions that state constitutions appear more fickle and concerned with more mundane detail. When we recognize the myriad informal changes to which the federal Constitution has been subject, the contrast in stability between the state and federal constitutions appears far less stark. As an empirical matter, the meaning of both the federal and state constitutions has changed with their changing political, economic, and social context.

In fact, even entrenchment theories, themselves, do not presume a constitution that can withstand changes for more than a matter of decades. As Robert Dahl has famously noted, a party or coalition that has entrenched its policies through a carefully selected court can expect that court to defend its policy preferences once it is out of power only until the new regime is able to appoint its own justices.[27] Certainly, then, more independent judiciaries will have a greater capacity for entrenchment, but even justices with life-tenure must eventually be replaced. Thus, even entrenchment theorists do not a view a constitution's malleability as an obstacle to its constitutionality.[28]

[27] Dahl, "Decision-Making in a Democracy: The Supreme Court as a National Policy-Maker."

[28] To be sure, some instances of constitutional drafting and change have been aimed at entrenching policies not just for a single generation, but forever. Such projects are often characterized by their goal of protecting the polity for all time from repeating a particularly egregious outcome. The guiding principle of this aversive constitutional drafting is often expressed by statements like "we will never allow that to happen again" or "we will never allow that to happen here." See Kim Lane Scheppele, "Aspirational and Aversive Constitutionalism: The Case for Studying Cross-Constitutional Influences through the Negative Model," *International Journal of Constitutional Law* 1, no. 2 (2003). A relatively high degree of constitutional stability does seem necessary if a constitution is to achieve this function. But it is even possible that a flexible constitution could set a government down a policy path from which deviation would become

Like many of their counterparts at the federal level, those who have labored to change state constitutions hoped that the provisions they enacted
would be lasting and politically meaningful despite the fact that the constitutions they sought to influence were undoubtedly subject to further revision. Part of the reason they did this was because state constitutions were,
despite their flexibility, still harder to change than their other lawmaking
option—statutes. But part of the reason they hoped these changes would be
politically meaningful, despite the fact that constitutions change, is that constitutions serve functions other than establishing a single, stable policy over
a long period. Because they structure the political system as a whole, constitutions can invite some branches of government into particular areas of
policymaking while simultaneously pushing others to the margins. This at-
tribute allows them to serve the judicialization function that entrenchment
theorists describe, but it allows constitutions to serve other functions as
well. Constitutional provisions can also de-judicialize particular conflicts.
Not only have constitutions been shaped by popular and legislative efforts
to remove policy questions from the judicial sphere (as labor organizations
generally intended), they have also been subject to popular efforts to force
policy questions onto the legislative agenda (as all three of the book's case
studies demonstrate). While many proponents of positive rights certainly
hoped that state governments would be forever forced to take action in
order to realize those rights, a constitution's agenda-setting capacity is also
independent of whether its meaning remains static. Thus, the relative rigidity of constitutional law is only one of its many attributes that cause people
to seek constitutional changes. By ignoring the others, we risk overlooking
several additional (and fundamentally different) routes to constitutional
development.

Constitutions' entrenchment capacity clearly raises interesting normative
and empirical questions, and just as clearly, these questions have received
significant scholarly attention. The resulting body of literature might well
lead one to believe that constitutions' only salient feature is their ability to
entrench, and that this feature alone explains why people write constitutions and seek to change them. However, constitutional law is also unique in
several other ways, each of which can also help to explain constitutional
development. By focusing on the immediate political problems that constitutions have been used to solve (rather than the long-term plans of their
authors), it becomes possible to disentangle the concepts of constitutionalism, entrenchment, and judicial review. Indeed, it is not only possible, but
also useful, to distinguish the practice of constitutional drafting or change

---

difficult, even if the constitution itself could subsequently change. Thus, even flexible constitutions might be useful to ensure that some horrible outcome will never occur. However, aversive
constitutionalism is only one mode of constitutional development, and is not necessarily the
primary one. As we have seen, constitutions have many other unique functions that do not require permanence over time.

from the desire to entrench existing policy because it allows us to recognize constitutional movements that are not aimed at long-term entrenchment or the judicialization of politics. As the case studies in this book will illustrate, entrenchment is not the only function constitutions can serve, and constitutional development may be driven by political actors seeking to exploit other properties of constitutional law.

Beyond Hegemons and Constraints

The strategic calculations of those in power play an important role in the development of constitutions that change mostly by way of judicial doctrine. Consequently, studies of such constitutions will almost certainly highlight the governing institutions that are responsible for appointing new judges, the parties that control those institutions, and the networks of lawyers that promoted new interpretations.[29] Because so many studies have focused on the U.S. Constitution and other national constitutions that change in similar ways, we know a great deal about elites' motivations and their roles in pursuing constitutional development. Ran Hirschl has even named his explanation for the origins of constitutional rights the "hegemonic preservation theory." As we have seen, however, elites have garnered such a prominent place in existing theories because these theories were built on observations of constitutional change through judicial decision-making.

State constitutions have evolved through textual revision as much if not more than through judicial doctrine. As a result, the study of state constitutions allows us to look beyond hegemons in our search for the origins of new rights, and to recognize that successful political parties are not the only ones that shape constitutions in order to advance their policy preferences. Given the right institutional structures, relative outsiders to the political process can also shape constitutions. For instance, when labor organizations found themselves thwarted by the courts, constitutions helped them shift policymaking power back into the legislatures. Similarly, when the common school movement found that legislatures were reluctant to establish or pay for public schools, they attempted to mandate this form of legislative action through constitutional provisions. These groups were certainly not the most marginalized members of society, but neither were they operating from centers of state power. Instead of using constitutions in attempts to maintain their hegemony, they used this form of law to speak to

---

[29] Gillman, "How Political Parties Can Use the Courts to Advance Their Agendas: Federal Courts in the United States, 1875–1891"; Balkin and Levinson, "Understanding the Constitutional Revolution"; Ginsburg, *Judicial Review in New Democracies: Constitutional Courts in Asian Cases*; Whittington, *Political Foundations of Judicial Supremacy: The Presidency, the Supreme Court, and Constitutional Leadership in U.S. History*; Epp, *The Rights Revolution: Lawyers, Activists, and Supreme Courts in Comparative Perspective*, 43.

their governments, demanding major changes in public policy through changes in state constitutions.

The study of state constitutional politics also points to a richer view of constitutions than simply constraints on political power. The movement leaders who decided to pursue political change through constitutional amendment certainly intended to limit government's choices through constitutions, but that was not their only goal. They also used constitutions to express their aspirations for change, to signal their political efficacy both to legislatures and to their own members, and to declare their equal membership in the political community. This is not to say that the positive rights they created are or were merely symbolic. On the contrary, the proponents of positive rights recognized the multiple roles of constitutional documents. At the same time that they sought to constrain legislatures and courts through clear and detailed mandates, these movements hoped that new constitutional texts would convince their members that their organizations were politically effective. Constitutional mandates for particular policies, ratified through a concrete demonstration of electoral strength, emboldened citizen groups to make even more forceful claims that they were entitled to the state's protection. Positive rights constrained government's discretion, while liberating activists to demand an expansion in government's scope.

The next three chapters describe sophisticated campaigns to add education rights (chapter 5), labor rights (chapter 6), and environmental rights (chapter 7) to state constitutions. Although each chapter examines a different kind of right, each makes the same two arguments about American constitutional development. The first is that, contrary to the conventional wisdom, Americans have successfully secured positive constitutional rights. The second is that there is more to the story of where rights come from than hegemons' attempts to entrench the status quo.

Education

A LONG TRADITION OF
POSITIVE RIGHTS IN AMERICA

It is the child's right to be educated; and it is not only his right
but it is our indispensable duty to provide for the education of
every child in the state.
Common School Advocate, 1847[1]

The Supreme Court has ruled unequivocally that "Education, of course,
is not among the rights afforded explicit protection under our Federal
Constitution."[2] States, however, have always played a far larger role than the
federal government in the provision of public education, and it is state constitutions that contain explicit education rights. In fact, every state constitution currently contains at least one constitutional provision regarding public
education. The Massachusetts constitution required the state to promote
education nearly a decade before the U.S. Constitution was drafted.[3] As
state governments built public school systems over the course of the nineteenth century, the organizations that promoted a robust public role in education directed their reform efforts at state law and state constitutions. As a
result, since the middle of the nineteenth century, many constitutions have
required that states establish and maintain free, public schools.

This chapter examines the origins of the education rights in state constitutions. In doing so, it makes two primary arguments. First, it establishes
that these provisions were positive rights. Next, it argues that the origins of

---

[1] "Editorial," *Common School Advocate*, 1847, Indianapolis, vol. 1, no. 7, 98.

[2] *San Antonio Independent School Dis. v. Rodriguez*, 411 U.S. 1 (1973).

[3] The earliest example of a state provision mentioning education was the Massachusetts
provision in the state's constitution of 1780. It began: "Wisdom, and knowledge, as well as
virtue, diffused generally among the body of the people, being necessary for the preservation of
their rights and liberties; and as these depend on spreading the opportunities and advantages of
education in the various parts of the country, and among the different orders of the people, it
shall be the duty of legislatures and magistrates, in all future periods of this commonwealth, to
cherish the interests of literature and the sciences, and all seminaries of them; especially the
university at Cambridge, public schools and grammar schools in the towns." Four years later,
this provision was copied almost verbatim into New Hampshire's constitution.

these education rights were often quite different from the ones that conventional theories about rights' origins would predict. To be sure, one reason that states added education rights to their constitutions was to satisfy Congress, and this motive does fit within the conventional, entrenchment, paradigm. However, these popular movements for positive rights have not typically conformed to existing theories about why people write and revise constitutions. Thus, after discussing the entrenchment of congressional preferences, I describe political motives for the creation of constitutional rights that are quite different from the desire to entrench the status quo. In particular, I focus on common school reformers' efforts to force the hand of the legislature through the creation of constitutional rights related to both school lands and school taxes. I then explain how reformers hoped to enforce these provisions even without recourse to courts. Next, I demonstrate that at least one of the constitutional education rights drafted during the nineteenth century was even created to keep courts out of the policymaking process. Finally, I describe the efforts of activists in the mid- to late-twentieth century to enable litigation through the drafting of new education rights. I conclude with a discussion of twentieth-century courts' willingness to enforce both new and old education rights and with the argument that we should not allow the detailed and relatively mundane phrasing of these rights to obscure their quintessentially right-like features or their place in our constitutional tradition.

EDUCATION PROVISIONS AS POSITIVE RIGHTS

It is important to note that few state constitutions actually use the phrase "the right to education."[4] Instead, state constitutions contain instructions, often in great detail, to state legislatures about education. One of the most common types of educational provisions is a mandate that the legislature establish free common schools. Some state constitutions also required legislatures to preserve and actively manage their school funds. Still other constitutional provisions obligated state governments to finance schools through particular forms of taxation and appropriation. All of these provisions are properly understood as positive rights. In order to recognize them as rights, however, it is helpful to understand the political circumstances under which they were added to constitutions.

The movement to add these provisions to state constitutions emerged in a political context that is difficult to imagine today. At the beginning of the nineteenth century, the entire concept of statewide and state-sponsored education was highly controversial. Simply bringing public school systems into existence was an enormous political challenge, one to which a group of

---

[4] Article 1 § 27 of the North Carolina Constitution of 1868 is the exception to this rule. It stated, "The people have a right to the privilege of education, and it is the duty of the State to guard and maintain that right."

nineteenth-century activists dedicated itself. These reformers often referred to themselves as "friends of education," and frequently dubbed their organizations "teachers' unions." Such organizations appeared in every existing state shortly before the Civil War.[5] They were primarily occupied with bringing public, or "common," school systems into being, and their movement for reform was consequently known as the common school movement. As school systems developed, their burgeoning existence created a group of professional educators whose members became some of the most vocal advocates of increased and better-funded schooling.[6] In fact, prominent leaders in these movements for public schooling often became county or state superintendents of public education, offices from which they regularly continued their attempts to build and strengthen statewide school systems.

Although they were organized at the state level, these groups stayed in continuous contact with one another. The leaders of state-level reform movements corresponded regularly, consulting one another on desirable policies as well as political strategies. They also communicated through the educational journals that many such organizations published.[7] These publications reported on educational developments across many different states, and allowed educational reformers to share ideas across wide geographic spaces. They reprinted one another's essays and reports, and many even printed lists of other state-level journals.[8]

The common school movement's newsletters and journals reveal that many educational leaders and constitutional activists identified education as a moral right. For instance, in 1847, the *Common School Advocate* declared, "*It is the child's right to be educated*; and it is not only his right but it is our indispensable duty to provide for the education of every child in the state."[9] Some even described the explicit instructions they placed in constitutions using the term "rights." For instance, Pennsylvania's constitution of 1874 limited legislative discretion about educational spending by declaring that the legislature "shall appropriate at least one million dollars each year" to support common schools. Shortly after its ratification, the *Pennsylvania School Journal* explained the significance of this mandatory appropriations clause, saying: "'Shall appropriate.'—This is obligatory and we must claim

[5] Lawrence A. Cremin, *American Education: The National Experience 1783–1876* (New York: Harper & Row, 1980), 177.

[6] Ibid., 176.

[7] Ibid., 177.

[8] Before New Mexico achieved statehood, for example, the *New Mexico Journal of Education* asked state superintendents of education from other states what they thought was the most desirable constitutional provision for education, so that they could print the results, and also use the knowledge to lobby their own constitutional convention. See "Extracts from Letters Concerning the Constitution," *New Mexico Journal of Education*, Sept. 15, 1910, Santa Fe, vol. 7, no. 1, 4–7.

[9] "Editorial," *Common School Advocate*, 1847, Indianapolis, vol. 1, no. 7, 98.

it as a right of the citizen."[10] The reason that the *Pennsylvania School Journal* described the phrase "shall appropriate" as a right is, as the *Journal* explained, that it rendered the appropriation "obligatory." In other words, it created a mandate on government. If, like the Pennsylvania appropriations clause, constitutional provisions were drafted to deny legislatures choices, by imposing duties or obligations on government, we must recognize these provisions as rights.

In fact, educational leaders and delegates to state constitutional conventions were entirely clear about their intention to create new governmental duties, or obligations, and they drafted constitutional provisions precisely for this purpose. For instance, Ohio's constitutional provision about education was created in direct response to educational activists' sense that the legislature must be constitutionally obligated to establish common schools. During Ohio's constitutional convention of 1850, the state's common school movement was so frustrated with the legislature's history of inaction that it decided to seek a constitutional provision that would leave the state legislature with no choice but to act.[11] In arguing on behalf of an explicit constitutional mandate, one delegate explained: "It has been said that we ought to trust the management of this interest to the General Assembly . . . [However] our system of common schools instead of improving in legislative hands, has been degenerating."[12] Another said, "I desire to lay a plan such as within certain limits the Legislature shall be bound to carry out."[13] As we know, this idea of binding the legislature, or limiting its discretion, defines constitutional rights. Ohio's common school movement championed these binding mandates in their attempts to ensure that governments would be forced to establish and support public schools.

Ohio was not the only state to add a mandate, or right, related to common schooling to its constitution. In fact, by the beginning of the twentieth century, most state constitutions included a provision that required government to establish or maintain common or public school systems. Table 5.1 describes the timeline over which state constitutions included their first provision mandating the establishment of a common or public school system. Each of these provisions is phrased in mandatory terms that direct the legislature to establish and/or maintain public schools.[14]

---

[10] "School Legislation Under New Constitution," *Pennsylvania School Journal*, Harrisburg, February, 1874, vol. 22, no. 8, 247.

[11] O'Brien and Woodrum, "The Constitutional Common School," 612.

[12] Ohio Constitutional Convention, Report of the Debates and Proceedings of the Convention for the Revision of the Constitution of the State of Ohio (Columbus: S. Medary, Printer to the Convention, 1851), 702. Also cited in O'Brien and Woodrum, "The Constitutional Common School."

[13] Ohio Constitutional Convention, Report of the Debates and Proceedings of the Convention for the Revision of the Constitution of the State of Ohio, 16.

[14] I compiled the data displayed in table 5.1 using the State Constitutions Project of the National Bureau of Economic Research. John Joseph Wallis, "National Bureau of Economic

TABLE 5.1. Common School Provisions First Added to State Constitutions

Years	Number of States	States
1816–25	2	**IN, ME**
1826–35	1	**MI**
1836–45	3	RI, LA, **TX**
1846–55	4	**IA, WI, CA,** OH
1856–65	7	**MN, OR, KS, WV, NV,** MD, MO
1866–75	12	**NE,** AR, GA, MS, SC, NC, FL, AL, VA, IL, PA, NJ
1876–85	1	CO
1886–95	9	**MT, ND, WY, SD, WA, ID,** KY, NY, UT
1896–1905	1	DE
1906–1915	3	**OK, NM, AZ**
1959	2	**AK, HI**

States' original constitutions are indicated in bold.

As we can see from table 5.1, many of these common school mandates were included by Southeastern states during Reconstruction or added to frontier states' original constitutions. I will discuss the significance of these events later in the chapter. For now, the thing to notice about table 5.1 is the large number of state constitutions that include mandates on state legislatures to establish public schools.[15]

It is important to note that the adoption of a common school provision in a state's constitution is not typically a good indication that the state actually created a public school system at the same time it ratified the provision. Some states did not create statewide common school systems until many years after their constitutions established the requirement. For instance, al-

Research / University of Maryland State Constitution Project," www.stateconstitutions.umd .edu. I supplemented this database with an older collection of state constitutions. See Francis Newton Thorpe, *The Federal and State Constitutions: Colonial Charters, and Other Organic Laws of the States, Territories, and Colonies Now or Heretofore Forming the United States of America,* 7 vols. (Washington, DC: GPO, 1909). I examined every iteration of every state's constitution to determine when states adopted these constitutional mandates to establish public schools.

[15] North Carolina and Pennsylvania included eighteenth-century provisions that mandated low-cost schooling or free schooling for the poor. These provisions are not included in table 5.1, since they did not require free schooling for all, and therefore did not mandate the establishment of a common or public school system.

though Indiana appears first on this list, the state's government would not actually establish a system of public schools until 1852.[16] In addition, some of these provisions, like New York's, were included in constitutions after the state's public school system had been in place for decades, simply to confirm that the provision of education was a state responsibility.[17] Thus, state constitutions were not always sufficient or even necessary to motivate a state to establish a public school system. Therefore, it would be a mistake to argue that the education provisions in state constitutions were responsible for the actual establishment of schools. Instead, I am making the far more modest claim that the texts of these provisions were understood and drafted in order to justify demands on government, and that as a result, we should recognize these provisions as rights.

But should we recognize them as positive rights? I think we must. Education provisions were crafted as mandates, not for governmental restraint, but also for active government intervention. In particular, these provisions were mandates for the type of intervention that would protect children not (or not primarily) from the threat of tyrannical government, but from the threats posed by their parents' poverty. These two attributes of constitutional education provisions are the features that distinguish positive from negative rights.

The constitutional provisions relating to education quite clearly call for government's activity, intervention, and increased expenditure, not governmental restraint. State constitutions require that states establish and fund entire free school systems for all children of the state. The constitutional mandates that established this requirement did not restrain the state from interfering with children's education. On the contrary, these provisions imposed an explicit duty on the state and its local governments to actively establish and fund systems of public education. As we saw in Ohio and Pennsylvania and as we will see throughout this chapter, reformers used constitutions to urge the state to take more action and intervene more forcefully. Thus, they created constitutional mandates to funnel state monies to public schools and to establish redistributive state taxes. Reformers consistently described the state's obligation to extend itself into social and economic life. For instance, after the New Mexico constitution was ratified, educational activists in that state argued that it established this interventionist principle: "It is the state's duty to see to it that every child has equal opportunity for an education, that after every district has done its utmost for the education of its children, the state should supply whatever else is needed

---

[16] Edward Reisner, *The Evolution of the Common School* (New York: The MacMillan Company, 1930), 343.

[17] John J. Dinan, "The Meaning of State Constitutional Education Clauses: Evidence from the Constitutional Convention Debates," *Albany Law Review* 70, no. 3 (2007): 942–3.

to bring equality of opportunity with richer districts."[18] In fact, many state constitutional mandates were drafted in order to ensure that government must supply whatever was necessary to give children educational opportunities, and in some cases to equalize their opportunities. These requirements that government act, rather than refrain from acting, render education rights positive, at least in this regard.

Positive rights are also distinguished from negative rights because they offer protection from threats that do not stem purely or directly from the state itself. Constitutional education provisions appear to be positive rights in this respect as well. In fact, members of the common school movement often described education provisions as necessary to protect children from poverty. For instance, in 1848, the *Western School Journal* declared, "The state protects the rights of individuals—it protects a man's property." It then asked, "Can it not also protect a child's interests—the right to be educated—which is to him more than property—which may determine his whole course in life? . . . Can he not look to the state for protection?"[19] Similarly, one delegate to the Pennsylvania constitutional convention of 1873 argued, "The child himself has a right to such training as will fit him for usefulness and enjoyment in life . . . when the parent fails and the child is about to die from physical want the state steps forward, *in loco parentis*, and gives him life. For what? To live in ignorance, in wretchedness, and in toil?"[20] These discussions of education provisions are emphatically not descriptions of constitutional rights that restrain the state to protect citizens from tyrannical government. On the contrary, they are arguments in favor of constitutional mandates for interventionist government to protect children from the more crippling consequences of poverty. As we will see, these arguments were typical justifications for the constitutional treatment of education. We should, therefore, understand these constitutional provisions as positive rights.

While constitutional education rights were often described as vehicles through which individual children could be protected from poverty, this was not the only justification for their drafting. In fact, advocates of public education generally justified their support for these rights by arguing that education is necessary to maintain a republican government. Anxiety about the character of the citizenry originated with the American Revolution itself and the sense that the new republic was engaged in a dangerous experiment,

---

[18] "Education and Equality of Taxation," *New Mexico Journal of Education*, Santa Fe, May 1912, vol. 8, no. 9, 5.

[19] "Public Schools," *Western School Journal: a Monthly Devoted to the Cause of Education in the Mississippi Valley*, November 1848, Cincinnati, vol. 2, no. 8, 125.

[20] Pennsylvania Constitutional Convention, *Debates of the Convention to Amend the Constitution of Pennsylvania: Convened at Harrisburg*, November 12, 1872, Adjourned, November 27, to Meet at Philadelphia, January 7, 1873 (Harrisburg: B. Singerly, 1873), vol. 6, 44.

which required an educated citizenry,[21] and the argument that an educated citizenry is essential to the preservation of the American republic has continued to surface in almost every public debate about education through the present day. In the mid-nineteenth century, however, this anxiety about the character of the citizenry took an explicitly anti-Catholic turn. Common school reformers equated Catholicism with a lack of civic virtue and independent political judgment, and common school advocates argued that increasing Catholic immigration rendered common schooling increasingly valuable. The book's conclusion discusses this exclusionary side to the common school movement in greater detail. Yet for purposes of this chapter, it is important to realize that public education in America has long been, and continues to be, understood not only as a means of elevating the individual and preparing him for the responsibilities of citizenship, but also of protecting the republic itself.

Because constitutional education provisions were often justified in terms of republican necessity, they appear somewhat different from our modern conception of rights. In today's discourse, rights are often associated with the welfare of individuals, and are frequently understood to be enforced even at the expense of the majority's wishes or the well-being of society as a whole.[22] Educational reformers certainly asserted that individuals would benefit from statewide school systems, but they often focused on the social value of school systems, rather than (or in addition to) the individual's claims on society. Constitutional education rights and the arguments offered in their support do have a somewhat different character from many more familiar rights, like the rights to free speech and assembly, which are understood to protect individual liberty even at the cost of social harmony. However, this emphasis on social rather than individual good does not render constitutional provisions any less obligatory. Many of their champions described these provisions as rights, but even when they did not, they were clear about their desire to impose duties on government, thereby limiting legislative discretion. The rest of the chapter examines the political origins of these rights, and compares their development to existing theoretical accounts of constitutional emergence and change.

ENTRENCHMENT OF CONGRESSIONAL PREFERENCES

The standard account of rights' development tells us that ruling coalitions create constitutions and write new rights in order to ensure that, even when they no longer hold the reigns of political power, their preferred policies will

---

[21] Gordon Wood, *The Creation of the American Republic, 1776–1787* (New York: Norton, 1969), 120–23.

[22] Mary Ann Glendon, *Rights Talk: The Impoverishment of Political Discourse* (New York: Free Press, 1991).

continue to endure. Given this explanation for rights' emergence, we should expect to see ruling coalitions write new rights shortly before they are forced out of power. This account applies quite well to Congress's role in shaping state constitutions and ensuring that these constitutions contained education rights.

Through its enabling acts and its acts to readmit former Confederate states to the Union, Congress encouraged the addition of educational mandates to state constitutions. In this way, Congress hoped to ensure that its preferences would continue to shape states' policies even after the federal government could no longer control the states' domestic policies. This motive for the creation of constitutional rights is a clear case of entrenchment. In 1876, for instance, Congress debated whether every state's constitution should be required to guarantee the establishment of a free school system as a condition of its readmission to the Union.[23] The primary advocate of this requirement explained its logic by asserting that Congress had the unusual opportunity to set Southern states on a virtuous course. He argued that "during this transition period, permanent governments might be matured on safe foundations and the people educated to a better order of things."[24] He expressed his hope that school systems would take the place of the federal troops in maintaining Northern influence throughout the former confederacy: "As the soldier disappears his place must be supplied by the schoolmaster. The muster-roll must be exchanged for the school register, and our headquarters must be in a school-house. Do not forget the grandeur of the work in which you are now engaged. You are forming states."[25] This rhetoric epitomizes the logic of entrenchment. As Congress prepared to relinquish its political and military dominance over the former Confederacy, it attempted to extend its influence into the future in order to guard its preferred policies against the differing wills of future political decision makers. This proposal was ultimately defeated, but it lost by an extremely narrow margin, and its near-victory provided delegates to Southern constitutional conventions with a sizeable incentive to demonstrate their commitment to public education through their new constitutions.[26]

---

[23] The most vocal advocate of the amendment to require an educational guarantee in the constitutions of Southern states was the Massachusetts Senator, Charles Sumner. He argued that Southern states should be put on notice that Congress would not re-admit them to the Union without constitutional provisions pledging to create public schools. Sumner explained , "I submit that it is important that we should declare this in advance, so that when their constitutions come here and are submitted for our approval they may not complain if we object to them because they do not provide free schools. My proposition is in the nature of notice to all these States that if they expect their constitutions to be approved they must insert in those constitutions a provision for free schools." *Congressional Globe*, March 16, 1867, 169.

[24] Ibid.,165.

[25] Ibid.,167.

[26] Tyack and Lowe, "The Constitutional Moment: Reconstruction and Black Education in the South," 244.

Congress also used state constitutions to exert continuing influence over states' systems of financing public education. Many of the earliest statewide school funds were created using the revenue of lands that the federal government gave to states.[27] However, state legislatures often diminished their school funds, either by selling lands at low prices (often to speculators), by investing the funds in speculative internal improvement projects, or simply by diverting the funds for other purposes.[28] Because many states had mismanaged the federal lands that were supposed to finance education, and squandered any proceeds that those lands did produce, Congress drafted increasingly complicated and detailed conditions for states wishing to acquire federal lands for purposes of school funding and even began to write these conditions into its enabling acts for new states.[29] The enabling acts for Ohio, Indiana, Illinois, Alabama, and Missouri were approved between 1802 and 1819, and granted land to these new states using the same system that Congress employed in the Northwest Ordinance. Sections of each township were reserved to the town government for support of its schools. Other conditions included the instruction that these lands support common schools, not simply subsidize private educational institutions, and specifications to prevent state governments from squandering the resources they were about to receive. These conditions are represented by the columns in table 5.2.[30] The authors of these enabling acts hoped that state constitutional provisions would allow them to extend their political influence beyond the period in which Congress had formal power to dispose of the lands it was giving to states. In fact, the enabling act for New Mexico and Arizona even specified that it was the duty of the attorney general to enforce the land provisions of the enabling act in federal court. This use of constitutions also embodies the logic of entrenchment theory.

As table 5.2 indicates, congressional enabling acts specified that particular sections of land must be reserved to finance common schools, that common schools would be guaranteed to exist, that a permanent school fund must be formed, and provided binding instructions for its investment. They also established conditions upon which school lands could be leased or sold. For instance, they required public auctions, and established minimum prices

[27] Twenty-nine of the forty-eight continental United States received land grants for education, most of them upon admission to the union. No grants were made in the original thirteen states or to Maine, West Virginia, Kentucky, Vermont, or Texas, primarily because the federal government did not own any land in those states. However, in 1836, Congress adopted the policy of distributing the surplus proceeds from federal lands in these states. John Mathiason Matzen, *State Constitutional Provisions for Education; Fundamental Attitude of the American People Regarding Education as Revealed by State Constitutional Provisions, 1776–1929* (New York: Teachers College, Columbia University, 1931), 105.

[28] Fletcher Harper Swift, *Federal and State Policies in Public School Finance in the United States* (Boston: Ginn and Company, 1931).

[29] Ibid., 60.

[30] This table exclude states for which no congressional enabling act was written and states that wrote a constitution before the passage of their congressional enabling act.

TABLE 5.2. Enabling Acts and State Constitutions on the
Management of School Lands and Funds

State (year)	(A)	(B)	(C)	(D)	(E)	(F)	(G)	(H)	(I)	(J)	(K)	(L)
OH (1802)	E.A.											
LA (1811)												
IN (1816)	E.A.											
MS (1817)												
IL (1818)	E.A.											
AL (1819)	E.A.											
MO (1820)	E.A.											
IA (1845)		Con.	Con.									
TX (1845)		Con.	Con.				Con.					
WI (1846)	E.A.	Con.	Con.									
MN (1857)	E.A.	Con.	Con.	Con.								
NV (1864)	E.A, Con.	Con.	Con.		Con.							
NE (1864)	E.A.	Con.	Con.			Con.						
CO (1875)	E.A.	Con.	E.A., Con.	E.A.		E.A.						
ND (1889)	E.A.	E.A., Con.	E.A., Con.	E.A., Con.	Con.	E.A., Con.	E.A., Con.	E.A.				
SD (1889)	E.A.	E.A., Con.	E.A., Con.	E.A., Con.	Con.	E.A., Con.	E.A., Con.	E.A., Con.				

(continued on next page)

(cont. from previous page)

TABLE 5.2. Enabling Acts and State Constitutions on the
Management of School Lands and Funds

State (year)	(A)	(B)	(C)	(D)	(E)	(F)	(G)	(H)	(I)	(J)	(K)	(L)
MT (1889)	E.A.	E.A., Con.	E.A., Con.	E.A.	Con.	E.A.	E.A.	E.A.				
WA (1889)	E.A.	E.A., Con.	E.A., Con.	E.A., Con.		E.A.	E.A.	E.A.		Con.		
UT (1894)	E.A.	E.A., Con.	E.A., Con.		Con.							
OK (1906)	E.A.	E.A., Con.	E.A., Con.	E.A.			E.A.,		E.A., Con.	E.A.		
NM (1910)	E.A., Con.	E.A., Con.	E.A., Con.	E.A.	E.A., Con.	E.A., Con.	E.A.				E.A.	E.A.
AZ (1910)	E.A.	E.A., Con.	E.A., Con.	E.A., Con.	E.A.	E.A.	E.A., Con.				E.A., Con.	E.A, Con.

Columns: (year) year of enabling act; (A) Sections reserved for schools; (B) Guarantee of common schools; (C) Permanent school fund; (D) Sale / lease at public auction / to highest bidder; (E) Investment instructions; (F) Minimum price; (G) Max. length of lease; (H) Max. size of leased parcel; (I) $5 million held in trust; (J) Max. size of sold parcels; (K) Establish separate funds for land grants; (L) Attorney general will enforce land provisions.

Cells: E.A.—Provision is included in state's enabling act; Con.—Provision is included in state's constitution.

on land and maximum parcels in which land could be sold or leased. Several enabling acts required states to establish a separate fund for each of the objects for which federal grants were made, and prohibited the movement of money between them. Oklahoma's enabling act required that at least $5 million be held in trust for purposes of public schooling, and several other enabling acts described the state's relationship to its common school resources as a trustee. State constitutions incorporated many of the explicit conditions for the use of school lands contained in their enabling acts.

While congressional enabling acts do seem to have shaped the school land provisions in constitutions, state constitutional conventions also included instructions to legislatures without the pressure of an enabling act. In fact, after 1845, almost every state ratified at least one constitutional requirement about school lands or funds that was not required by its enabling act. Toward the end of the nineteenth century, constitutional conventions created many mandates for legislatures that were never included in congressional instructions. These included timelines for the sale of school lands, which were designed to guarantee that the lands were not sold too quickly, instructions for how public auctions must be advertised, in what form the state would accept payment for lands, and guarantees that the state must replace any money lost to the school fund for any reason. These additional provisions suggest that constitutional mandates about educational funding were not simply a response to congressional efforts at entrenchment.

FORCING THE LEGISLATURE'S HAND: SCHOOL LANDS AND FUNDS

State constitutions were not only subject to congressional pressures, but also to pressures from the educational groups that organized both within and across individual states. Many of the education provisions in state constitutions were placed there at the behest of state-level organizations for educational reform as part of the common school movement. In states with no public school systems, common school advocates sought to establish school systems. In states where a system of schools already existed, members of the common school movement pushed to render them entirely free to students, and where free schools existed, the movement focused its energies on improving the quality of teachers and schoolhouses and increasing the resources available to the school system.[31]

Because common school activists sought political change, they were not solely, or even primarily, concerned with their constitutions' ability to entrench particular policies. While existing theories of constitutional development describe rights as products of legislative majorities' attempts to guard the policies they have already established from tampering by future majorities, the common school movement attempted to create constitutional education rights for a different, and almost opposite, purpose. Members of the common school movement were frustrated with existing legislative outcomes and hoped that new constitutional provisions would help them bring about political change. These organizations believed that constitutional provisions would enable them to change existing policies by forcing legislatures to take the kinds of actions they had been unwilling to take in the absence of constitutional provisions. These groups certainly hoped their preferred policies would endure over time, but they were not seeking to maintain their existing dominance over the state's policymaking process. In other words, the constitutional rights they championed were not elite tools to entrench the status quo. Instead, many of the education rights in state constitutions stemmed from the efforts of these relative outsiders to force the legislatures of their states into new kinds of behavior.

[31] Reisner, *The Evolution of the Common School* , 341

In some states, educational reformers sought constitutional provisions in direct response to their own legislatures' mishandling of school funds. For example, in Kentucky, the state legislature's abuse of the school fund was one of the central concerns of the state's educational professionals and reformers. Although Kentucky did not receive lands from the federal government to establish its original school fund, at the behest of common school advocates, the legislature nonetheless established a state fund with which to finance common schools. The state legislature, however, regularly used the funds that had been set aside for schools to fund internal improvements or aid banks, so that little of the money from this school fund actually ever trickled through to schools.[32] While the legislature technically borrowed from the fund to finance these other endeavors, in 1845, the legislature simply passed legislation that canceled all its obligations to repay the state's debts to the fund.[33] The school fund was eventually rebuilt through the efforts of the state superintendent of common schools, who in 1847 convinced the legislature to levy special taxes for that purpose. Experience, however, had taught Kentucky's common school movement that the legislature might easily disregard the intended purpose of this fund.[34]

When a constitutional convention was called in 1849, Kentucky's superintendent of common schools and many educational activists saw in the convention an opportunity to control the legislature, and lobbied the convention's delegates accordingly.[35] One delegate to the constitutional convention reported that "If there was any one subject on which I was thoroughly and fully instructed, it was to rescue from the vacillation of the legislation of the state, the common school fund . . . and place it beyond the control of the legislation of the commonwealth and its changeable character."[36] Another delegate made his intention to force the hand of the legislature even more explicit. In response to the charge that a detailed provision about how to manage the school fund reflected a lack of faith in the legislature, he replied, "Said he, are you afraid to trust the legislature?—I am. He asked it with great emphasis and confidence—I answer it in the same spirit—I am afraid to trust the legislature; and the reasons for that distrust, I will give, drawn

---

[32] William Connelley and E. M. Coulter, *History of Kentucky*, vol. 2 (Chicago and New York: American Historical Society, 1922), 759. In 1836, the federal government adopted a policy of distributing the surplus revenues from the sale of public lands to various state governments. Kentucky was expected to receive $2 million, a million of which the legislature designated as a common school fund. Despite the existence of this million-dollar fund, by 1845 only $2,500 had been paid to schools. Ibid., 759–65.

[33] Ibid., 765.

[34] Ibid., 767.

[35] Ibid.

[36] Kentucky Constitutional Convention, *Report of the Debates and Proceedings of the Convention for the Revision of the Constitution of the State of Kentucky*, ed. Richard Sutton (Frankfort, KY: A. G. Hodges & Co., 1849), 893.

from legislative records on this subject."[37] He then recounted the state legislature's history of misappropriating and dissipating the school fund. The constitutional convention ultimately adopted an extremely detailed provision about the state's school fund, specifying the amount of the principal and mandating that the current fund, along with any future additions, should be "held inviolate" for the purpose of sustaining a system of free common schools and could be appropriated for no other purpose. It also mandated that the school fund and its dividends must be invested in a safe and profitable manner, and gave instructions for the distribution of these funds to county schools.

Although Kentucky's constitutional provision was only about the management and distribution of the school fund, and did not include sweeping statements about educational rights, its proponents nonetheless identified these constitutional provisions with the creation of education rights. For instance, one delegate to Kentucky's constitutional convention declared, "It is the duty of a republican government to educate its children. It is said by all writers upon republics, that education is the birthright of every child born in a republic. Leave this subject to the legislature, judging from the past, the schools will never go into operation, and the funds will be squandered and resquandered."[38] The delegates who were most committed to preserving the school fund also bridled at the suggestion that the matter was not appropriate for inclusion in the constitution and ought to be left to the legislature to manage. One such delegate asked:

> Am I to be told that we must look to the legislature for our rights; and that we are to be denied protection of the Constitution? . . . Are we of the mountains, who are poor, to be taxed to improve the rivers and roads of you who are wealthy? And then, sir, when the general government has set apart a fund, for the purpose of general and equal education . . . is it right for us to be told that there is no constitutional security for us, and that our rights are to be disregarded?[39]

Although the school fund might appear to be too mundane an administrative detail to warrant constitutional treatment, this comment demonstrates how closely even these provisions were associated with the right to an education. This delegate argued that only by placing detailed instructions for the legislature in the constitution itself could those in need of public education feel secure in the knowledge that the legislature would attend not only to projects that further advantaged the wealthy, but also to those that benefited the poor. Kentucky's activists were not alone in this conviction.

By the end of the nineteenth century, it was widely recognized that many state legislatures had significantly diminished their school funds by misman-

[37] Ibid., 889.
[38] Ibid., 895.
[39] Ibid., 887.

aging the public lands from which those funds were to be drawn. Consequently, education activists routinely sought to establish constitutional safeguards for school lands, even in the absence of mismanagement in their own states. The educational activism of the Dakota territories exemplifies this phenomenon. Although the Dakota territories did not achieve statehood (and therefore did not possess federal land grants for education) until 1889, members of the statehood movement began to talk about the need for a constitutional amendment to safeguard school lands as early as 1882. Dakota's "friends of education" argued that school lands of other states had been victims to the maneuverings of "combinations and fraudulent schemes."[40] For instance, in North Dakota, the territorial superintendent of schools, William Beadle, led the campaign to safeguard school lands. Beadle believed a constitutional provision to be necessary because of the history of other states' school funds. In 1880, in a self-published pamphlet about the question of school lands, he wrote: "There has been abundant evil experience in the several States in the handling of these school lands and we should profit fully by all of it . . . The burden of discussion in the educational reports of many states has been, or still is, the waste of the school lands." Describing particular problems in Wisconsin and California, he said, "Every state has found cause to regret any early indifference."[41] To guard against these dangers, Beadle proposed that the new constitution should require that the state set a minimum price of $10 per acre for the sale of school lands.[42]

North Dakota's friends of education also explicitly linked the successful management of school lands and funds with the right to education. The North Dakota Educational Association issued a resolution stating:

> That the school lands and every gift of property to the cause of public education, constitute a peculiarly sacred trust, and we call upon all legislators and others who have at any time the immediate care and control of such funds or resources, to exercise the utmost vigilance in effectually securing, in wisely managing, and in faithfully transmitting the same, with its legitimate increase undiminished and inviolate, as the just inheritance and indefeasible birthright of the children of the commonwealth through all generations.[43]

[40] Jon Lauck, "'The Organic Law of the Great Commonwealth': The Framing of the South Dakota Constitution," *South Dakota Law Review* 53, no. 2 (2008): 234.

[41] William Henry Harrison Beadle, *Source Materials in South Dakota History of Education: Three Important Contributions by General W. H. H. Beadle, Who Was the Champion of Public Schools During Territorial and Early Statehood Days* (s.n., 1884), 6–7.

[42] At the time, public lands in Iowa were selling for $2.50 to $4.00, and no state had ever established such a high minimum price. Lauck, "'The Organic Law of the Great Commonwealth': The Framing of the South Dakota Constitution," 234–5.

[43] Resolution of the North Dakota Educational Association held in 1888, published in the *Dakota Educator*, February 1889, Scotland, Dakota, 9.

TABLE 5.3. First Constitutional Mandates Regarding the
Management of School Lands or Funds

Years	Num. states	States
1816–25	5	**IN, MS, CT, AL, NY**
1826–35	2	TN, **MI**
1836–45	6	**AR, FL, RI, NJ, LA, TX**
1846–55	5	**IA, WI, CA**, KY, OH
1856–65	7	**MN, OR, KS, WV, NV**, MD, MO
1866–75	6	NE, GA, SC, NC, VA, IL
1876–85	1	CO
1886–95	7	**MT, ND, WY, SD, WA, ID, UT**
1896–1905	1	DE
1906–1915	2	**OK, AZ**

States' original constitutions are indicated in bold.

Two elements of this statement warrant special attention. The first is the active role it describes for the state in the management and preservation of school funds. Notice that the state legislature is not simply supposed to refrain from pillaging the school fund, but also to take active steps to protect and increase it. These provisions do not merely impose restrictions on squandering of lands, but also create legislative duties to manage them well and for the benefit of the public school students. The second telling feature of this statement is that this constitutional mandate to preserve the school fund was understood to secure children's right to a publicly funded education.

Many state constitutions contain this particular form of education right. Table 5.3 describes the period in which each state with a constitutional provision relating to the management of its school lands and/or fund first included such a provision in its constitution.[44] As this list demonstrates, the idea that constitutions ought to protect school funds against legislatures persisted into the twentieth century, shaping the constitutions of states across the continent. These constitutional rights were drafted to control legislatures.

Of course, the idea that constitutional development is motivated by a desire to force the hand of the legislature raises an immediate and obvious question: if common school activists possessed sufficient political power to

---

[44] This table excludes New Hampshire, which first added a constitutional mandate regarding school funding in 1990, well after the period covered by this chapter.

achieve constitutional changes, why were they unable to influence the legislative process in the first place? One answer is that, unlike legislatures, constitutional conventions (especially in the nineteenth century) were often called in response to a sense that the legislature had led the state astray.[45] Thus, these conventions were generally engaged in the explicit and self-conscious project of addressing the state's most stubborn problems. Even when constitutional conventions had not been called for this purpose, the knowledge that a new constitution was being drafted often increased the salience of policies, like education, devoted to the common good and to the state's long-term flourishing. For instance, one study, conducted at the end of the nineteenth century, concluded that state constitutions offered a solution to the problem of state lands because "when a constitution is framing, then and then only, is any popular interest in the subject likely to be manifested."[46] Since popular interest in school lands and funds was often generated or dramatically increased by the establishment of a constitutional convention, it could subsequently be harnessed to create constitutional instructions that would force legislatures to act as careful stewards of school lands and the revenues they produced. This feature of conventions may have allowed them to adopt different policies from the legislatures of their states, policies targeted directly at changing the legislative behavior that common school activists found problematic and had struggled to change through other means. Another difference between state legislatures and constitutional conventions was that convention delegates did not need to seek reelection to their offices. This difference may have been particularly important with respect to school taxes.

Forcing the Legislature's Hand: School Taxes

Electoral incentives made it difficult for the members of many state legislatures to establish or raise school taxes. Consequently, state legislatures were not only prone to neglecting and mismanaging school funds, they were also reluctant to establish stable and equitable tax policies to support public schools. The idea that public education ought to be a centrally financed, and therefore redistributive, governmental function originated in the first half of the nineteenth century and gained popularity over the course of the nineteenth and early twentieth centuries. Members of the common school movement often argued that the property of the state should educate the children of the state, meaning that local governments should not be left to establish

---

[45] Tarr, *Understanding State Constitutions*, 111–12.
[46] George Knight, *History and Management of Land Grants for Education in the Northwest Territory*, 3 vols., vol. 1, Papers of the American Historical Association (New York: G. P. Putnam's Sons, 1885), 164–5.

and finance schools with whatever revenues they happened to find at their disposal.[47]

By the beginning of the twentieth century, the idea that states must not only facilitate education by establishing and supervising schools across the state, but also centralize educational finance and thereby equalize educational opportunity, had become a primary concern of education activists and constitutional drafters. The more centralized a school tax (or the greater the percentage of revenue that the state provides to its public school system), the more equalizing and redistributive that tax generally is. As a result, centralized state taxes often faced significant political opposition and could prove difficult for legislatures to enact. Consequently, the common school activists in many states insisted that constitutional rights were necessary to ensure that legislatures fulfilled their moral obligation to establish redistributive educational policies.[48]

Concern that the legislature would not raise taxes, for example, motivated a vigorous campaign for constitutional education rights in California. By 1920, district-level taxation began to outpace taxation at both the county and state levels. The California Teachers' Association spearheaded a movement to amend the constitution to further centralize school financing. The state superintendent of public instruction explained, "A vote for this amendment will uphold the principle that money for schools shall be raised where

[47] One member of the common school movement argued for constitutional education provisions in this way: "All [Ohio's] youth have a God-given right to such an education . . . and therefore, they have a claim, not only upon their parents, and the State, but upon the entire property of the State." O'Brien and Woodrum, "The Constitutional Common School," 611.

[48] For instance, when New Mexico was on the verge of statehood and drafting its first constitution, educational activists began to express concern over the territories' rural schools and their lack of resources. The New Mexico Journal of Education explained the need to constitutionalize this policy of centralized school financing. "We prate about equal rights, but has not one person as much right to an education as another? . . . The man of wealth can educate his child without the aid of the state, and therefore resent paying for the education of those of his less fortunate neighbor . . . It is for this fundamental reason that we advocate that education become the agency of the state rather than some particular portion of it." See "The Constitution and Education: What Provisions Should Fundamental Law of New Mexico Contain?" New Mexico Journal of Education, 1910, Santa Fe, New Mexico, vol. 7, no. 2, 5. Similarly, a friend of the common school system, writing a series of articles on education in the new state constitution (under the pseudonym "Delta"), in the Weekly Indiana State Journal explained, "A general system of education—a system of free schools—has not been established. Why is it so? Will circumstances not permit it? Possibly there are those who, blinded by avarice or influenced by interested men doubt the right of legislatures to impose a tax upon property for this purpose. There may be men of wealth, and consequently of influence, who say 'my money, my lands, my merchandise are mine, and may I not do what I will with my own?' Were it not for the perception that with increased privileges must come increased taxation, the individual who pleads the cause of free schools would carry every audience." See Delta, "Common School No 1," Weekly Indiana State Journal, Indianapolis, May 11, 1850.

income is, and distributed where children are."[49] It was precisely this redistributive feature of the increased state tax that convinced educational advocates to seek a constitutional amendment rather than simply lobbying the legislature for new statutory law.

California's educational leaders were convinced that, without a constitutional mandate on the subject, the legislature was unlikely to support an increased and redistributive school tax. The *Sierra Educational News*, official journal of the California Teachers' Association, explained, "The heavy taxpayers in any community, or in any state, those who can best afford to pay taxes, are those, usually, who offer most objection to increased rates. Politicians, too, often fear to take an aggressive stand, if thereby it means increase in the tax rate."[50] The same article also quoted another author on the subject, who wrote: "We cannot have schools without teachers. We cannot have teachers without reasonable salaries to enable them to discharge their duties. This means taxes, and politicians are as bold as lions in all matters but one, and that is taxes."[51] The virtue of a constitutional amendment was that it would force the legislature to adopt a tax policy that would otherwise have been difficult to enact.[52] The California Teachers' Association printed a primer on school finance, which argued in favor of the amendment by emphasizing its function as a mandate for action: "unless we compel the state to do its fair share in supporting education, the very life of the nation is imperiled. . . . This proposed amendment will force the state and the county to provide an equal share and an adequate share of the cost of elementary education and will thereby restore educational opportunity."[53] Here again, educational reformers pursued constitutional provisions in order to force the legislature to make the kind of political change that it was otherwise reluctant to make.

This desire to force the hand of the legislature was a particular motivation among the Reconstruction conventions of Southeastern states, where the "friends of education" had been active since the 1850s, but had generally been less successful in achieving reform than their Northern counterparts.

[49] Will C. Wood, "Argument for Constitutional Amendment Relative to Increase of School Funds," *Sierra Educational News*, San Francisco, September, 1920, vol. 16, no. 7, 412.

[50] Arthur Henry Chamberlain, "Proposed Constitutional Amendment," Sierra Educational News, San Francisco, May, 1920, vol. 16, no. 5, 268.

[51] Ibid.

[52] Educators' conviction that the legislature would be unlikely to raise taxes was not merely conjecture. In fact, as the state superintendent of public instruction reminded voters shortly before the referendum on the constitutional amendment, in its 1917 session, the state legislature had already attempted to abolish the minimum rate at which counties were required to levy taxes for the support of schools. He explained that a constitutionally mandated tax would "make similar attacks on the elementary and high schools impossible." See "School Funds in California," *School Review*, Chicago, 1921, vol. 29, no. 1, 2.

[53] "Primer of Education and School Finance," *Sierra Educational News*, San Francisco, September 1920, vol. 16, no. 7, 409.

Many Southern states lacked public school systems until after the Civil War, when Reconstruction governments created them.[54] Thus, during the nineteenth century, the South's education activists worked to include mandatory taxation in constitutions in a context of deep popular skepticism, and often as a last resort. These reformers typically hoped that constitutional mandates would help to overcome the significant popular resistance they observed to the idea of public education.[55] For instance, although Baltimore developed a fairly extensive free school system in tandem with many more northern cities, the state of Maryland did not develop a common school system until the Union party seized control of state government during the Civil War.[56] By 1864, when a constitutional convention was called, the Union party had managed to disenfranchise many of the Democratic Confederate sympathizers, who typically opposed state-sponsored education.[57] As a consequence, opposition to public schooling was so diminished among delegates to the 1864 Convention that the Union delegates were able to include a provision mandating the establishment of tax-supported schools.[58]

The delegates at the constitutional convention who argued in favor of tax-supported public schools explained that a constitutional mandate was necessary to overcome legislative opposition to school taxes. One delegate reported that "for the last fifteen years, I believe, there has been a constant effort made to obtain such legislation, and at every session of the legislature that effort has failed."[59] This delegate had, himself, served in the legislature in 1856, and labored on the committee that drafted common school legislation. He described the major obstacle to its passage this way: "I was told by men from counties, where there was no system of public education, that they would never consent to have their property taxed to educate 'the brats of poor white men.'" He went on to say, "I am very glad this committee has made such a report as this, taking the matter out of the hands of the legislature, and providing by a vote of the people of the state to give us a system of public instruction by which 'the brats of poor white men' may get an education."[60]

[54] Cremin, *American Education: The National Experience 1783–1876*, 177.

[55] Some of the reluctance to support public stemmed from racist opposition to the education of black citizens. However, the idea of tax-supported schooling was controversial even when the state only proposed to educate white children.

[56] William Hunter Shannon, "Public Education in Maryland (1825–1968): With Special Emphasis Upon the 1860's" (Ed.D. thesis, University of Maryland, 1964), 165.

[57] Blanche Leora Jenkins, "Public Education in Maryland, 1863–1875" (Master's thesis, University of Maryland, 1940), 4–5.

[58] Shannon, "Public Education in Maryland (1825–1968): With Special Emphasis Upon the 1860's," 175.

[59] Maryland Constitutional Convention, *The Debates of the Constitutional Convention of the State of Maryland: Assembled at the City of Annapolis*, Wednesday, April 27, 1864, ed. Wm Blair Lord and Henry M. Parkhurst (Annapolis: R. P. Bayly, 1864), 1221.

[60] Ibid.

In order to establish public schools, it obviously seemed necessary to "take the matter out of the hands of the legislature." To this end, the constitutional convention drafted a provision which stated that if the legislature failed to enact a system of common schools after the state superintendent had made a report on the most desirable system, the superintendent's proposed system would simply become law. This provision was quite controversial, and in its defense, a delegate offered this justification: "I ask you what probability there is that in any ordinary session of your legislature you will find a uniform system of free public education passed through . . . you might have reiterated in the ears of this legislature until the judgment trump should sound, without any effect."[61] The provision ultimately passed, and was included in the constitution. The subsequent legislature levied a statewide tax for the support of a system of common schools. By 1867, Democrats had regained control of the state government and a new constitutional convention was held. The delegates to this convention were solidly Democratic, and the public school system was widely unpopular among the delegates.[62] It was clear to most observers that the forceful education mandate of the previous constitution would not be allowed to stand.

In response to the constitutional changes that seemed likely to emerge from the 1867 convention, the Maryland State Teachers Association submitted a last-minute plea to the convention, which it printed in the *Maryland Educational Journal*. It stated that, "in order to establish and maintain a system of public instruction worthy of the state of Maryland it will . . . be necessary to insert in the organic law of the state a provision for a *general* school tax." The appeal explained the necessity of a constitutional provision, arguing that "unless such a constitutional tax is provided, the whole question of free public schools will be left to accident or to the varying judgments of successive legislatures."[63] Given the tone of the convention and the legislative history of public schools, it was fairly clear that the "varying judgment of successive legislatures" would leave little room for a tax-supported public school in the near future.

These taxation and appropriation provisions were intended to compel state governments to play a redistributive role through the financing of their public schools. Legislatures may, and certainly did, levy taxes in the absence of constitutional mandates. However, constitutional mandates were intended to limit legislative discretion on the questions of taxation and

[61] Ibid., 1226.

[62] One described the school system as "infamous." He declared that "it was forced upon the people of Maryland against their will, and was being used in the interests of the enemies of the people of Maryland, and should be wiped out as soon as possible." Maryland Constitutional Convention of 1867, *Debates of the Maryland Constitutional Convention of 1867* (as Reprinted from Articles Reported in the *Baltimore Sun*), ed. Francis A. Richardson and Philip B. Perlman (Baltimore: Hepbron & Haydon, 1923).

[63] "Memorial to The Constitutional Convention," *Maryland Educational Journal: A School and Family Monthly*, August, 1867, Baltimore, Vol. 1, no. 4, 122. Italics in original.

spending, thereby serving as a guarantee that the state would finance public education. In 1865, Maryland's superintendent of public instruction interpreted the state's constitutional provision this way: "The duty of citizens in each section of the state is to have an earnest and active solicitude for the welfare of all within the limits of the state . . . This is to be accomplished by making the property of the whole state bear the expense of educating every child in the state."[64] In this explanation of the constitution's taxation provision and in the many others like it, we can recognize the logic of positive rights, that is, the recognition (and legal creation) of a collective duty to protect each citizen from the consequences of his socioeconomic position. The constitutionalized state tax was a means of guaranteeing that the state government would play that redistributive role.

Even when the proponents of a constitutionalized tax did not use the term "rights" to describe the education provisions they championed, their arguments make it entirely clear that these provisions were intended to operate as positive rights. In other words, the mandatory taxation provisions were designed to require that government act to raise money even in the face of majoritarian opposition. Especially in the face of widespread hostility to taxation, proponents of statewide public schools felt that it was necessary to constitutionalize the school tax, so that the question of taxation would not be left in the hands of the legislature. At the Texas Constitutional Convention of 1875, for instance, the state's "friends of education" insisted that a constitutional article which guaranteed a state system of schooling, but did not guarantee a tax, was little more than a "farce."[65] One delegate explained the major objection to a proposed education provision that did not include a mandatory tax: "it sets aside no specific sum; it does not positively commit the State to the principle of taxation for educational purposes, but leaves it optional with the Legislature to do or not to do."[66] In this description, we can again recognize the essential feature of constitutional rights. From the perspective of common school activists, the virtue of constitutional provisions on this subject was precisely that they rendered this form of redistributive state activity mandatory, rather than optional, in a time and place where public schooling was politically unpopular.[67]

[64] L. Van Bokkelen, *Report of the State Superintendent of Public Instruction to the General Assembly of Maryland* (Annapolis, MD: Richard P. Bayly, Printer, 1865), 12.

[65] Texas Constitutional Convention of 1875, *Debates in the Texas Constitution of 1875*, ed. Seth Shepard McKay (Austin: University of Texas, 1930), 232–3.

[66] Ibid., 342.

[67] Frederick Eby, *The Development of Education in Texas* (New York: MacMillan Company, 1925), 163. When the Republican-run government established a school system during the 1870s, it met with enormous resistance from the state's white population. Many found the highly centralized control of the schools militaristic and usurpatious, particularly since education had once been considered primarily a familial and local prerogative. The fiercest opposition to this new system of state-supported schools, however, was focused on the property taxes levied to finance it. After the establishment of the tax in 1871, taxpayers throughout the state

Table 5.4. First Constitutional Provisions Mandating Taxation
or Minimum State Appropriations for School Support

Years	Centralized	Local	Total States
1840s	TX	WI	2
1850s	VA		1
1860s	WV, NV, MD, AR, MS, SC, FL, AL	WV, FL, TX	9
1870s	PA, AL, MO	SC	4
1880s	SD		1
1890s	DE		1
1900s			
1910s	NM	NM	1
1920s	CA	CA	1

Many Southern states first acquired mandatory constitutional taxation
or appropriation provisions immediately after the Civil War. In fact, this
type of provision was most prevalent in the Reconstruction constitutions of
Southern states. While many of these taxation provisions mandated centralized state taxes, some instructed the legislature to require localities to tax
themselves for the support of schools, and others did not specify the type of
taxation required. Still other state constitutions mandated poll taxes during
the 1860s and '70s, specifying that poll tax revenues must be used for public
school support. Table 5.4 lists the first constitutional provisions mandating
taxation or minimum state appropriations for school support.[68]

While many state constitutions specify that the state must provide for a
system of common schools "through taxation or otherwise," and some even
specify that revenues from school taxes will make up the school fund, the
states in table 5.4 all made school taxes and/or appropriations mandatory.

Since common school activists were devoted to constitutional change as
a means to their larger end of establishing statewide systems of free schools,
they did not stop their work when a new constitution had been ratified.
Instead, they continued their attempts to shape public sentiment and demand legislative change. The fact that constitutional activists followed the
enactment of highly detailed constitutional rights with further legislative
lobbying highlights another difference between the origins of education
rights and the explanations of constitutional change provided by entrenchment theories.

---

began to meet in order to protest the tax. A general taxpayer's convention was held in Austin,
where protesters even advised those present to simply refuse to pay school taxes.

[68] The constitutions of Alabama, Arkansas, California, Louisiana, Mississippi, South Carolina, Tennessee, Texas, and West Virginia also mandated that the state levy poll taxes, and specified that the proceeds of the poll taxes were to be placed in the state's school fund.

ENFORCEMENT WITHOUT COURTS

As we saw in chapter 4, the existence of courts that will enforce constitutional rights against legislatures is key to most existing explanations of why people write constitutions. Entrenchment theories posit that legislative majorities constitutionalize their favorite policies so that courts will enforce those policies even after new legislative majorities, with different policy preferences, have emerged.[69] While litigation may be a powerful and straightforward means of enforcing constitutional rights, there is little evidence that common school activists drafted constitutional provisions with an eye toward judicial enforcement. Yet they clearly understood the provisions they drafted as rights, or mandates. How, then, did the champions of education rights expect to enforce these mandates without recourse to the courts?

First, it is worth noting that at least some people (including judges) thought of constitutional education provisions as judicially enforceable, even in the nineteenth century. For instance, in 1874, California's highest court declared that California's constitutional provision, which directed the legislature to establish a system of free common schools, did create a judicially enforceable right:

> The opportunity of instruction at public schools is afforded the youth of the state by the statute of the state, enacted in obedience to the special command of the Constitution of the State, directing that the Legislature shall provide for a system of common schools . . . The advantage or benefit thereby vouchsafed to each child, of attending a public school is, therefore, one derived and secured to it under the highest sanction of positive law. It is, therefore, a right—a legal right—as distinctively so as the vested right in property owned is a legal right, and as such it is protected, and entitled to be protected by all the guarantees by which other legal rights are protected and secured to the possessor.[70]

This decision ultimately upheld California's system of segregated common schools. It was, therefore, not as great a victory for judicially enforced education rights as the previous excerpt alone might lead us to believe. However, this decision does demonstrate that even in the nineteenth century, a constitutional mandate to establish common schools was understood as a judicially enforceable right.

Despite the fact that these provisions did give rise to some lawsuits in the nineteenth century, it is nonetheless clear that most of the education provisions in state constitutions were neither written nor ratified to enable litigation.[71] Some scholars have consequently argued that these provisions are not

---

[69] Hirschl, *Towards Juristocracy: The Origins and Consequences of the New Constitutionalism*; Ginsburg, *Judicial Review in New Democracies: Constitutional Courts in Asian Cases.*

[70] *Ward v. Flood*, 48 Calif. 36 (1874).

[71] John J. Dinan, "The Meaning of State Constitutional Education Clauses."

really rights, or that they only became rights when courts became willing to enforce them.[72] And in fact, many theories of rights do assert that constitutional provisions must be judicially enforceable in order to be considered rights at all.[73] Proponents of this position would surely take issue with the claim that the educational mandates in state constitutions are actually rights. Can we really call these constitutional education provisions rights even though most were not written with the idea that citizens could enforce their individual claims through courts? Can mandates on government have any meaning unless courts are willing to enforce them?

While judicial review is certainly a potent enforcement mechanism for constitutional rights, it is certainly possible for political actors other than judges to interpret educational provisions and demand legislative changes. One obvious source of extra-judicial enforcement was the organizations of educational reformers who had often lobbied to have these provisions included. Since these organizations were devoted to constitutional change as a means to their larger end of establishing statewide systems of free schools, they did not stop their work when a new constitution had been ratified. Instead, they continued their attempts to shape public sentiment and demand legislative change. For instance, after Pennsylvania's new education provision was added to its constitution in 1872, prominent educators immediately drew up a revised school code that they presented to the legislature.[74] Similarly, after the passage of its amendment to centralize school taxes, the California Council on Education focused its efforts on lobbying for legislation to bring the provision into effect.[75]

Another way that education activists and constitutional conventions attempted to ensure that legislatures would obey their constitutional directives, even without the promise of court enforcement, was to draft extremely clear and detailed provisions. For instance, an education advocate in Indiana explained: "The Constitutional injunction is direct, positive, immediate, and coming with the authority and sanction of an immense majority of the people."[76] Thus, he concluded that "The question of free schools is no longer a question in Indiana . . . It is the sworn duty of the Legislature to carry out this great provision in the Constitution."[77] North Dakota's education provision in the Constitution of 1889 even stated, "This legislative requirement

[72] John C. Eastman, "Reinterpreting the Education Clauses in State Constitutions," in *School Money Trials: The Legal Pursuit of Educational Adequacy*, ed. Martin R. West and Paul E. Peterson (Washington, DC: Brookings Institution Press, 2007).

[73] Holmes and Sunstein, *The Cost of Rights: Why Liberty Depends on Taxes*.

[74] See the Forty-First Annual Report of the Superintendent of Common Schools, published in the *Pennsylvania School Journal*, January 1875, vol. 23, no. 7, 233.

[75] "The Legislative Situation," *Sierra Educational News*, San Francisco, February 1921, vol. 17, no. 2, 59.

[76] Read, Address on the Means of Promoting Common School Education: Delivered in the Hall of the House of Representatives, at Indianapolis, on the Evening of Dec. 30, 1851: 7.

[77] Ibid.

shall be irrevocable without the consent of the United States and the people of North Dakota." The provision went on to specify that the legislature must establish schools "at their first session after the adoption of this constitution." Education provisions did get much longer and more detailed over time. By the end of the nineteenth century, one scholar of the education clauses in state constitutions described them this way: "Even constitutional conventions that have refrained from legislation in relation to schools, have often spoken a firmer voice than before. Indefiniteness makes room for clearness, and permission gives way to command."[78]

The hope was that it would be embarrassing for legislators to ignore such explicit commands and that if legislators were to thwart these provisions, it would harm their electoral prospects. This electoral threat was particularly demonstrable because constitutions and new provisions were often ratified by statewide vote. For instance, in Indiana, the same activist who noted the need for a detailed provision explained: "By the Constitution, which has been adopted by such an overwhelming majority, and which is now the fundamental law of this commonwealth, it is made the duty of the Legislature to provide by law for a general and uniform system of common schools, wherein tuition shall be without charge and equally open to all."[79]

Education activists promoted the drafting of detailed constitutional instructions about states' specific responsibilities in part so that their demands would be harder for legislatures to ignore. They attempted to enforce these directives through popular pressure, and often without recourse or reference to courts. As we have seen, the champions of these detailed mandates on government consistently justified them as necessary to impose legal obligations on the state and thereby limit legislative discretion. In other words, they used the language and logic of rights to describe these provisions, even when they did not expect to enforce the provisions in court.

Entrenchment theories of constitutional development focus on constitutions' capacity to usher the judiciary into particular conflicts in order to maintain the status quo. The common school movement's pursuit of positive rights differs from the entrenchment theorists' account in two important ways. First, common school activists seek change rather than preservation of the status quo. Second, they created rights even without plans to rely on judicial enforcement. Thus, the origins of education rights reveal a new reason for the creation of constitutional rights: forcing the legislature into action. Entrenchment theories certainly explain the origins of some constitutional rights, and even some education rights, but the common school movement's activism demonstrates that a desire for entrenchment through judicial enforcement is not the only motive that has prompted the creation of new constitutional rights.

[78] B. A. Hinsdale, *Education in the State Constitutions* (n.p., 1889), 12–13.
[79] Read, Address on the Means of Promoting Common School Education: Delivered in the Hall of the House of Representatives, at Indianapolis, on the Evening of Dec. 30, 1851: 7.

Preempting Litigation

In the case of some political conflicts, rights campaigns have actually grown out of activists' desire to exclude the judiciary. While constitutions can create the basis for litigation, they can also ensure that those courts are unable to rule particular statutes unconstitutional. Thus, interest groups and social movements may draft constitutional rights not only to judicialize conflicts, but also to insulate particular kinds of statutes from courts' power to nullify them. Reformers' desire to insulate educational policies from potentially hostile judiciaries led to the creation of education rights as well. For instance, it is clear that the education provision in Pennsylvania's 1874 constitution was written in part to protect common school legislation from the charge that it was unconstitutional.

Like many of the common school activists discussed earlier, Pennsylvania's educational reformers hoped to compel legislative action through the drafting of highly detailed, mandatory provisions about educational spending. To this end, they established the constitutional requirement that the legislature appropriate $1 million each year for the support of schools. One delegate to Pennsylvania's constitutional convention explained, "The failure of the legislature to make such appropriations as would equalize the burthens [sic] of supporting the system is therefore, I take it, a reason why this proposition is inserted."[80] At the annual meeting of the state teachers association, Superintendent J. P. Wickersham described a similar purpose for this provision: "Heretofore, the amount appropriated depended largely upon the liberality of the Legislature, or the degree of personal effort made to secure the money. It might be a certain sum one year, and a larger or a smaller one the next. The whole matter was governed by circumstances in which caprice oftentimes played quite as prominent a role as wisdom."[81] However, Wickersham also went on to explain that these appropriations were valuable not only to insulate educational funding against the whims of the legislature, but primarily to demonstrate the state's commitment to education in extremely concrete terms. He explained that, even more important than the legislative compulsion it created, was the fact that the new provision gave "the sanction of the convention that framed the Constitution and of the Constitution itself to the policy of a system of public education in the most emphatic manner."[82] This sanction was not merely symbolic, but was also strategically valuable.

---

[80] Pennsylvania Constitutional Convention, *Debates of the Convention to Amend the Constitution of Pennsylvania: Convened at Harrisburg*, November 12, 1872, Adjourned, November 27, to Meet at Philadelphia, January 7, 1873: vol. 7, 679.

[81] J. P. Wickersham, "Education Under the New Constitution," *Pennsylvania School Journal*, Harrisburg, September 1874, vol. 23, no. 3, 107.

[82] Ibid.

It was important to educational activists that Pennsylvania's constitution explicitly sanction the state's existing system of education because that system had been challenged in court. In 1851, the Pennsylvania Supreme Court had considered the constitutionality of the state's public school system. The previous constitution declared that the "the legislature shall, as soon as conveniently may be, provide by law for the establishment of schools throughout the sate in such a manner that the poor may be taught gratis." In 1849, the legislature required (via statute) that every township establish a common school. Opponents of this law argued that it was unconstitutional because the legislature only had the constitutional authority to establish free schools for poor students, not common schools for all.[83] The court ruled that no part of the law contravened any part of the constitution. However, this vindication of the legislature's authority to establish public schools was apparently insufficient to quell further debate on the subject. The *Pennsylvania School Journal* explained: "Under the operation of a common school system, the poor are taught gratis, and, therefore such a system is not contrary to the Constitution, and the Supreme Court has so decided; but a common school system goes much beyond this . . . For this extension of authority it should have better constitutional warrant."[84] Superintendent Wickersham also explained that, while the state's highest court had sanctioned its school system, "Many legal minds . . . [had] always remained in doubt as to the soundness of this decision."[85]

Wickersham believed that the new constitutional provision would protect the state's future educational institutions from the charge that they were unconstitutional, and in several of his writings on the subject, he celebrated his belief that the new constitution would also protect an even more expansive school system than currently existed. He wrote: "We have now a firm foundation, embedded in the organic law of the state, on which to erect the grand educational structure of the future."[86] In part, Wickersham seems to have been thinking about the establishment of public high schools. After the adoption of the new constitution, he specified that, under the new provision, high schools would be safe from constitutional challenge. He wrote, "No constitutional objection will hereafter stand in the way of the establishment of schools of the highest grade . . . This surely is solid ground."[87] This "solid ground" was important to Wickersham not because it would usher courts into policy battles over the school system, but because it would ensure that

[83] Mahlon Hellerich, "Public Education and the Pennsylvania Constitutional Convention of 1873," *History of Education Journal* 9, no. 1 (1957): 3.

[84] J. P. Wickersham, "Thirty-Ninth Annual Report of the Superintendent of Common Schools," *Pennsylvania School Journal*, Harrisburg, January 1873, vol. 21, no.7, 233.

[85] J. P. Wickersham, "Forty-First Annual Report of the Superintendent of Common Schools," *Pennsylvania School Journal*, Harrisburg, January 1875, vol. 23, no. 7, 232.

[86] J. P. Wickersham, "Education Under the New Constitution," *Pennsylvania School Journal*, Harrisburg, September 1874, vol. 23, no. 3, 107.

[87] Ibid.

courts could not undo legislative programs. Despite the fact that this provision was created to keep courts out, rather than usher them in, Wickersham described this constitutional mandate as a right: "If my son or daughter attains the legal minimum education . . . I will have a right to demand that the system be such that such further or higher education can be had. The schools must be provided."[88]

From our vantage point in the twenty-first century, without any context for this explanation, we might well imagine that Wickersham intended to enforce his new right to education in court. As we have seen, however, the opposite was true. One of the virtues of the constitutional education right, from Wickersham's perspective, was that it would insulate high schools from judicial nullification. In fact, opponents of public high schools often argued (like the opponents of Philadelphia's common schools) that state legislatures lacked the constitutional authority to establish any state-supported schools beyond the elementary level. Controversy over this issue continued from 1860 to nearly the end of the nineteenth century in every region of the country, though it was most widespread in the Northeastern and Midwestern states.[89] This controversy even culminated in state supreme court cases in at least seven states between 1871 and 1907.[90] Although state courts generally ruled in favor of public high schools, they did entertain challenges to these extensions of state common school systems. Constitutions could be used to forestall such challenges by explicitly authorizing or even mandating the legislative creation of common school systems.

Clearly, the entrenchment theories that explain the creation of rights as a result of their creators' desire to enable litigation do not apply particularly well to the education rights created in the nineteenth century. Instead of enabling litigation, educational provisions were intended to force legislatures into action. Many education activists planned to enforce their rights without recourse to courts and, at least in Pennsylvania, constitutional rights were understood as a way of keeping courts out of this policymaking arena. Consequently, educational activists in the nineteenth century crafted detailed policy instructions and placed these instructions directly in their states' highest laws. They clearly understood these constitutional provisions to impose obligations on government, and it was precisely their desire to impose these obligations that prompted common school activists to seek

[88] J. P. Wickersham, "School Legislation Under New Constitution," *Pennsylvania School Journal*, Harrisburg, February 1874, vol. 22, no. 8, 246.

[89] B. Jeannette Burrell and R. H. Eckelberry, "The High-School Controversy in the Post-Civil-War Period: Times, Places, and Participants," *School Review* 42, no. 5 (1934): 335.

[90] *Charles E. Stuart and others v. School District No. 1 of the Village of Kalamazoo*, 30 Mich. 69 (1874); *Frederick Richards v. Samuel Raymond*, 92 Ill. 612 (1879); *Roach v. The Board of President and Directors of the St. Louis Public Schools* 77 Mo. 484 (1883); *Newman v. Thompson*, 9 Ky. L. Rptr. 199 (1887); *Koester v. Board of County Commissioners of Atchison County*, 44 Kan. 141 (1890); *Board of Sup'rs of Bedford County v. Bedford High School*, 92 Va. 292 (1895); *Evers v. Hudson*, 36 Mont. 135 (1907).

constitutional change in the first place. Consequently, we should recognize these detailed education provisions as constitutional rights. We should also recognize that these rights had different origins than those envisioned by entrenchment theorists.

ENABLING LITIGATION

Most of America's constitutional education rights were created during the nineteenth century. As we have seen, the authors of these provisions described plans for their enforcement without reference to courts. However, some attempts to change the education provisions of America's state constitutions have been intended to invite the judiciary into educational policymaking. These provisions were drafted during the late twentieth century, and were spurred largely by the burgeoning litigation movement to equalize states' systems of public school financing. Proponents of these provisions hoped that, by drafting education rights, they could enable state courts to order the state to spend more money on public schools or find a more equitable way to raise and distribute money for public education.

Well before the 1960s, education activists pointed to state constitutional provisions when arguing that the government should change its system for financing education. For instance, in 1921, the *Indiana Farmer's Guide* ran an opinion piece entitled "Our Public Schools." It argued that "some sections [of the state] that are favorably located and wealthy [are] paying a small tax, and having the best of schools with fine buildings and equipment, while other and poorer sections get along as best they can with unsuitable building and equipment and short-term schools, for which they are compelled by the state to pay a high local tax." Consequently, it asserted that Indiana's school financing system violated the state's constitutional guarantee of educational equality. The piece rhetorically asked its readers: "Is this the 'free and equal' opportunity for education decreed by the state constitution?"[91] The education refinance litigation of the late twentieth century employed this identical reasoning.

The innovation of the late twentieth century was to use courts in an attempt to reshape states' systems of educational financing. This reform effort began with an attempt to advance the claim that the federal Constitution contained the right to an education. In the 1960s, academics and poverty-focused lawyers began constructing arguments about the meaning of the Fourteenth Amendment's Equal Protection Clause as it related to school finance. While still a graduate student at the University of Chicago, Arthur Wise published an article claiming that the Fourteenth Amendment guaran-

[91] Charles Strange, "Our Public Schools," *Indiana Farmer's Guide*, Huntington, February 5, 1921, vol. 33, no. 6, 33.

teed that the quality of education within a given state could not depend upon a student's home address or his wealth.[92] Meanwhile, John Coons, a Berkeley Law professor, along with two of his students, William Clune and Stephen Sugarman, were developing a more modest interpretation. They claimed that the Equal Protection clause required states to enable school districts that were willing to tax themselves at the same rate to raise equal amounts of money. Any state system that lacked this feature, they argued, discriminated unconstitutionally on the basis of wealth, and deprived the poor of the fundamental right to education. This argument was initially successful in a string of state and lower federal court decisions, most famously before the California Supreme Court in the 1971 case *Serrano v. Priest*.[93]

However, in 1973, the U.S. Supreme Court definitively rejected the idea that the U.S. Constitution contained the right to an education. Justice Powell's majority opinion first dispensed with the notion that the Equal Protection clause of the U.S. Constitution rendered Texas's system of school financing unconstitutional. It then declared that change might be necessary, but asserted that such change could not come through the Supreme Court or the Fourteenth Amendment.[94] The Court's unequivocal rejection of a federal right to education, coupled with its holding that school financing systems that consistently disadvantaged poor districts were constitutionally permissible, was a major disappointment for those who hoped to end the current regime of state financing for education through judicial interpretation of the Equal Protection Clause. One such academic declared, "The point to be made is this: For the foreseeable future, the federal courts must be considered closed to those who seek to overturn educational finance systems through the federal Equal Protection Clause."[95] Yet, advocates of educational equality did not abandon litigation. Instead, education activists responded to the setback by challenging systems of education financing on state constitutional grounds and in state courts.

The potential for litigation under state constitutions gave rise to a new wave of textual education rights. In several states, proponents of educational equality attempted to re-draft constitutions in order to facilitate legal challenges to school financing systems, this time on state constitutional grounds. For instance, Montana's Constitutional Convention of 1972 not only addressed the problem of providing an education for students in poor districts, but actually re-drafted the state's education article explicitly to facilitate litigation that could address the problem. The report of the committee on education introduced its proposed changes with the explanation that

---

[92] J. S. Berke, "Recent Adventures of State School Finance—Saga of Rocket Ships and Glider Planes," *School Review* 82, no. 2 (1974): 187.

[93] *Serrano v. Priest*, 487 P.2d 1241 (1971).

[94] *San Antonio Independent School Dis. v. Rodriguez*, 411 U.S. 1 (1973).

[95] Berke, "Recent Adventures of State School Finance—Saga of Rocket Ships and Glider Planes," 191.

"Montana's school financing system is similar to those declared unconstitutional in the states where challenges have been made. The same vast discrepancies in tax burdens and educational support exist in Montana as exist elsewhere."[96] The educational article was intended to fix these discrepancies primarily by empowering the state court. The final education article adopted by the convention required the legislature to "fund and distribute in an equitable manner to the school districts the state's share of the cost of the basic elementary and secondary school system," and declared that "equality of educational opportunity is guaranteed to each person of the state." Critics at the constitutional convention argued that adding this provision would be akin to putting the *Serrano* opinion directly into the Constitution, and its advocates did not challenge that characterization. The education provision in Montana's 1972 constitution was clearly drafted precisely to enable Montana's courts to issue a ruling like the *Serrano* decision.[97]

In Florida, the activists who pushed for constitutional change on behalf of educational equality also hoped that such changes would enable (or force) the judiciary to overturn existing systems of school financing. The changes that were most clearly intended to serve as the basis for litigation were prompted by an instance of unsuccessful litigation within the state. In the 1996 case of *Coalition for Adequacy and Fairness in School Funding v. Chiles*, education activists challenged the state's system of school funding, arguing that it violated the constitution's mandate to provide an adequate system of free public schools. The Florida Supreme Court ruled against the plaintiffs, arguing that they had not demonstrated the existence of an "appropriate standard for determining 'adequacy' that would not present a substantial risk of judicial intrusion into the powers and responsibilities of the legislature."[98]

The state's educational activists immediately attempted to supply such a standard in the form of a constitutional amendment. Since the Florida constitution allows for amendments through the initiative and referendum process, they could accomplish this change largely without the help or cooperation of the state legislature that had crafted the financing system they wished to dismantle. Toward this end, a group of education organizations drafted

[96] Montana Constitutional Convention of 1971–2: 722–3.

[97] Several other constitutional conventions explored the idea of drafting education provisions so that their new constitutions would serve as more effective bases for school finance litigation. Through his careful work on state constitutional conventions, John Dinan has demonstrated that the New York convention of 1964, as well as the Texas and New Hampshire conventions of 1974, also entertained the idea of including such amendments. In Texas and New York, these clauses were written into new constitutions, which, as a whole, were never ratified. The New Hampshire convention simply rejected the new education clause. Dinan, "The Meaning of State Constitutional Education Clauses: Evidence from the Constitutional Convention Debates."

[98] *Coalition For Adequacy and Fairness In School Funding, Inc., et al. v. Lawton Chiles*, 680 So. 2d 400, 23 (1996).

an initiative entitled "requirement for adequate public education funding," which defined adequacy by requiring the state to appropriate a minimum of 40 percent of its annual revenues to education. Part of the procedure for adopting a constitutional amendment through initiative is to request that the state attorney general ask the state supreme court for an advisory opinion about whether the proposed change fulfills the constitutional requirement that a citizen initiative embrace only one subject. The Florida supreme court ruled that, because this type of constitutional provision would have such a far-reaching impact on all kinds of budgetary decisions, it embraced more than one topic. This decision effectively quashed this constitutional initiative, but not the movement for constitutional change.

When the state created a constitutional revision commission in 1998, education activists once again worked to place a justiciable standard of educational adequacy directly into the state's constitution. This new proposal, which came to be known as Revision 6, required the state to provide an "efficient, safe, secure and high quality education." Other state courts had already ruled these particular terms to be a justiciable standard of adequacy. As one law review article supporting the amendment explained: "Revision 6 is a conscious response to the *Coalition for Adequacy Case*, attempting to give meaningful definition to 'adequacy' under Article IX, and provide a measurable standard for the legislature's duty to support education."[99] Unsurprisingly, the successful passage of this amendment was followed almost immediately by further litigation. As in Montana, the champions of this constitutional provision were primarily interested in enabling litigation, and in forcing courts to invalidate existing litigation.

The Virginia Constitution was also revised with the idea of facilitating educational litigation. Although it occurred during the late 1970s, this change to the state's education article was largely a response to the state's widespread resistance to desegregation, during which county governments chose to close their schools rather than integrate them. Despite Virginia's constitutional provision requiring that the state maintain common schools, the Virginia Supreme Court declared such closures were constitutionally permissible.[100] The 1978 constitutional revision commission revised the education article with this ruling firmly in mind, and hoped to remove all doubt about the obligations of the state and local governments. The executive director of the commission explained that state courts ought to interpret their new article far more forcefully than its predecessor:

> The new education article replaces provisions in the old Constitution which, as interpreted by the courts, had virtually no force. The old Constitution had been construed as permitting the Commonwealth

[99] Jon Mills and Timothy McLendon, "Strengthening the Duty to Provide Public Education," *Florida Bar Journal* 72, no. 9 (1998).

[100] *County School Board v. Griffin*, 133 S.E.2d 565 (1963).

and the localities alike simply to opt out of the business of running public schools—despite language in the old Constitution which might have seemed to require a proper system of public education. The new Constitution changes this. Its legislative history makes unmistakably clear the constitutional mandate on the General Assembly and the localities alike to support a meaningful system of public education.[101]

Virginia's new provision seems to have been both backward- and forward-looking. On the one hand, it was an immediate response to the state supreme court decisions that had allowed localities to resist integration. On the other hand, its drafters also seem to have anticipated the impending controversies about education financing and equality. For instance, the executive director of the revision commission also explained that "the mandate on the localities to provide their share of school money, as determined by the general assembly is explicit. Implicit, but equally important to the whole plan, is the corollary duty on the General Assembly to put up sufficient money to meet the prescribed standards of quality education in those localities lacking the wherewithal to do the job from local resources."[102]

In contrast to their nineteenth-century predecessors, these twentieth-century provisions do seem to have been drafted with an eye toward judicial interpretation and enforcement. Consequently, their origins look far more similar to the process the entrenchment theories describe. However, even these provisions, which were indeed crafted to promote litigation, were not intended to entrench the status quo or to maintain a hegemon's influence. On the contrary, these provisions were drafted to challenge the entrenched system of educational finance with the hope that courts would help to un-entrench them. Thus, even these twentieth-century provisions demonstrate that constitutional rights can come into existence through channels other than those described by the existing (i.e., entrenchment) theories.

CONCLUSION

Entrenchment theories tell us that constitutional development occurs when those in power try to extend their power by placing the policies they have already enacted in constitutions that will outlast their own political dominance. Thus, entrenchment theories portray the creation of constitutional rights as an inherently conservative enterprise; for entrenchment purposes, constitutions' most salient feature is their ability to keep things the same well into the future. Congress clearly influenced state constitutions with the hope that constitutions would entrench particular policies even when Con-

---

[101] A. E. Dick Howard, "Education in Virginia's New Constitution," *Compact* 5, no. 2 (1971).

[102] Ibid.

gress was no longer in a position to insist on them. However, the case of education rights offers additional and importantly different explanations for why people write new constitutional rights.

Educational activists certainly hoped that their policies would endure, and that was no doubt part of the appeal of constitutional politics. However, they also hoped that constitutional change would have short-term benefits, and that new rights would bring about immediate change. After all, these activists were not in a position of legislative dominance that constitutional change might allow them to extend, but were instead relative outsiders to the legislative process, who experienced ongoing frustration with their state legislatures. As a result, a different feature of constitutional politics appealed to them. Constitutions were not useful to them because they could entrench existing policies with the help of a friendly judiciary, but because those rights might facilitate changes to educational practices that were already deeply entrenched. When legislatures would not establish statewide schools, manage school funds wisely, or levy the taxes necessary to provide adequate or redistributive school funding, common school activists attempted to force legislatures into these kinds of actions through the creation of positive constitutional rights. Furthermore, they hoped that constitutional rights would help them to bring about change even in the absence of judicial enforcement. Even when twentieth-century reformers drafted new education rights to enable litigation and waged litigation campaigns under both new and old provisions, their use of the judiciary was not intended to protect the status quo or maintain the policies of the dominant regime. They did use constitutional rights to usher courts into policymaking battles, but like nineteenth-century activists, they did so in the interests of change.

Ultimately, state supreme courts did enforce both new and old education provisions, and consistently identified even the nineteenth-century common school provisions as education rights. By 2007, state high courts had considered the constitutionality of state systems of public school financing in all but seven states, and the challenges to state financing for education prevailed in twenty-six of these cases.[103] These legal victories cannot be dismissed as small judicial forays into state policy or as rulings that only affected educational financing on the margins. On the contrary, many state courts issued sweeping and highly consequential opinions, often placing themselves at the center of the policymaking process. For instance, in the same year that the U.S. Supreme Court declared that the U.S. Constitution did not guarantee the right to an education,[104] New Jersey's highest court ruled that the state constitution did. In 1973, the New Jersey Supreme Court found that the state's constitutional mandate, created in 1875, to establish a "thorough and efficient" system of free public schools, could "have no other

[103] Michael Paris, *Framing Equal Opportunity : Law and the Politics of School Finance Reform* (Stanford, CA: Stanford Law Books, 2010), 46.

[104] *San Antonio Independent School District v. Rodriguez*, 411 U.S. 1 (1973).

import" but to mandate that the state create an equal educational opportunity for all children.[105] The court then cited the efforts of the state's common school reformers to centralize the system of taxation for education.

As we have already seen, common school reformers argued that the less centralized taxation for schooling was, the less equal the state's educational opportunities would be. On this issue, New Jersey's highest court declared itself in firm agreement with the state's nineteenth-century reform movement:

> [I]t is . . . difficult to understand how the tax burden can be left to local initiative with any hope that statewide equality of educational opportunity will emerge. The 1871 statute embraced a statewide tax because it was found that local taxation could not be expected to yield equal educational opportunity. Since then the State has returned the tax burden to local school districts . . . There is no more evidence today than there was a hundred years ago that this approach will succeed.[106]

Consequently, the court ruled that the state's system of school financing violated the "thorough and efficient" clause of the state constitution, and continued, "Whatever the reason for the violation, the obligation is the State's to rectify it. If local government fails, the State government must compel it to act, and if the local government cannot carry the burden, the State must itself meet its continuing obligation."[107] The New Jersey court is not alone in having issued such a strong defense of the positive right to education in the state's constitution.

When the Kentucky Supreme Court was asked to interpret its state's common school provision in 1989, it too declared the state's entire system of school financing unconstitutional. Like the common school reformers of the nineteenth century, Kentucky's highest court understood the constitutional instructions to "provide for an efficient system of common schools throughout the State" to impose a duty on state government. Thus, the court explained, "The obligation to so provide [for a system of common schools in Kentucky] is clear and unequivocal and is, in effect, a constitutional mandate."[108] To support this assertion, the Court quoted extensively from the records of the state's 1890 constitutional convention, and cited delegates' statements about both the obligatory and redistributive nature of the constitution's common school mandate. The court explained that it must enforce that mandate. These well-known cases, and the many others like them, exemplify high courts' willingness to demand, on the basis of constitutional rights, that states allocate their resources differently and that state govern-

---

[105] *Robinson v. Cahill*, 287 A. 2d 187, 519 (1972).
[106] *Robinson v. Cahill*, 287 A. 2d 187, 516 (1972).
[107] *Robinson v. Cahill*, 287 A. 2d 187, 519 (1972).
[108] *Rose v. Council for Better Education*, 790 S.W.2d 186, 205 (1989).

ments intervene more forcefully in the lives of their states in order to create functional public school systems.

The Kentucky court even went on to address the question of whether it had the authority to enforce this positive right, or as the court put it, "to stick our judicial noses" into this arena of legislative policymaking. Its answer was an unequivocal yes. The court explained that it had little choice but to become involved:

> It is our sworn duty, to decide such questions when they are before us by applying the constitution. The duty of the judiciary in Kentucky was so determined when the citizens of Kentucky enacted the social compact called the Constitution and in it provided for the existence of a third equal branch of government, the judiciary . . . To avoid deciding the case because of "legislative discretion," "legislative function," etc., would be a denigration of our own constitutional duty. To allow the General Assembly (or, in point of fact, the Executive) to decide whether its actions are constitutional is literally unthinkable.[109]

Although school financing formulas are just the sort of decisions about the allocation of public resources that courts are supposedly unwilling to challenge,[110] the Kentucky court actually characterized it as "literally unthinkable" that it would do anything else.

Not only have courts enforced the education rights in state constitutions, but their decisions seem to have facilitated real reform. Douglas Reed has examined changes in levels of educational inequality after state supreme courts have decided education refinancing cases. He found that, in states where courts have enforced positive education rights, interpreting these provisions to declare state systems of public school financing unconstitutional, educational inequality either stayed at the same level or (more frequently) decreased dramatically. Where Supreme Courts declined to nullify their state's systems of school financing, educational inequality generally increased. In light of these findings, Reed argues that "the lesson we should learn from court-initiated school finance equalization is that it generally achieves results."[111] America's constitutional education rights have a recent legacy of judicial enforcement and meaningful reform.

Even if they lacked this legacy of judicial enforcement, however, the education provisions in state constitutions would still be clear examples of positive rights in American constitutions. As we have seen, common school activists described these provisions as legal mandates for state action on behalf of the poor. On their own accounts, they sought constitutional change precisely so that they could trump legislatures, forcing their reluctant govern-

---

[109] *Rose v. Council for Better Education*, 790 S.W.2d 186, 209 (1989).

[110] See, for example, David M. Beatty, *Human Rights and Judicial Review: A Comparative Perspective* (Norwell: Kluwer Academic Publishers, 1994), 348.

[111] Reed, *On Equal Terms: The Constitutional Politics of Educational Opportunity*, 191.

ments into the active steps necessary to build statewide systems of free schools. Many also described these mandates as necessary to ensure not only that government extend itself, but also that it extend itself on behalf of those who, without the help of government, would not have had access to an education. Like the twentieth-century reformers who pursued litigation for this purpose, common school activists were quite explicit in their goal of creating constitutional obligations to intervene in the course of social and economic life in order to protect people from the consequences of the threats stemming from poverty.

It may seem strange to build an argument for the existence of America's positive-rights tradition by examining seemingly mundane, administrative details like the management and sale of school lands, the preservation and investment of school funds, and the structure of state taxation. However, we should not allow the specificity of these mandates to fool us into ignoring the sustained and widespread movement on behalf of these constitutional provisions. The champions of constitutional education provisions consistently argued that protections for private property were not morally sufficient and that the state must also protect those born without it. They insisted that the state ought to intervene on behalf of poor children in order to shield them from the life-long consequences of their parents' inability to pay for their education. Thus, the origins of these provisions not only tell us something new about where constitutional rights come from, they also demonstrate that, at the state level, Americans have used their constitutions to demand protective and interventionist government. In other words, when we look at state constitutions, we can see that even since the middle of the nineteenth century, America has had positive constitutional rights.

Workers' Rights

CONSTITUTIONAL PROTECTIONS WHERE (AND WHEN)
WE WOULD LEAST EXPECT THEM

> Labor's Bill of Rights . . . should be made the ultimate test by
> which we are to measure the work of the Constitutional Con-
> vention. Nothing short of that will answer the social and indus-
> trial needs of a growing and progressing state for a generation
> to come. Organized labor stands for human rights.
> *The Garment Worker*, 1915[1]

In the previous chapter, I argued that America has positive constitutional
rights to education. In light of these positive education rights, it is surely
mistaken to characterize American rights as exclusively negative and America's constitutional tradition as exceptional in this regard. Yet the case of
education may be a particularly easy one. Perhaps education is, itself, the
exception to American exceptionalism. It seems quite possible that even
America's liberal hegemony might point toward active government where
children are concerned. After all, the idea that people's opportunities should
not be circumscribed by the circumstances of their birth might be said to be
one of the tenets of liberalism. In addition many believe that, when it comes
to education, civic republicanism, which places a particularly strong emphasis on education and on the state's role in educating, has dominated American political development from the very beginning.[2] Perhaps, then, there is
something special about education that allowed this one type of positive
right to find its way into American constitutions. We might still suspect that
negative rights have dominated American constitutional development in all
other domains. Therefore, before we can dispense with claims of American
constitutional exceptionalism, we must examine a harder case, one in which
American liberalism is agreed to have reached its fullest flower and in which

---

This chapter was previously published as Emily Zackin, "'To Change the Fundamental Law
of the State': Protective Labor Provisions in U.S. Constitutions," *Studies in American Political
Development* 24, no. 1 (2010): 1–23.

[1] "Labor's Bill of Rights," *The Garment Worker*, New York, September 17, 1915, 5.

[2] Wood, *The Creation of the American Republic, 1776–1787*, 120–23, 426.

liberal ideology would have counseled strongly against protective or interventionist government.

The quintessential arguments about America's exceptional liberalism and its uniquely negative-rights culture have focused on its labor movement. Most famously, Louis Hartz argued that America's Lockean liberal ideology exerted a hegemonic influence on American political development.[3] Instead of demanding governmental aid and protection, the American labor movement is frequently said to have insisted only that government leave unions free to bargain privately. Thus, Hartz's influential account of American liberalism asserts that the labor movement was a participant in, not a rival of, the dominant economic and ideological regime. Because American labor participated unconsciously in the nation's liberal tradition, he argues, the movement never developed a salutary sense of class-consciousness, and consequently failed to demand the creation of a powerful and protective state, like those in Western Europe. Hartz famously declared that, "Far from inheriting the earth, all [the American laborer] wanted to do was to smash trusts and begin running the Lockian race all over again."[4]

American political development (APD) scholars and labor historians have challenged Hartz from many directions, with some arguing that liberalism was not so hegemonic as a matter of either ideology or law, and others claiming that the distinctive network of the nation's political institutions, and not ideology, was responsible for labor's failure to bring about a socialist democracy.[5] However, in its relationship to constitutional law, the prevailing picture of the American labor movement still remains one of negative rights and anti-governmental voluntarism. Even those who have challenged Hartz's take on American labor have nonetheless shared his assessment of American rights. For instance, William Forbath's preeminent treatment of the AFL's rights consciousness argues that the AFL was not duped by America's pervasive ideology, but consciously and strategically chose to reject governmental intervention in labor's affairs. Because judicial

---

[3] Hartz, *The Liberal Tradition in America; an Interpretation of American Political Thought since the Revolution.*

[4] Ibid., 223.

[5] Rogers Smith Smith, *Civic Ideals: Conflicting Visions of Citizenship in U.S. History*, has famously demonstrated the influence of multiple ideological traditions in American political thought. In addition to liberalism, these include ascriptive hierarchical thinking (or racism) and republicanism. Sean Wilentz has documented the strong influence of republican ideology on American labor. See Sean Wilentz, *Chants Democratic: New York City & the Rise of the American Working Class, 1788–1850* (New York: Oxford University Press, 1984). While Karen Orren has argued that pre–New Deal American labor law was actually feudal, rather than liberal. See Karen Orren, *Belated Feudalism: Labor, the Law, and Liberal Development in the United States* (Cambridge: Cambridge University Press, 1991). Ruth O'Brien has argued for the importance, not of liberal individualism, in shaping New Deal labor policies, but instead of the corporatist theory of responsible unionism. Ruth O'Brien, *Workers' Paradox: The Republican Origins of New Deal Labor Policy, 1886–1935* (Chapel Hill: University of North Carolina Press, 1998).

rulings often criminalized the AFL's activities and undercut its legislative gains, the AFL abandoned its former arguments in favor of interventionist government and began to demand only that government leave it alone. Thus, according to Forbath, by the 1890s, the AFL had adopted "a rigid and anti-statist liberalism."[6]

Victoria Hattam has similarly argued that American labor was not ideologically stunted, but that it rejected governmental intervention in response to its institutional and political environment. In fact, she demonstrates that American labor was no less militant than European labor, and argues that what requires explanation is not why labor never tried to improve its lot, but why its militancy in the industrial realm was accompanied by a marked moderation in the political realm.[7] She explains this bifurcation as the result of the institutional structure in which American labor organizations found themselves and the conclusions they drew about that structure. Because the judiciary was able to undermine many of its legislative victories, the AFL ultimately shifted tactics away from law and toward private bargaining. Thus, Hattam argues that American labor was exceptional, not because it was less radical, but because it had fewer incentives to bring that radicalism to bear in the legal arena. Current scholarship, like that of Forbath and Hattam, has largely undermined Hartz's account of American labor as simply blinded to the potential value of an active and protective state. However, these authors still emphasize labor's withdrawal from the political realm and its abandonment of positive-rights claims.

In light of the belief that American labor had to give up on positive rights, the existence and origins of the protective labor rights in state constitutions are particularly illuminating. American constitutions not only contain positive education rights, they also contain positive protections for labor. While labor's demands for positive rights are not evident in the federal Bill of Rights, they are reflected in state constitutions. For example, state constitutions guarantee the right to an eight-hour day, a minimum wage, and protection from blacklisting practices and private armies. These constitutional provisions demonstrate that education rights are not alone in the American constitutional tradition.

Just as we saw with educational mandates, the proponents of protective labor regulation understood the constitutional provisions they championed as positive labor rights, even when they did not use those terms. The statements of labor leaders, progressive lawyers, and constitutional convention delegates make it clear that these provisions were intended to create obligations on government to intervene, placing itself between employers and laborers, and providing protection from the often brutal conditions market

---

[6] Forbath, *Law and the Shaping of the American Labor Movement*, 130.

[7] Hattam, *Labor Visions and State Power: The Origins of Business Unionism in the United States*, 9.

capitalism had created. These justifications for constitutional labor protections, like arguments in favor of educational mandates, embody the defining features of positive rights.

The origins of constitutional labor rights, like those of education rights, also compel us to augment the standard explanation for the creation of new constitutional rights. As we will see, labor organizations were not interested in using constitutions to usher courts into policymaking, as entrenchment theories predict. On the contrary, they were primarily interested in prompting legislatures to pass protective regulations and in insulating that legislation from courts. Laborers and their advocates argued that constitutional rights would insulate protective labor laws from charges that those laws were unconstitutional, thereby excluding unfriendly courts from particular areas of policymaking. The proponents of labor rights also argued that constitutional provisions could be used to force recalcitrant legislatures to pass protective statutes, and finally that constitutional provisions would facilitate political organizing within their own social movement. Thus, education rights are not the only rights whose origins do not fit neatly with entrenchment theories, nor are they America's only positive rights. Even where we might least expect to find them, in the area of labor markets, American constitutions contain positive rights.[8]

I begin this chapter by arguing that many of the labor provisions in state constitutions are properly understood as positive rights. Next, I describe the efforts of state-level labor leaders to add these rights to constitutions. The rest of the chapter addresses what the advocates of protective labor regulations hoped to gain by seeking constitutional, rather than merely statutory, changes. First, I argue that they pursued constitutional change in order to reverse court decisions that nullified labor laws and to preempt similar rulings where they had not yet been issued. I then address the relationship of these state-level legal questions to the U.S. Supreme Court and its infamous Lochner Era. Next, I argue that labor organizations were not only motivated to create positive rights in order to address their problems with the judiciary, but also in order to compel reluctant state legislatures to enact protective statutes and finally to help them organize. All of these motives are different from those that entrenchment theories describe. Thus, just as with

---

[8] James Pope has noted that labor movements staged a "constitutional insurgency in this period, assailing current constitutional understandings. Rather than rejecting the Constitution, however, Pope explains that laborers turned to the Constitution to justify their claims to a right to strike, grounding it in the Thirteenth Amendment. Although Pope's excellent study focuses on a constitutional right to strike, grounded in the federal Constitution, and this book is focused on other labor rights found in state constitutions, they both find a similar pattern. Laborers attacked existing constitutional understandings, but not constitutionalism as a whole. Instead, they sought to reshape constitutions to better reflect their vision of constitutional rights, often circumventing the most traditional political channels in order to effect these changes. James Gray Pope, "Labor's Constitution of Freedom," *Yale Law Journal* 106, no. 4 (1997).

education rights, the origins of constitutional labor rights should cause us to re-think not only the standard view of American rights, but also the reigning theory about where constitutional rights come from.

LABOR PROVISIONS AS POSITIVE RIGHTS

In order to demonstrate that state constitutions contain positive labor rights, it is first necessary to describe the relevant provisions. Although there are a multitude of state constitutional provisions related to employment, if we are interested in positive rights, I believe we should focus on provisions that directly addressed labor or laborers and that mandated active government intervention in their workplaces and relations with employers.[9] These provisions relate to laborer's liens, the number of hours in a legal workday, the safety of workplace conditions, the minimum wage, and the form of those wages. They also outlawed, or called for the legislature to outlaw, contracts that released employers from liability for workplace injuries, and established the constitutionality of workmen's compensation programs. Some called for the state to outlaw blacklists and provide protection from employers' private armies. These labor provisions were rarely universal—often relating only to women, people in particularly dangerous industries, and public employees. They were almost always written with only white workers in mind, and as the conclusion demonstrates, labor organizations were often quite clear about their desire to exclude immigrant labor from eligibility for public works projects. Some labor organizations even attempted to bar immigrants from residing in their state, and states in which labor organizations created the most robust constitutional protections for laborers were frequently states in which anti-immigrant sentiment proved strongest. Despite the fact that the labor rights documented here were not universally protective, these constitutional provisions did address many of the central concerns of labor organizations during the time of their passage. Table 6.1 summarizes the provisions by topic.[10] Table 6.2 offers a chronology of their

---

[9] Although many state constitutions required or enabled legislatures to regulate railroads, banks, and other corporations, I excluded these provisions if they did not specifically address employment. I also excluded child labor provisions, provisions that address the right to work or the right to unionize and strike, as well as provisions that merely required the establishment of a labor commission or created a new office. While the creation of bureaus of labor and offices of inspectors were often the first steps to the passage of regulation, provisions that merely created these institutions but did not require or even empower them to regulate employment seemed significantly different from constitutionalizing protections themselves. Because the protections to work and unionize are often aimed at stopping government from interfering with labor relations, I have not included them in this list of protections that government must actively provide.

[10] I compiled a list of state constitutional amendments that require active government protection of laborers. I did this by reading the text of every state constitution, including all of their

TABLE 6.1. Constitutional Labor Provisions by Topic

Topic	Number	States
Working conditions	15	AZ, AR, CA, CO, ID, IL, MI, NE, NM, NY, OH, OK, UT, WA, WY
Hours	14	AZ, CA, CO, ID, LA, MI, MT, NE, NM, NY, OH, OK, UT, WY
Employer liability	12	AZ, CO, MS, MT, NM, NY, OK, SC, TX, UT, VA, WY
Laborers' liens	8	CA, FL, GA, ID, LA, NC, OH, TX
Workmen's compensation	9	AR, AZ, CA, NY, OH, PA, TX, VT, WY
Protection from private armies	8	AZ, ID, KY, MT, SC, UT, WA, WY
Wages	7	CA, KY, LA, NE, NY, OH, UT
Blacklisting	4	AZ, MS, ND, UT

TABLE 6.2. Chronology of Constitutional Labor Provisions

Years	Number of States to Add at Least One Labor Protection	States
1864–1865	1	LA
1866–1870	4	GA, NC, TX, IL
1871–1875	1	AR
1876–1880	4	TX, CO, CA, LA
1881–1885	1	FL
1886–1890	6	MT, ND, WY, WA, ID, MS
1891–1895	2	KY, UT
1896–1900	1	SC
1901–1905	5	ID, VA, CO, MT, NY
1906–1910	2	OK, MI
1911–1915	7	CA, NM, AZ, OH,* VT, NY, PA
1916–1920	3	CA, MI, NE*
1921–1925	1	OH
1926–1930	0	
1931–1935	1	UT
1936–1940	4	MT, TX, NY, AR

States that wrote labor provisions into new constitutions appear in bold.

*Ohio and Nebraska revised their constitutions though a convention, but the resulting changes were approved as individual amendments to the existing constitution.

addition, by state.[11] Both tables exclude broad declarations of labor rights that lack specific policy content, like Utah's declaration that "The rights of labor shall have just protection through laws calculated to promote the industrial welfare of the State."[12]

Table 6.1 describes the variety of labor protections added to state constitutions during the Gilded Age and Progressive Era. In general, provisions relating to laborers' liens, employer liability, and workplace safety (particularly for mines and railroads) dominate the early provisions. Provisions outlawing private armies and blacklisting were mostly constitutionalized in the 1890s (although both appear in Arizona's original constitution of 1912). Provisions relating to the hours and wages of labor are scattered throughout the period, while states began adding workmen's compensation to their constitutions only in 1911.

The individual states that appear more than once in table 6.2 either added new provisions in succeeding years or expanded existing provisions after the original inclusion of a labor provision. As table 6.2 demonstrates, protective labor provisions were steadily added to constitutions throughout the entire period from 1864 to 1940. (Although certain five-year periods saw more labor amendments added to constitutions than others, the appearance of discrete bursts of activism is largely due to the relatively small increments into which table 6.2 divides this period.) However, in general, the earliest instances of constitutional change did differ from those in the middle and at the end of the period. The years following the Civil War saw the constitutionalization of labor provisions through the rewriting of many Southern constitutions. With the exception of Louisiana, which included a provision about the regulation of hours and wages, all of the protective labor provisions added to Southern constitutions in the 1860s established laborers' liens. The labor provisions written at the end of the nineteenth and beginning of the twentieth century were largely included through the writing of new Western states' original constitutions. Many of these provisions addressed the concerns of miners. Finally, the Progressive Era saw the most coordinated attempts to establish protective legislation related to hours,

---

amendments. Since most states have ratified multiple constitutions, it is often challenging to acquire the text of constitutions and their amendments now that those documents have been superseded. I obtained every constitution and amendment of 39 states from the NBER State Constitution Project. Because the NBER project is still incomplete, I also referred to an earlier compilation of state constitutional texts. See John Wallis, "National Bureau of Economic Research / University of Maryland State Constitution Project"; Thorpe, *The Federal and State Constitutions: Colonial Charters, and Other Organic Laws of the States, Territories, and Colonies Now or Heretofore Forming the United States of America.*

[11] Rather than determining an a priori time period for this examination, I allowed the timing of the addition of these amendments to establish the historical period over which I examined labor organizations' constitutional activities.

[12] Utah Constitution, Article XVI, Section 1.

wages, working conditions, and workmen's compensation, and witnessed attempts to safeguard this type of legislation through constitutions.

Several constitutional provisions were phrased in classic rights language. For instance, the Wyoming constitution of 1889 read, "The rights of labor shall have just protection through laws calculated to secure to the laborer proper rewards for his service and to promote the industrial welfare of the State."[13] Other provisions simply declared the state's obligation to provide protection. For instance, the Illinois constitution of 1870 proclaimed it the "duty of the general assembly to pass laws as may be necessary for the protection of operative miners by providing for ventilation and the construction of escapement shafts as may secure safety in all coal mines."[14] Another way that constitutions established legal obligations on governments to provide a particular labor protection was by including the protective regulation directly in the text of the constitution. For example, Arizona's constitution of 1912 declared, "Eight hours and no more, shall constitute a lawful day's work in all employment by, or on behalf of, the state or any political subdivision of the State." By establishing these protective policies through constitutions, constitutional provisions removed democratic and legislative discretion on these issues, thereby creating a right. In total, thirty-six labor protections (in nineteen different states' constitutions) contained this kind of direct declaration of state policy. This group was primarily composed of provisions relating to laborers' liens, employer liability, maximum hours, private armies, and blacklists. Some of the earliest constitutional labor rights were phrased this way, and this phrasing was employed through the late 1930s. In addition, seven more provisions (in six states' constitutions) included a direct declaration of state policy followed by a statement that the legislature would enact the necessary laws to put the provision into effect and establish penalties for its violation.

Another way that constitutions created recognizable rights was by mandating legislative action on a particular issue. For instance, the New Mexico Constitution of 1911 declared, "The legislature shall enact laws requiring the proper ventilation of mines, the construction and maintenance of escapement shafts or slopes, and the adoption and use of appliances necessary to protect the health and secure the safety of employees therein." Some provisions also described a state policy first and then demanded that the "legislature shall" write laws to enforce the provision. This type of mandatory language also meets our definition of a right. If the constitution says that the legislature "shall" or "must" do something, then that constitutional provision serves as the basis for a demand that the state do it, regardless of the preferences of the state's democratic majorities. Twenty labor provisions used this mandatory language. Provisions that employed this phrasing re-

---

[13] Wyoming Constitution of 1889, Article 1 § 22.
[14] Illinois Constitution of 1879, Article 4 § 29.

lated primarily to workers' safety and laborers' liens and were added to constitutions between 1868 and 1912.

The next question is whether we ought to consider these mandates to be "positive rights." Remember that positive and negative rights are generally distinguished from one another along two distinct dimensions. First, positive rights are defined by the active intervention they require of government, while negative rights are characterized by the fact that they require governmental restraint. Second, negative rights protect people from dangers posed by a tyrannical or overbearing state, while positive rights also protect citizens from dangers that do not stem directly from government. As Forbath and Hattam have demonstrated, labor organizations certainly saw government as a threat, especially when the state hindered their ability to organize and strike. Though they recognized the dangers that government could pose, state-level labor organizations still continued to lobby for government intervention to protect them from their employers and from the brutal working conditions that laborers often encountered. Many state labor organizations demanded that, rather than allowing market forces to govern employment relationships and workplace practices, the state should intervene to offer laborers protection. In addition to the regulation of particularly dangerous workplaces, they petitioned for other sorts of regulations, including maximum hours legislation, minimum wages, and the creation of laborers' liens on the products of their labor (see table 6.1). By adding mandates for this kind of state intervention to constitutions, the advocates of protective labor legislation hoped to leave the state with no choice but to intervene in the interests of protecting workers. The constitutional provisions they drafted were intended to protect people from the practices of their employers, rather than the threat of interventionist government.[15] These features of constitutional labor provisions are the hallmarks of positive rights.

In the case of provisions outlawing the use of private armies and blacklists, these regulations protected laborers from the union- and strike-breaking practices of their employers. Workmen's compensation provisions are another clear example of the state extending itself through the creation of a statewide program and often a monetary fund for the protection of injured laborers. These provisions comprised the tail-end of a larger constitutional campaign to reform the governmental response to employer liability for workplace injuries. The employer liability provisions in state constitutions

---

[15] While some of the labor provisions that regulated hours, wages, and workplace safety related only to public employees. In the case of these provisions, the threat from which the constitution protected laborers was the state itself, rather than a private employer. However, these constitutional rights regulated the state in its capacity as employer, rather than its capacity as government. Such provisions were also intended as a wedge that would help to establish similar working conditions or wages throughout private industry. Despite the fact that these provisions technically protected people from government, therefore, they behave like positive, rather than negative, rights, and are included in this study.

protected workers from the necessity of signing contracts which guaranteed that their employers could not be held liable for workplace injuries. Several constitutions even abrogated the judicial doctrine known as the "fellow servant doctrine," which held that employers could not be held responsible for injuries resulting from the actions of another employee. These clauses spoke directly to the judiciary and, by eliminating the legal barriers to collecting compensation from employers, participated in the establishment of a more protective role for states in the lives of injured workers.

In discussing the creation of these constitutional labor provisions, the champions of these provisions were frequently quite explicit about their goal of requiring state intervention to protect laborers. For instance, one delegate to the Illinois Constitutional Convention of 1869 exhorted his fellow delegates this way: "Let us take care of the poor working man. Capital is most abundantly able—somewhat too able, in many instances, for the interests of humanity—to take care of itself."[16] A delegate to the Ohio Constitutional Convention of 1906–7 expressed a similar sentiment:

> We should provide for the health and safety of the miners in the coal mines and protect them from the evils and dangers to which in the past they have been subject. In the interests of labor on railroads and other public works we should provide for a regular day's labor of eight hours, and that no railroad or other corporation shall be allowed to compel an employee to work more than sixteen hours in any one day . . . It is true that the farmer, who can go to work and quit when he pleases without losing his job, does not need an eight-hour law, but the laborer on the railroad does. On the road running through my town, Tishomingo, why I have known one crew being compelled to work continuously for sixty-five hours without sleep. These people must have our protection. We must provide also that where a railroad corporation, mine operators or others, require of a laborer the signing of a contract, which would exempt him from damages in case of death or injury, that such contract shall be null and void. We shall provide for the protection of all laborers, whether in mines, factories or on the railroad.[17]

Clearly, these delegates wanted to "provide for the protection of laborers" by requiring the state to intervene, altering (through regulation) the conditions that the labor market had created.

---

[16] Illinois Constitutional Convention, *Debates and Proceedings of the Constitutional Convention of the State of Illinois: Convened at the City of Springfield, Tuesday, December 13, 1869,* 264.

[17] Oklahoma Constitutional Convention, *Proceedings of the Constitutional Convention of the Proposed State of Oklahoma: Held at Guthrie, Oklahoma, November 20, 1906 to November 16, 1907* (Muskogee: Muskogee Printing Co., 1907), 20.

While regulation is arguably not as active a role for the state as the provision of education or medical care, it is an instance of the state extending itself, rather than restraining itself from intervening. In fact, many conservatives of the period described this type of regulation not only as active state intervention in social and economic life, but as illegitimate intervention, the very sort of overreaching that courts consistently deemed to be a violation of the due process clauses of the federal and state constitutions. In the name of enforcing negative rights that protected people's freedom to establish whatever kinds of contracts they desired, courts consistently nullified protective labor laws. Laborers and their advocates responded to these assertions of negative rights by claiming that the world was changing, and that new economies required the creation or recognition of a different kind of right. There is a hint of this type of argument in the Oklahoma delegate's assertion that "the farmer, who can go to work and quit when he pleases without losing his job, does not need an eight-hour law, but the laborer on the railroad does." Many advocates of positive labor rights were even more explicit about this contrast.

Laborers and their advocates repeatedly asserted that traditional rights to freedom of contract and private property were useless to them, and they needed a new kind of right. Although labor organizations did not generally use the term "positive rights" to describe the active protection they sought, they regularly contrasted existing (negative) constitutional rights with the (positive) ones they hoped to add to constitutions. For instance, the debates about mining safety at the Illinois Constitutional Convention reflect a clear distinction between positive and negative rights. In arguing for the inclusion of a mining safety provision, one delegate noted that miners did not ask the convention for more traditional property rights because, he argued, that sort of protection was largely irrelevant to the laborer, who often had little in the way of property. Instead, a different sort of right was necessary to protect the laborer. He explained, "The class it affects come not before us asking that their property or their material interests be protected at our hands. This protection they do not require, for to them has been allotted no considerable portion of this world's wealth. They come to ask that, instead thereof, we protect their all—made up of their lives, their limbs, and their health."[18] Miners did not request constitutional restraints on government to protect their property from government itself, but instead desired active legislation and regulation to protect them from the dangerous conditions under which they labored. Because miners desired rights to ensure the safety of their workplaces, the sort of rights that could protect the laborer would force the state legislature to require that mining companies add escapement shafts and proper ventilation to their mines. While state policies may ultimately

[18] Illinois Constitutional Convention, *Debates and Proceedings of the Constitutional Convention of the State of Illinois: Convened at the City of Springfield, Tuesday, December 13, 1869*, 265.

have been responsible for the condition in which miners found themselves, the threats to their lives did not stem directly from government action and could not be remedied by further government inaction. Instead, the most immediate dangers in miners' lives resulted from the conditions of their workplaces and the practices of their employers. Laborers and their advocates requested active government intervention to mitigate them.

Many discussions of the labor provisions in state constitutions echoed the distinction between the types of rights that prevented government from regulating contracts or taking property and the types of rights that would force government to regulate on behalf of the worker. For instance, one delegate to the Virginia constitutional convention of 1901 argued, "Surely, if it is necessary to put in the Constitution some provision to protect a man's property, if you find the whole tendency or doctrine of the courts is to allow a man's life to be taken without due compensation, it is necessary to have a Constitutional protection to stop that evil also."[19] In 1913, the *American Review of Labor Legislation* echoed this critique: "We must abandon the idea that we have either a legal or a moral right to buy labor in the cheapest market."[20] Negative rights protected people's liberty to buy or sell labor at whatever terms they agreed upon. Thus, negative rights prevented government from telling people what sorts of contracts they could enter into and what sorts of wages they could accept. The advocates of protective labor regulation wanted to replace these constitutional restraints on government with countervailing obligations on government to protect laborers by ensuring that they would not be forced to enter into particularly disadvantageous contracts or accept cruelly inadequate wages.

To underscore the uselessness of rights that restrained government from intervening in employment contracts or working conditions, advocates of protective labor legislation often described the rights they demanded as belonging to a different category of rights. One commentator described the need for new "industrial" rights, and contrasted those rights with the existing liberties of contract. He described a judicial ruling that nullified a protective regulation on the grounds that it deprived a young, female employee of due process right to freedom of contract. Then he explained why this type of right was so useless to her:

Instead of giving this girl the actual and substantial right which the statute provided for her,—instead of declaring that she had a right to work in safety,—[the court] gave her an academic right, the right to work in danger, to accept danger and suffer by it without redress. In a state in which, every year, there are more than twice as many persons killed in industrial establishments as were killed in the Spanish war;

[19] Quoted in Dinan, *The American State Constitutional Tradition*, 190–91.
[20] George Anderson, "General Discussion," *American Labor Legislation Review* 3, no. 1 (1913): 93.

in which, in addition to the killed, forty thousand employees are an-
nually crippled, maimed, or wounded, such a decision, guaranteeing to
working men and women the right to endure unnecessary danger,
and effectually denying their right to safety in their work, is bound
to create some dissatisfaction among the working classes . . . The
counterfeit liberty is no more satisfactory to its recipient than is the
counterfeit dollar.[21]

The author of this article argued that we should replace this counterfeit
liberty with real and meaningful industrial rights. Similarly, a prominent
advocate of protective legislation and well-known factory inspector, Florence Kelley, described the right to maximum hours legislation as "the right
to leisure," and argued that this right was absolutely fundamental to human
flourishing.[22] Labor union publications made similar distinctions. For example, in 1912, The *Toledo Union Leader* declared, "The right to live is inherent . . . The right to live comes first . . . and he [the workingman] can't
surrender that right by listening to the senseless drivel and sugar-coated
preachments of smug respectables well clothed and housed, who talk of
their 'inherent rights' [to property and freedom of contract]."[23] In this context, it is clear that the right to leisure and the right to live required government intervention in labor markets and workplaces. Restraints on state
regulation in these areas would only allow laborers to remain in danger.
Thus, state-level labor organizations placed mandates for protective state
intervention directly in their constitutions. While they did not name these
mandates "positive rights," they were quite clear about how different these
mandates were from those that restrained legislatures to guard subjects'
property from the state.

It is important to note that, because of their phrasing, not all constitutional labor provisions can be considered rights. Thirty of the labor provisions included in table 6.1 simply authorized or empowered legislatures to
implement labor legislation, but did not mandate that the state provide the
protection. For example, the Texas constitution was amended in 1936 to
read: "The legislature shall have the power to provide for workman's compensation insurance for . . . . State employees."[24] This permissive phrasing
was particularly prevalent among workmen's compensation provisions. The
New York Constitution was similarly amended in 1913 to read: "nothing in
this constitution shall be construed to limit the power of the legislature to set
up a system of workmen's compensation." Although the permissively phrased
provisions in state constitutions do not seem to create obligations on govern-

---

[21] George W. Alger, "Some Equivocal Rights of Labor," *Atlantic Monthly* 1906, 365.
[22] Kelley, *Some Ethical Gains through Legislation*.
[23] "The Right to Live," *Toledo Union Leader*, Toldeo, August 9, 1912.
[24] Texas Constitution of 1876, Article 3 § 59.

ment, the political struggles surrounding their adoption reveal that they were nonetheless drafted as directives to both legislatures and courts about the purposes and expectations of government. Constitutional labor provisions like these were phrased as grants of authority not because those amending the constitution hoped to give the legislature choices about whether or not to protect labor, but often because they were responding to court decisions that had explicitly denied permission to legislatures.[25] Thus, these permissive provisions were often included in state constitutions with the understanding that they would allow, and in some cases prompt, legislatures to pass protective legislation. These permissions were aimed at overcoming the political obstacles that hindered the passage of protective labor laws. After all, the U.S. Constitution reserves to states all the powers that it does not (explicitly or implicitly) deny them. Therefore, state legislatures would not have needed permission to enact labor legislation unless some obstacle stood in their way.

We may not consider permissive constitutional provisions rights, since they are not mandates. However, by studying the movements that led to the drafting and ratification of these provisions (as well as their mandatory counterparts), it is possible to shed light on why labor organizations sought constitutional rather than merely statutory protections. The rest of this chapter demonstrates that labor organizations mobilized around the inclusion of labor rights (and permissive provisions) in state constitutions and then examines the reasons that laborers and their advocates pursued constitutional changes.

LABOR ACTIVISM AND CONSTITUTIONAL CHANGE

Like the educational activists that the common school movement comprised, laborers, labor leaders, and other advocates of protective regulation devoted significant resources to the creation of constitutional protections. The earliest instance I have identified of a protective labor provision added to a state constitution called on the legislature to establish a nine-hour workday and a minimum wage for laborers on public works in Louisiana. In 1864, while the constitutional convention was composed largely of delegates who were themselves white laborers, thousands of the state's white laborers formed an informal lobby to ask that their policy preferences be written into the new

---

[25] A delegate to the Nebraska Constitutional Convention of 1921 even explained his use of permissive language: "It seems to me that the decision of our court in *Lowe v. Rees Printing Company* makes this word 'may' particularly applicable. That was law which intended to fix the hours of labor and compensation. That is just what this proposal opens the way for. . . . The word 'may' thus becomes co-ordinate with those other constitutional inhibitions." Quoted in John J. Dinan, "Framing a People's Government: State Constitution-Making in the Progressive Era," *Rutgers Law Journal* 30, no. 4 (1999): 979.

fundamental law. They prefaced their petition to the Louisiana constitutional convention with the words, "The undersigned, citizens of the state of Louisiana, beg leave to memorialize you honorable body in behalf of our claims, feeling that this being the only liberty-loving body, composed purely of the laboring class, that has ever convened in the State of Louisiana for the promotion of the interests of mankind in general, their appeal will not be in vain."[26] Constitutional conventions represented an opportunity to influence state law and extract a visible and public promise of governmental protection for more formally organized groups as well. The Knights of Labor, the Western Federation of Miners, the California Workingmen's Party, as well as many state chapters of the American Federation of Labor all lobbied for the addition of protective labor provisions to state constitutions. Women's organizations, such as local chapters of the Women's Trade Union League, and progressive social reformers also supported (and sometimes spearheaded) the inclusion of protective labor provisions.[27] These organizations both lobbied to amend existing constitutions and to add provisions during the writing of new constitutions by constitutional convention.

Constitutional conventions often created a sense of opportunity among labor leaders and organizations, prompting them to pursue the creation of a new constitutional provision when they might not have otherwise. Amy Bridges' description of the delegates to constitutional conventions applies equally well to the reasoning of the labor leaders: "The opportunity to legislate group preferences might well not reappear in state assemblies, encouraging them to seize the time . . . When would there be another gathering of such hard working delegates, with so much public attention, and afterwards,

---

[26] Louisiana Constitutional Convention, *Debates in the Convention for the Revision and Amendment of the Constitution of the State of Louisiana: Assembled at Liberty Hall, New Orleans, April 6, 1864* (New Orleans: W. R. Fish, Printer to the Convention, 1864), 418.

[27] The labor organizations and progressive reformers who were primarily concerned with the welfare of working women tended to support protective legislation and constitutional amendments. For instance, in her capacity as Illinois' chief factory inspector, Florence Kelley bemoaned the fact that the state supreme court had based its decision to nullify an eight-hour law in part on the federal constitution. Kelley explained in her third annual report that, if the court had only based its decision on the state constitution, that constitution could have been altered to allow for a reenactment of the law. See Kathryn Kish Sklar, *Florence Kelley and the Nation's Work: The Rise of Women's Political Culture, 1830–1900* (New Haven: Yale University Press, 1995), 238. Similarly, the Women's Trade Union League (WTUL) was an early advocate of protective legislation and broadly supportive of the state constitutional amendments. For instance, the WTUL's official journal, *Life and Labor*, discussed a Wisconsin court's nullification of a workmen's compensation law predicting "there will also be a constitutional amendment which will guarantee the enforcement of these humanitarian laws as well as a curtailment of the prerogatives of the supreme court judges." See "Wisconsin Compensation Law," *Life and Labor*, Chicago, vol. 4, no. 2, February 1914, 2. A Los Angeles branch of the WTUL also worked energetically to secure a constitutional amendment to California's constitution in the hopes that the amendment would protect existing minimum wage laws for women. Sherry Katz, "Socialist Women and Progressive Reform," in *California Progressivism Revisited*, ed. William Francis Deverell and Tom Sitton (Berkeley: University of California Press, 1994).

so great a claim to popular mandate?"[28] For instance, in 1910, when it became clear that the Arizona territory would begin writing a state constitution, the many labor organizations of the state convened a large conference to discuss the provisions that they hoped would be included in the new constitution and to formulate plans for the pursuit of their inclusion. The *Arizona Daily Star* reported: "All organizations are urged to be present at the conference. The working class, if it only utilizes it, has the power to make the constitution to its own liking, and if it is properly drafted, our economic struggles of the future will be greatly simplified and our opportunities of bettering our conditions rendered much easier."[29] Similarly, in 1915, the Tennessee State Federation of Labor urged its members to vote affirmatively in the upcoming referendum on whether to hold a state constitutional convention, saying, "This is the first real opportunity we have had to place ourselves in a position to get substantial relief." They declared, "if we grasp the opportunity and handle it intelligently the benefits cannot be estimated."[30]

Labor leaders tried to ensure that sympathetic delegates would be elected to constitutional conventions. For instance, the Twin Territories Federation of Labor refused to support the election of any delegates to the Oklahoma constitutional convention who would not pledge in writing to support the inclusion of a list of labor protections. The Federation of Labor then hired a paid lobby to attend the convention to ensure that these delegates served labor as they had promised.[31] Similarly, Utah unionists decided to support only candidates to the state constitutional convention who promised to accede to their list of demands. And, when George Meany was president of the New York Federation of Labor, he spent an intensive week lobbying the New York constitutional delegates when they threatened to reject the labor article proposed for the New York Constitution.[32]

In some cases, labor organizations even tried to elect constitutional convention delegates from among their own ranks. For example, the *Michigan Union Advocate* explained that members of the Michigan Federation of Labor were "determined to take matters into their own hands and 'pass up' the alleged reformers." Instead, "the labor unionists of this city and county decided to put up their own candidates for the constitutional convention."[33] Also feeling that they had "not obtained any satisfactory 'recognition' at the

[28] Amy Bridges, "Managing the Periphery in the Gilded Age: Writing Constitutions for the Western States," *Studies in American Political Development* 22, no. 1 (2008): 42.

[29] Anthony McGinnis, "The Influence of Organized Labor on the Making of the Arizona Constitution" (Master's thesis, University of Arizona, 1930).

[30] Cited in "Want Constitution Changed," *The Garment Worker*, New York, December 10, 1915, 8.

[31] Keith L. Bryant, Jr., "Labor in Politics: The Oklahoma State Federation of Labor During the Age of Reform," *Labor History* 11, no. 3 (1970): 263.

[32] "Laws Committee Votes a Labor Bill," *New York Times*, New York, July 12, 1928, 10.

[33] "Labor Unionists Have Put Candidates in the Field," *Michigan Union Advocate*, Detroit, July 19, 1907, 1.

hands of either political party," New York labor organizations discussed the need for "strenuous efforts to secure direct representation in the Constitutional convention [of 1893]."[34]

When labor organizations succeeded in inserting their provisions into the proposed constitutions, they then mobilized their members in an effort to ensure that their states' voters ratified these documents. For instance, because it was satisfied with the labor rights embodied in the Ohio Constitution of 1912, the Ohio Federation of Labor called a statewide meeting of labor leaders to "devis[e] ways and means to stimulate interest in the new constitution and secure a full vote for its adoption at the special election by arousing workers to its importance."[35] The *Toledo Union Leader* then announced that "labor unions throughout the state, working under the direction of the Ohio Federation of Labor, and co-operating with various progressive organizations, will begin an active campaign for the adoption of the proposed constitutional amendments."[36]

In addition to influencing the drafting of new constitutions, laborers also organized to amend existing constitutions. Just as they had lobbied constitutional conventions, labor organizations lobbied legislatures to introduce pro-labor amendments. They also ran statewide "get out the vote" efforts to attract both union members and non-union members to the cause, circulated letters about the need to garner support for their amendments, and published numerous pro-amendment editorials in their journals.[37] Before 1900, only Minnesota added a labor provision to an existing constitution. The other twenty states that included protective labor provisions in their state constitutions did so while drafting entirely new documents. However, in the twentieth century, there were twenty-five different instances in which

[34] "Workingmen and the Convention," *New York Times*, New York, October 24, 1893, 4.

[35] "Constitution Makers Finish Labors," *Toledo Union Leader*, Toledo, May 17, 1912, 1.

[36] "To Urge Constitution: Ohio Federation of Labor Plans Campaign for Adoption of Laws to Help Workers," *Toledo Union Leader*, Toledo, July 28, 1912, 1.

[37] For example, the Montana Federation of Labor promoted a 1936 constitutional amendment about hours regulation by contacting labor unions throughout the state, urging them to support the amendment, and publishing many editorials, which responded to the charges leveled against the amendment by its opponents. For the entire month of October, the *Montana Labor News* published the slogan "Vote for the Eight-Hour Amendment" on its front page, above the paper's nameplate. The paper also recounted the efforts of the state federation of labor as well as the state Mining Council of Montana, writing "The State Mining Council of Montana, which includes representatives of all mining and smelter organizations in the State of Montana, vigorously urged the necessity of the passage of the 8-Hour Amendment at its last meeting and notified the Central Labor Body of Butte of its action. The State Mining Council also praised the efforts of the Montana State Federation of Labor in arousing the people to the need of passing the proposed amendment. Nothing that has come up before the people in recent years, according to the report of the Council, is so vital to their interest as the passage of this 8-hour law." See *Montana Labor News*, Butte, October 8, 1936, 1. After the amendment passed, the *Montana Labor News* ran a long column thanking those labor advocates and union leaders who "fought for the amendment and spent their time and money." See the *Montana Labor News*, Butte, November 12, 1936, 1.

labor provisions were added to a state constitution (though several were in the same states, albeit in different years), and in only eight of these instances were the provisions included in new constitutions (see table 6.2).

Whether they pursued constitutional changes during conventions or as amendments, it is clear that labor organizations did not seek constitutional rights alone, but as part of larger campaigns to change state policy. Like education rights, constitutional labor provisions were understood to supplement, not substitute for, protective legislation. When a particular organization was attempting to influence the shape of its state's constitution, it often devoted significant resources to that endeavor, publishing newspaper articles, influencing constitutional conventions, lobbying state legislatures, and/or creating statewide support for its proposals. However, once they had succeeded (or even failed) to influence the constitution, labor organizations typically returned to their other political activities, which included lobbying for the passage of protective legislation and working to ensure that existing legislation was enforced.

Like educational reformers, laborers' advocates were committed to building a new statutory regime. As with educational activists, then, we might ask why laborers bothered to promote constitutional changes at all. If labor organizations were really interested in new statutes, why did they believe that constitutional rights were likely to advance their cause? Even if the existence of a constitutional convention prompted labor organizations to seek constitutional changes, those organizations still deemed it worthwhile to devote resources to the acquisition of constitutional protections. The remainder of this chapter explores why they did this. In explaining the reasons that labor delegates sought constitutional change in addition to new statutes, it lists the advantages that labor delegates believed constitutional change held over and above the potential benefits of statutory law alone. As we saw with educational reformers, traditional entrenchment theories do not do a very good job of describing the origins of these positive labor rights.

OVERTURNING COURTS

One major advantage that the creation of constitutional labor rights held over the passage of statutes only was that constitutional protections could potentially overcome the hostile stance of state courts toward labor. Some scholars have questioned the degree to which state courts ultimately hampered the development of protective legislation.[38] Yet, regardless of how

[38] Melvin Urofsky, "State people to the need of passing the proposed amendment. Nothing that has come up before the people in recent years, according to the report of the Council, is so vital to their interest as the passage of this 8-hour law." See *Montana Labor News*, Butte, October 8, 1936, 1. After the amendment passed, the *Montana Labor News* ran a long column thanking those labor advocates and union leaders who "fought for the amendment and spent

many protective statutes were actually overruled by state courts, labor legislation passed during the Gilded Age and Progressive Era was constantly challenged through litigation. Consequently, labor organizations of the period were convinced that judicial decisions posed a formidable obstacle to their legislative agenda. AFL founder Samuel Gompers concluded that: "The power of the courts to pass upon the constitutionality of a law so complicate[d] reform by legislation as to seriously restrict the effectiveness of that method."[39] This anxiety about the constitutionality of labor legislation transformed labor's desire for protections that could simply have been enacted as statutes into demands for constitutional rights.[40]

One reason constitutional rights seemed superior to mere statutes is that they enabled labor to work around adverse court decisions by widening the scope of conflicts about the constitutionality of a particular law.[41] By increasing the number of people engaged in the conflict over the legitimacy of labor legislation, it was possible for labor to change the ratio of its allies to its opponents. This tactic was particularly important when state supreme courts struck down protective labor legislation. Because no appeal to a higher court was legally possible, when the state supreme court nullified a piece of labor legislation, advocates of the legislation often attempted to reinstate the legislation by removing the conflict from the court and shifting it to a different venue.[42] Once constitutions clearly authorized legislatures to

---

their time and money." See the *Montana Labor News*, Butte, November 12, 1936, 1. "Courts and Protective Legislation During the Progressive Era: A Reevaluation," *Journal of American History* 72, no. 1 (1985).

[39] Quoted in Forbath, *Law and the Shaping of the American Labor Movement*, 41.

[40] As William Ross describes, judicial rulings on labor questions also created a more general fervor for curbing the power of the courts. See William G. Ross, *A Muted Fury: Populists, Progressives, and Labor Unions Confront the Courts, 1890–1937* (Princeton, NJ: Princeton University Press, 1994). These protective labor provisions were part of the larger movement to use state constitutions in an effort to rein in courts. On these movments see John J. Dinan, "Court-Constraining Amendments and the State Constitutional Tradition," *Rutgers Law Journal* 38, no. 4 (2007); Douglas S. Reed, "Popular Constitutionalism: Toward a Theory of State Constitutional Meanings," *Rutgers Law Review* 30, no. 4 (1999).

[41] E. E. Schattschneider, *The Semisovereign People: A Realist's View of Democracy in America* (Hinsdale, IL: Dryden Press, 1975).

[42] Jed Handelsman Shugerman, *The People's Courts: Pursuing Judicial Independence in America* (Cambridge, MA: Harvard University Press, 2012), 164. As Shugerman's study of judicial elections has demonstrated, proponents of protective labor legislation also reacted to adverse state court rulings by voting the judges that issued those decisions out of office. For instance, the New York judge William Werner lost his office soon after striking down the state's workmen's compensation law in 1911. Another Progressive Era strategy for overcoming judicial hostility to progressive labor legislation was, famously, the push for judicial recall, but as Shugerman points out, "most states already had their own form of judicial recall: judicial elections to relatively short terms." Ibid. Another strategy some progressive reformers advocated to deal with obstructionist courts was to require a supermajority vote for the state's high court to strike down legislation. Ohio, North Dakota, and Nebraska all amended their constitutions to adopt this requirement. Ibid., 166.

pass particular pieces of protective legislation, there could be little question about the constitutionality of that legislation (at least on state grounds). Thus, these amendments effectively returned questions about whether protective legislation should exist to state legislatures.

New York's Constitution was amended in 1905 for just this purpose. Since its founding in 1865, the primary goal of the New York Workingmen's Assembly was to promote the passage of protective labor legislation in New York State. The eight-hour workday was one of its earliest legislative demands, and by 1897, it had succeeded in convincing the legislature to pass a law limiting the workday on public works to eight hours and requiring that laborers must be paid at the prevailing rate.[43] In a series of state supreme court cases, this regulation was challenged and declared unconstitutional and completely void.[44]

In order to reestablish the regulations, New York State labor leaders attempted to amend the state's constitution. In his 1906 article about New York's eight-hour movement, political scientist George Groat explained: "The only way out of the difficulty was to change the fundamental law of the state in such a way as to overcome the objections of the court against the law."[45] Groat was pointing out that, because the state supreme court had ruled the eight-hour law unconstitutional, the only way to address their problems with the courts and to reestablish the law was to change the constitution itself.[46] Groat then described the New York Federation of Labor's

[43] George Groat, "The Eight Hour and Prevailing Rate Movement in New York State," *Political Science Quarterly* 21, no. 3 (1906): 418–19.

[44] *People ex rel. Rodgers v. Coler*, 59 N. E. 716 (1901); *People ex rel. Treat v. Coler*, 59 N. E. 776 (1901); *People v. Orange County Road Construction Company*, 67 N. E. 129 (1903); *People ex rel. Cossey v. Grout*, 72 N. E. 464 (1904).

[45] Groat, "The Eight Hour and Prevailing Rate Movement in New York State," 428.

[46] It is instructive to compare this constitutional response to the invalidation of legislation to labor's responses to its other major complaint against courts in this period: their continued issuance of injunctions to end strikes and hamper labor organizing. Unlike state courts' constitutional rulings on constitutional grounds, which could only be overcome by amending the constitution itself, labor injunctions were typically grounded in either common law or antitrust legislation. Thus, it seemed possible to prevent the courts from issuing anti-labor injunctions through legislation alone, that is, without a constitutional amendment. As Felix Frankfurter explained in a 1929 law review article: "Reform of abuses revealed by the use of labor injunctions therefore presents a variety of problems for legislative solution. Legislation might immunize activities of organized labor from all tort liability—pecuniary responsibility, as well as restraint of conduct—or merely define the conduct that is to be deemed wrong. Again, legislation might withdraw from the scope of injunctive relief activities normally prevalent in labor controversies, or merely fashion a procedure especially suitable to injunctions in such cases. Legislation has entered all these fields." Felix Frankfurter, "Legislation Affecting Labor Injunctions," *Yale Law Journal* 38, no. 7 (1929): 880. This is not to say that labor organizations never tried to address their injunction problem through constitutions. The Arizona constitutional convention of 1910 considered the addition of an anti-injunction provision to its constitution, but ultimately rejected these proposals. See Paul Mandel, "Labor Politics, Hayden Style," in *American Labor in the Southwest: The First One Hundred Years*, ed. James C. Foster (Tucson:

response: "The machinery of the state organizations was accordingly at once set in operation to accomplish this result. The state federation became the champion of the cause."[47] Groat also discusses the reason that the labor advocates did not simply address themselves to changing composition of the state supreme court. With only changes in personnel, he explained, the constitutionality of the law would always remain in doubt and subject to changes on the bench. By contrast, a constitutional amendment would settle the issue permanently.

The New York chapter of the American Federation of Labor shepherded a resolution proposing a constitutional amendment through both houses of the state legislature, then publicized the amendment and called on all of its members to vote for its ratification. In October 1905, the president of the state chapter sent a letter to every labor organization in the state. It explained, "This [amendment] means if it is adopted that the Legislature of this state will have constitutional authority to pass laws in the interest of wage-earners, and the courts will not have the former excuse of nullifying our laws on the ground of unconstitutionality as has been the case, especially in the eight-hour and prevailing rate laws." It then urged each labor organization to "take immediate steps to notify each individual member and see to it that he is not permitted to forget his duty on election day."[48] The eight-hour amendment was adopted in 1905 and took effect on the January 1, 1906. That same year, the eight-hour law was reenacted, and, in 1908, was upheld by the state Supreme Court. In its opinion, the court explained that the constitutional amendment required the court to reverse itself and uphold the eight-hour law.[49] Thus, the eight-hour constitutional amendment shifted the ultimate authority to establish (or decline to establish) the eight-hour day from the state courts to the state legislature.

Karen Orren's seminal work argues that American labor had to fight to establish liberalism as a replacement for the older and less advantageous feudalism, which permeated American employment law.[50] She characterizes America's original system of labor law as feudal, rather than liberal, because it treated the laborer not as an equal of his employer's, but as a member of a rigid social hierarchy. Feudalism treats the laborer's status as an inalienable personal characteristic, outside of the sphere of politics. The judiciary, first

---

University of Arizona Press, 1982), 208. In addition, the New York constitution was amended in 1938 to include the statement that "Labor of human beings is not a commodity nor an article of commerce and shall never be so considered or construed." This declaration was taken directly from the Clayton Act of 1914, a piece of congressional legislation designed to prevent courts from issuing labor injunctions on the basis of antitrust laws. However, the availability of legislative remedies for labor's injunction problem drove labor activists and their advocates to pursue legislative remedies at both the federal and state levels.

[47] Groat, "The Eight Hour and Prevailing Rate Movement in New York State," 428.

[48] John J. Pallas, "To the Organized Labor Forces of the State of New York, Greetings," *Official Proceedings of the Workingmen's Federation of the State of New York*, 1906, 7.

[49] *People ex rel. Williams Engineering & Contracting Co. v. Metz*, 85 N.E. 1070 (1908).

[50] Orren, *Belated Feudalism: Labor, the Law, and Liberal Development in the United States*.

TABLE 6.3. Amendments in Direct Response to a
Supreme Court Case within the State

Year	State	Topic	Case Name
1902	California	Hours on public works	Ex parte Kubach (1890)
1902	Colorado	Hours in mines	In re Morgan (1899)
1905	New York	Hours on public works	People v. Orange County Road Const. Co. (1903)
1913	New York	Workmen's compensation	Ives v. South Buffalo Ry. Co. (1911)
1913	Ohio	Hours on public works	City of Cleveland v. Clements Bros. Const. Co. (1902)
1920	Nebraska[1]	Women's hours and wages	Lowe v. Rees Printing Company (1894)

[1] The Nebraska amendment about women's hours and wages followed a Nebraska state court decision that overturned a regulation for both men and women. In fact, while delegates passed this constitutional amendment in response to a state supreme court case overturning an eight-hour law for both men and women, a similar law for women alone was actually passed and even upheld by the state supreme court before the constitutional revision of 1920. Consequently, an examination of records from the constitutional convention was necessary to reveal that this constitutional amendment was proposed in response to this case. This suggests that even more amendments than are evident from my survey alone may have been proposed in response to supreme court cases within the same state.

through its common law jurisprudence and then through constitutional rulings that invalidated government regulations on behalf of workers, continually maintained this feudal understanding of the workplace. Consequently, Orren sees the shift from feudal relationships to liberal ones as both defined and accomplished by a shift in venue. The state became liberal precisely when legislatures began (and courts ceased) to direct the development of labor law. Orren has already described labor's attempt to wrest control of labor relationships from the courts and locate that control in elected legislatures. The neglected element of this story is that labor employed constitutional protections in its efforts to achieve this switch from courts to legislatures.

I have identified six instances in which an amendment to a state's constitution was proposed in order to overturn a decision by that state's supreme court (table 6.3).[51] Because my survey of state court cases only includes

[51] I identified these instances using a survey of state supreme court cases related to labor statutes using the Westlaw keynumber system combined with my survey of constitutional labor protections from the NBER state constitutions project. Wallis, "National Bureau of Economic Research / University of Maryland State Constitution Project." I looked for labor provisions that were added to state constitutions after a supreme court case in the same state declared a labor law on the same topic unconstitutional, and I consulted primary and secondary sources

supreme courts, I could not identify amendments that were prompted by lower court decisions. Because table 6.3 does not include amendments passed in response to adverse rulings of lower courts, it is quite likely that other constitutional amendments were also created in an attempt to overturn a specific court ruling.

In California, both New York cases, and Ohio, the type of protective law that the court struck down was restored following the passage of the constitutional amendment (see table 6.3). These amendments, therefore, allowed for the reestablishment of particular labor regulations.[52]

In New York, when the eight-hour law was reestablished after the constitution's amendment, the law's opponents challenged its constitutionality yet again. When asked to rule on the constitutionality of the newly reestablished eight-hour law, New York's highest court explained that the new constitutional amendment forced it to reverse its earlier decision:

> The power to fix and regulate the hours of labor upon public work was intrusted to the Legislature by the amendment which took effect on the 1st of January, 1906. Prior to that date the power did not exist, and hence certain decisions made under the Constitution before it was thus amended do not now apply. . . . We had held that the Legislature had no power to pass the labor law of 1897, and the amendment was designed to authorize a law of that kind. The Legislature acted under the amendment and re-enacted the precise law the overthrow of which by the courts made the amendment necessary. . . . Unless the amendment did this it did nothing, and the Constitution is the same in effect as it was before. The presumption is that the people in exercising their supreme power did not do a vain act, but effected a definite purpose.[53]

The people's purpose was, of course, to ensure that there would be no doubt about the constitutionality of the eight-hour law. Thus, the court announced that it could no longer prevent the legislature from establishing an eight-hour day. One could view this case as a sort of *Jones and Laughlin Steel* for New York State. Like *Jones and Laughlin Steel*, it recognized, and helped to reify, a change in the constitutional order. Thanks to the constitutional amendment about labor, the legislature was finally free to intervene in this area of employment relations. In states with high courts that already

to verify that the amendments I identified were actually passed in direct response to the state supreme court's ruling.

[52] Nebraska was a more complicated case since the constitutional amendment passed so long after the court case to which it was responding and did not pertain to an identical policy. While delegates passed this constitutional amendment in response to a state supreme court case overturning an eight-hour law for both men and women, a similar law for women alone was actually passed and even upheld by the state supreme court before the constitutional revision of 1920.

[53] *People ex rel. Williams Engineering & Contracting Co. v. Metz*, 85 N. E. 1070 (1908).

nullified labor legislation, this type of judicial reversal was the very outcome for which proponents of labor regulation designed positive constitutional rights.

PREEMPTING LITIGATION

Labor rights were not only created to overturn particular court decisions, but were also introduced to preempt possible court decisions. Thus, we even see these provisions in the original constitutions of newly admitted states. For instance, Colorado, Wyoming, North Dakota, Montana, Washington, Idaho, Utah, Oklahoma, New Mexico, and Arizona all included labor protections in their original constitutions. Though a state's first constitution could not have been a response to the state's own supreme court, it does seem quite likely that labor provisions were added to these state constitutions in response to the opinions of other states' courts. For instance, Florence Kelley explained Utah's inclusion of labor rights in its first constitution with reference to an Illinois Supreme Court case that declared it unconstitutional for the state to regulate the hours of women's employment. "The people of Utah, instructed by the supreme court of Illinois in 1895, showed by their action in 1896 that they had learned their lesson . . . they incorporated in their own constitution of 1896 an article dealing explicitly with the rights of labor."[54] In this article, Kelley then advised other states to follow Utah's example by including specific labor rights in their constitutions. In this way, Kelley explained, state legislatures could be made to pass such legislation and state courts could be prevented from overturning it. Even in brand new states, therefore, constitutional labor protections appear to have stemmed in part from the national sense that such provisions would facilitate the passage of labor legislation and secure this legislation from nullification by potentially hostile courts.

Constitutional labor rights had the potential to preempt constitutional challenges to statutory labor protections because, if these protections were actually contained in a state's constitution, it seemed much less likely that they could be declared to violate that constitution. The champions of positive labor rights in both old and new states, therefore, hoped that these constitutional provisions would take certain questions off of the political agenda. For instance, in 1904, Montana added a provision to its constitution establishing an eight-hour workday for miners, smelters, and state employees. Two years later, the state Supreme Court upheld similar legislation. However, over the next three decades, the legislature passed many more eight-hour laws that were not protected by this constitutional amendment.

---

[54] Florence Kelley, "The United States Supreme Court and the Utah Eight-Hours' Law," *American Journal of Sociology* 4, no. 1 (1898): 25–6.

These included eight-hour laws for laborers employed in strip mining, sugar refineries, cement and hydroelectric plants, and retail stores. Statutes also existed establishing an eight-hour day for bus drivers and female employees.[55] In 1935, a law regulating the hours of firemen was ruled unconstitutional by the state Supreme Court.[56] In addition, two lower courts ruled the law regulating store clerks' hours unconstitutional.[57] Even before these decisions were handed down, labor advocates desired a constitutional amendment that would establish a universal eight-hour day. They made several attempts to have the legislature place the eight-hour amendment on the ballot for ratification by the electorate.[58] Once this amendment was on the ballot, the Montana State Federation of Labor campaigned aggressively on its behalf. Its newspaper, the *Montana Labor News*, ran a series of articles about the need to constitutionalize the right to an eight-hour day. One headline read: "All of these laws will be in danger if the eight hour amendment is defeated by the people November 3." The article explained:

> Let us try and understand this picture presented by the proposed 8-hour amendment. Only a few industries are governed in hours by the Constitution of the state of Montana, namely underground workers and work performed by various units of the government. These people are protected. Other people who are enjoying 8 hours have gained this advantage by laws passed by the legislature and not through the Constitution. These people include clerks in stores and women in industry. Sugar beet workers, coal strip miners and others. All of these latter laws that have been passed by the Legislature are subject to challenge by the courts as to their constitutionality. All of these 8-hour laws may be destroyed by the corporations unless you pass this 8-hour amendment. Usually, the courts function in the interests of the corporations; so does the legislature."[59]

One primary purpose of the new eight-hour amendment clearly was to preempt an adverse court decision and protect these laws from courts. In fact, in 1938, two years after the passage of the eight-hour amendment, the state's Supreme Court did entertain a challenge to an eight-hour law for store employees, and citing "the work of the people" in amending the state's constitution to include an eight-hour day, it found the law to be constitutionally permissible.[60]

[55] "All These Laws Will Be In Danger If The Eight Hour Amendment Is Defeated By The People November 3," *Montana Labor News*, Butte, October 29, 1936, 1.

[56] *State ex rel. Kern v. Arnold*, 49 P.2d 976 (1935).

[57] "History of the Shorter Working Day Constitutional Amendment in Legislature," *Montana Labor News*, Butte, October 22, 1936, 1.

[58] Ibid.

[59] "All These Laws Will Be In Danger If The Eight Hour Amendment Is Defeated By The People November 3," *Montana Labor News*, Butte, October 29, 1936, 1.

[60] *State v. Safeway Stores*, 76 P.2d 81 (1938).

Interestingly, Montana's eight-hour provision was not only designed to protect hours regulations from courts, but also to guard the shorter work-day against any future legislative action. This intent was reflected in the text of the amendment itself, which read, "the legislative assembly may by law reduce the number of hours constituting a day's work whenever in its opin-ion a reduction will better promote the general welfare, but it shall have no authority to increase the number of hours constituting a day's work beyond that herein provided." This provision denied the legislature the authority to increase the legal workday, thereby allowing any future legislatures to con-tinue shortening the workday while simultaneously securing the current eight-hour maximum. Because constitutions control all branches of govern-ment, labor organizations hoped to use constitutional change to exclude courts and control legislatures simultaneously.

Labor organizations were not the only bodies that crafted new constitu-tional provisions in order to preempt constitutional challenges to protective legislation. State legislatures also employed this strategy on occasion. For instance, in 1914, the California legislature initiated a change to the state Constitution, authorizing the legislature to establish a minimum wage for women and minors, to regulate on behalf of the "comfort, health, safety, and general welfare of any and all employees," and to confer on "any commis-sion now or hereafter created such power and authority as the legislature may deem requisite to carry out the provisions of this section." The addition of this provision was motivated primarily by the desire to establish preemp-tively the constitutionality of the Industrial Welfare Commission that the legislature had created the previous year and endowed with the power to regulate wages, hours, and working conditions.[61]

The Commission's power to establish minimum wages for women seemed particularly likely to provoke a constitutional challenge. In addition, it was quite controversial, even among California's labor organizations. The Cali-fornia State Federation of Labor had officially declared its opposition to minimum wages in 1912, and its official journals published editorials vehe-mently opposing the establishment of a state commission empowered to set wages. Labor opposition to minimum wages stiffened still further when Samuel Gompers weighed in on the question.[62] By the California Federation of Labor's annual convention of 1914, the state's labor leaders were sharply divided on the desirability of a minimum wage for women.[63] The strongest

[61] Joseph R. Grodin, Calvin R. Massey, and Richard B. Cunningham, *The California State Constitution: A Reference Guide*, Reference Guides to the State Constitutions of the United States (Westportct: Greenwood Press, 1993).

[62] Norris Hundley, "Katherine Philips Edson and the Fight for the California Minimum Wage, 1912–1923," *Pacific Historical Review* 29, no. 3 (1960): 274.

[63] While there were movements among both male and female labor leaders for the adoption of gender-neutral minimum wage laws, led by Gompers, the AFL was staunchly opposed to minimum wage laws for men and women, believing that labor would be better served by estab-lishing a family wage for male breadwinners directly through their employers. The National

support for these laws came from progressive social reformers who were committed to protectionist policies for women. One such activist, Katherine Edson, a special agent for the Bureau of Labor Statistics for Southern California, advocated a preemptive amendment to the state constitution even before the legislature had passed the relevant law. Several women's organizations, including the newly established Women's Trade Union League of Los Angeles, organized a campaign to convince voters to support the minimum wage bill and to ratify the constitutional amendment.[64]

Two years earlier, members of the Vermont legislature (like its counterpart in California) had been so concerned about preempting a conflict over the constitutionality of a proposed workmen's compensation law that they sought a constitutional amendment on the subject before even passing the law. The state Republican Party included workmen's compensation legislation as a plank in its 1912 platform. Once elected, however, legislators became so concerned about the constitutionality of this legislation that, instead of passing a workmen's compensation law, they refused to act before securing explicit constitutional authority. The voters approved the amendment in 1914, authorizing the legislature to create a system of workmen's compensation. Only then, in 1915, did the legislature pass a workmen's compensation law.[65] As we have seen, the desire to screen legislation from potential court decisions prompted both labor organizations and legislatures to pursue preemptive constitutional amendments.

Even when these provisions could not entirely preempt litigation, labor rights were at times capable of shielding labor laws from judicial nullification. In rulings upholding the constitutionality of labor regulations, state high courts did cite constitutional labor rights in explaining why protective labor regulations did not violate the state constitution. For instance, Kentucky's supreme court upheld the state's law that miners must be paid in lawful money against the charge that this was special class legislation, and therefore unconstitutional, by citing the state's own constitution. The Kentucky court explained: "The organic law makes the general classification in

---

Women's Trade Union League and middle-class female progressive reformers, like Florence Kelley, generally supported a minimum wage for both men and women, but settled for protective legislation for women, some out of the belief that protective legislation for women was better than no protective legislation at all, while some were motivated by maternalist sentiments, believing that women needed special state protection because of their role as mothers coupled with their relative weakness when compared to male laborers. See Vivien Hart, *Bound by Our Constitution: Women, Workers, and the Minimum Wage* (Princeton, NJ: Princeton University Press, 1994), 75–85.

[64] Katz, "Socialist Women and Progressive Reform," 131; Theda Skocpol, *Protecting Soldiers and Mothers: The Political Origins of Social Policy in the United States* (Cambridge, MA: Belknap Press of Harvard University Press, 1992), 415.

[65] Winston Allen Flint, *The Progressive Movement in Vermont* (Washington, DC: American Council on Public Afairs, 1941).

the first instance, and this fact cuts short all discussion of its constitutionality which might otherwise grow out of the special application to miners."[66] Similarly, the Utah supreme court declined to void an eight-hour law for miners, stating that such a law could not violate the state's constitution because the state constitution explicitly directed the legislature to pass laws providing for the health and safety of employees in factories, smelters, and mines.[67] The U.S. Supreme Court even cited Utah's constitution in its opinion affirming the state supreme court's decision.[68] When the Wyoming Supreme Court upheld the state's workmen's compensation statute against the charge that it violated the state's constitutions, it too described the "active and strenuous campaign by and on behalf of the workmen of the state and their organizations" to see the constitutional amendment enacted, and then explained that the workmen's compensation law could not possibly be said to violate the constitution or deprive workmen of their constitutional rights: "The act in question . . . is in accord with the system of workmen's compensation acts that were in the minds of the people adopting the constitutional amendment . . . And any and all provisions of the [state] Constitution that might have been construed as preventing the Legislature from passing such an act are modified or repealed as far as they would effect such an act."[69] The Wyoming court's characterization of the "the mind of the people" when they enacted the constitutional right to workmen's compensation applies to labor activists in states across the country. Whether the advocates of positive labor rights championed these provisions in order to overturn rulings their own state courts had already issued, or in order to stop courts from ever overturning legislation, their purpose was to modify or repeal any aspects of their state constitutions that might have been used to nullify protective labor legislation.

Entrenchment theories tell us that rights are born of elite efforts to switch courts on, ushering them into policy battles in order to protect the status quo. As we have seen, however, labor rights were created for an almost entirely opposite purpose. The champions of constitutional labor rights were generally political reformers, who were frustrated with courts' conservatism. They pursued the creation of positive labor rights in order to switch courts off, thereby insulating legislative change from judicial scrutiny.

---

[66] *Commonwealth v. Hillside Coal Co.*, 58 S.W. 441 (1900).

[67] The state supreme court explained that the state constitution "makes it the duty of the legislature to 'pass laws to provide for the health and safety of employees in factories, smelters and mines.' And we are not authorized to hold that the law in question is not calculated and adapted in any degree to promote the health and safety of persons working in mines and smelters. Were we to do so, and declare it void, we would usurp the powers intrusted by the constitution to the lawmaking power." *Holden v. Hardy*, 14 Utah 71 (1896).

[68] *Holden v. Hardy*, 169 U.S. 366 (1898).

[69] *Zancanelli v. Central Coal & Coke Co.*, 173 Pac. Rep. 981 (1918).

What About Lochner?

Although state legislatures were the primary sources of labor regulation before the New Deal, it is still important to consider the federal government, and federal courts, when discussing the politics of labor rights in the Gilded Age and Progressive Era. For instance, it still would have made little sense for labor organizations to focus on the content of their state constitutions if the U.S. Supreme Court had declared all labor legislation unconstitutional on federal constitutional grounds. After all, the federal Supreme Court of this period is best remembered for its declaration, in *Lochner v. New York*, that a state law limiting the working hours of bakers violated the Due Process Clause of the federal Constitution.[70] If protective labor regulations were understood as a violation of the federal Constitution, state constitutions would have been powerless to protect these statutes from judicial review and nullification. Consequently, the "Lochner Era" (during which the Supreme Court was best known for its opposition to labor regulations on federal constitutional grounds) poses a problem for my claim that state-level rights were designed to protect labor laws from state courts.

Scholars of American political development, however, have begun to challenge the conventional understanding of the Supreme Court's doctrine during the so-called "Lochner Era." First, relatively recent scholarship has begun to dispel the myth that the Court struck down all labor legislation simply to protect the "liberty of contract" it saw implied in the Fourteenth Amendment. Instead, as Howard Gillman has demonstrated, the Court was also concerned about whether it was constitutional to pass legislation that applied only to a single class of people, rather than applying equally to all members of the polity.[71] This mode of decision making was significantly different from a jurisprudence that required the Court to strike down any statutes that limited contractual freedoms, and it left room for the Court to uphold protective labor legislation when its application to a single class appeared justifiable in the name of public welfare. This re-interpretation of Lochner-era jurisprudence helps to explain the second type of revisionist scholarship, which argues that the Supreme Court was not a major impediment to the establishment of labor regulations. More often than not, the Court ruled that statutes regulating the hours and conditions of work could be justified, despite the fact that they singled out one class of citizens, because these laws fell under the state's police power to regulate in the interests of the health and order of the community. Between 1897 and 1937, forty-three Supreme Court rulings rejected substantive due process objections to employment regulations, while declaring employment regulations

---

[70] *Lochner v. New York*, 198 U.S. 45 (1905).

[71] Howard Gillman, *The Constitution Besieged: The Rise and Demise of Lochner Era Police Powers Jurisprudence* (Durham: Duke University Press, 1993); Keith E. Whittington, "Congress before the Lochner Court," *Boston University Law Review* 85, no. 3 (2005).

unconstitutional in only twelve.[72] Consequently, many advocates of labor legislation argued that state supreme courts posed an even more serious threat to labor legislation than the federal courts. State courts posed this threat through their interpretations of the due process clauses of state constitutions.

Many protective labor provisions were added to state constitutions before it was even clear that the U.S. Supreme Court would hinder the enactment of labor legislation. Initially, state courts were the only institutions overturning protective legislation. In 1898, when the Supreme Court finally did rule on these questions, its first ruling actually affirmed the constitutionality of the state labor law.[73] Even after the Court's famous *Lochner* decision in 1905, the Court did not strike down a significant number of labor regulations until the 1920s.[74] This period of active judicial review occurred in the final third of the period during which states added labor amendments to their constitutions (see table 6.2).

During the Progressive Era, several legal experts noted that state courts posed a far larger threat to protective labor legislation than the U.S. Supreme Court. For instance, in a *Columbia Law Review* article published in 1913, the prominent Progressive and law professor Charles Warren argued that, with the notable exception of *Lochner* itself, the Supreme Court's attitude toward progressive legislation had been markedly sympathetic.[75] The previous year, a political scientist published a similar assessment and noted that the public was widely frustrated with the opposition of state courts to labor legislation. He went on to explain: "While this [frustration] is the feeling towards many state courts, it is not to-day the feeling towards the Supreme Court of the United States. There is, I am glad to say, a very general belief that that Court, as now constituted, is in reasonably close touch with the desire of the people for social and economic legislation."[76] These observers characterized the federal Supreme Court as progressive at the height of the period now known as the Lochner Era. Their analyses suggest that, although a federal case lent the period its name, state supreme courts may have played at least as large a role as their federal counterpart in distressing labor legislation's advocates.

Because the state courts did not always interpret the due process clause of state constitutions in the same way that the U.S. Supreme Court interpreted the identical clause in the Fourteenth Amendment, labor legislation had to

---

[72] Michael J. Phillips, *The Lochner Court, Myth and Reality: Substantive Due Process from the 1890s to the 1930s* (Westport, CT: Praeger, 2001), 57.

[73] *Holden v. Hardy*, 169 U.S. 366 (1898).

[74] Phillips, *The Lochner Court, Myth and Reality: Substantive Due Process from the 1890s to the 1930s*, 57.

[75] Charles Warren, "The Progressiveness of the United States Supreme Court," *Columbia Law Review* 13, no. 4 (1913): 295.

[76] William Draper Lewis, "A New Method of Constitutional Amendment by Popular Vote," *Annals of the American Academy of Political and Social Science* 43 (1912): 325.

overcome two distinct sets of restrictions on government power. One delegate to the Nebraska constitutional convention in 1919 explained: "I want to say that the Supreme Court of the United States has construed laws of this character more with reference to the public welfare clause of our national Constitution than to the inhibitory clause as to due process of law, and therefore the necessities under the federal Constitution are quite different from ours."[77] Similarly, in a discussion of workmen's compensation laws, one political scientist explained: "No state compensation act can be effective which violates the Fourteenth Amendment; But on the other hand, satisfying the Fourteenth Amendment will not insure the validity of the act. The state constitution must also be satisfied."[78] Even if state constitutional change could do nothing to alter the federal constitutional threat, it could certainly neutralize the threat that state courts posed in the interpretation of state constitutions.

Legal scholars and labor advocates of the period discussed the need for labor legislation to conform to dual due process clauses—those in both the state and federal constitutions. For instance, in its brief about the need to add more protective labor provisions to the New York Constitution, the American Association for Labor Legislation explained:

> There have been since 1868 two due process clauses to which New York legislation must conform—one authoritatively and finally interpreted by the United States Supreme Court, the other finally and authoritatively interpreted by the New York Court of Appeals. If these two tribunals always agreed as to what due process requires in connection with labor legislation . . . no harm would have resulted from this repetition . . . But it is notorious that the courts have not agreed.[79]

It appeared clear that labor regulations had to overcome two separate hurdles—one found in the federal Constitution, and one in the state constitutions.

The significance of this system of dual due process clauses became clear to Colorado's labor leaders when they tried to enact legislation providing an eight-hour workday for miners and smelters. In 1895, the Colorado Supreme Court issued an advisory opinion stating that it would consider the eight-hour law unconstitutional on both state and federal grounds.[80] How-

[77] Nebraska Constitutional Convention, *Journal of the Nebraska Constitutional Convention: Convened in Lincoln December 2, 1919*, 2 vols. (Lincoln: Kline Publishing Co., 1921), 1714–15.

[78] Thomas I. Parkinson, "The Future of the Workmen's Compensation Amendment," *Proceedings of the Academy of Political Science in the City of New York* 5, no. 2 (1915): 98.

[79] Committee on Labor Legislation and the Constitutional Convention of New York State, *Constitutional Amendments Relating to Labor Legislation and Brief in Their Defense Submitted to the Constitutional Convention of New York State* (New York: American Association for Labor Legislation, 1915).

[80] *In re Eight-Hour Law*, 39 P. 328 (1895).

ever, in 1898, the federal Supreme Court upheld a Utah law that was virtually identical, stating that such limitation did not violate the Fourteenth Amendment.[81] Encouraged by the federal Supreme Court's decision, the Colorado legislature then enacted the eight-hour law. In cases such as these, in which the U.S. Supreme Court upheld protective legislation from one state, opponents of such legislation would sometimes issue reminders that, regardless of what the Supreme Court had to say about the Fourteenth Amendment, their state's constitution still forbade such legislation. For instance, one lawyer who argued against the constitutionality of an eight-hour law in New York responded to a U.S. Supreme Court decision upholding an extremely similar law in Kansas, saying, "The Court of Appeals of this state held that the eight-hour law was not only a violation of the Constitution of the United States, but of the Constitution of the state of New York as well and that was a material difference."[82] In fact, when the Colorado Supreme Court reviewed the constitutionality of the eight-hour law, it employed this very logic, declaring the Supreme Court's ruling insufficient to render the law constitutional. The Colorado court explained that the U.S. Supreme Court's ruling could not validate Colorado's law:

> It goes without saying that if a federal question were involved in the case at bar, and had been passed upon by that tribunal [the federal Supreme Court], our duty in the premises would be clear. But the petitioner does not invoke the protection of any provision of the national Constitution. He maintains that his sacred rights of liberty, and freedom of contract embraced in his right of property, and his exemption from arbitrary and unjust discriminations, all of which are guaranteed to him in the sections of our constitution . . . , are violated by this act.[83]

By "our constitution," of course, the court was referring to the state constitution. This ruling illustrates the importance of both state and federal due process clauses. Without an amendment to its state constitution, even the Supreme Court's interpretation of the federal Constitution could not protect Colorado's labor laws. Accordingly, in 1902, Colorado's labor unions responded by organizing a successful campaign to add such a provision to the Colorado Constitution.[84] While this state constitutional amendment could not protect labor legislation from the charge that it violated the federal Constitution, the amendment could guard against the claim that protective leg-

[81] *Holden v. Hardy*, 169 U.S. 366 (1898).

[82] "Eight Hour Law Decision: Labor Men and Lawyers Anxious to See Text of Opinion," *New York Times*, New York, December 3, 1903, 7.

[83] In re Morgan, 58 P. 1071, (1899).

[84] David L. Lonsdale, "Chicanery in Colorado," Red River Valley Historical Review 4, no. 3 (1979): 33–5; John P. Enyeart, " 'The Exercise of the Intelligent Ballot': Rocky Mountain Workers, Urban Politics, and Shorter Hours, 1886–1911," *Labor: Studies in Working-Class History of the Americas* 1, no. 3 (2004): 63–5.

islation violated the state constitution. In this case, the charge of unconstitutionality on state grounds was the more dangerous one.

As Colorado's experience demonstrates, the advocates of protective labor
legislation sometimes amended state constitutions to address the very real
possibility that labor laws would be deemed to violate the state constitution,
and the state constitution alone. This phenomenon was also evident in California. In 1914, the California constitution was amended to include a minimum wage for female employees. A state assemblyman explained that this
amendment was necessary to guard against charges that the minimum wage
laws for women violated the state constitution. He explained that the U.S.
Supreme Court was unlikely to rule the minimum wage law unconstitutional on federal grounds, writing: "A similar law has been sustained by the
Oregon courts and is now before the United States supreme court . . . It is
expected that the United States supreme court will hold as it has with the
eight hour law [that the minimum wage law is] 'legislation that is not in
conflict with the federal constitution, but is an extension of police power of
the state.'" Yet, even this favorable ruling by the U.S. Supreme Court would
not have been sufficient to settle questions about the constitutionality of the
minimum wage law. Even if the Supreme Court saw no conflict between the
statute and the federal Constitution, it was still entirely possible that the law
could be deemed to violate the state constitution. To address this threat to
the minimum wage law, it was necessary to amend the state constitution.
Thus, the assemblyman urged the state's voters: "To be sure that nothing in
our state constitution will prevent this great act of justice and mercy being
done to protect the women of this state, vote 'Yes' on Assembly Constitutional Amendment No. 90."[85] This concern about state rather than federal
constitutionality demonstrates that, even in 1914—at the height of the
Lochner Era, state constitutional law mattered. By writing labor regulations
directly into state constitutions, the advocates of protective labor regulations hoped either to overturn unfavorable state court rulings or even to
preempt a constitutional challenge on state grounds.

Forcing the Legislature's Hand

Although entrenchment theories tell us that rights are created by legislative
majorities who want to extend their dominance over time and through
courts, labor organizations did not want to get into courts, and in fact used
constitutions in their attempt to keep courts at bay. Like the education re-

[85] "Minimum Wage" in Amendments to Constitution and Proposed Statutes with Arguments Respecting the Same: To be Submitted to the Electors of the State of California at the
General Election on Tuesday November 3, 1914, Certified by the Secretary of State and Printed
at the State Printing Office, 1914, 29.

form groups described in chapter 5, labor organizations also pursued the creation of constitutional rights in their attempts to force the hand of state legislatures.[86] This use of constitutions highlights another difference between the origins of labor rights and the origin stories described by entrenchment theories. The champions of labor rights were not legislative hegemons, seeking to maintain their dominance over state policy, but frustrated reformers attempting to force new laws through frequently recalcitrant legislatures.

Labor organizations employed constitutional labor provisions not only in their attempts to overturn and exclude courts, but also in their larger efforts to lobby legislatures for protective statutes. As we saw with members of the common school movement, reformers created constitutional rights to push legislatures into building social safety nets, and as we saw in the case of public schooling, labor leaders felt that legislatures needed the push. State legislatures were often perceived as unscrupulous and on the payroll of corporations.[87] Thus, some labor amendments were passed with the express purpose of circumventing or controlling these corrupt legislative bodies. Constitutional conventions, whose delegates were often separate from the legislature and who did not need to consider reelection, sometimes wrote the labor-friendly policies that state or territorial legislatures had refused to enact. Furthermore, new constitutions or constitutional amendments often necessitated a statewide vote for ratification. Thus, when labor provisions were ratified by large margins or enacted through the initiative and referendum process, labor organizations then were able to point to these results to demonstrate their electoral strength and threaten any legislators who voted against protective legislation. When corrupt legislatures were able to keep labor regulations off the legislative agenda, the advocates of that regulation used constitution writing and revision to try to force legislatures to address their popular demands for regulation.

The Ohio Federation of Labor (OFL), for example, used the amendment of its constitution to demonstrate the extent of labor's electoral power within the state. In 1913, the Ohio State Constitution was amended to include provisions that established an eight-hour day on public works, created liens for laborers on the products of their labor, authorized the legislature to pass a workmen's compensation law, and empowered the legislature to reg-

[86] As George Lovell has demonstrated, Congress crafted seemingly protective labor legislation during this period in such a way that courts could then undermine its protective capacity and transformative potential. George I. Lovell, Legislative Deferrals: Statutory Ambiguity, Judicial Power, and American Democracy (Cambridge, New York: Cambridge University Press, 2003). Since legislatures may pass legislation with the aim of transferring real policymaking power to the courts, and have been shown to do this in the area of labor legislation, the goals of forcing legislatures into meaningful action and de-toothing courts may be entirely complementary, and perhaps even overlapping.

[87] Dinan, "Court-Constraining Amendments and the State Constitutional Tradition."

ulate the hours, wages, and working conditions of all employees. In the OFL convention that followed the adoption of these amendments, labor leaders explained that they planned to redouble their efforts to achieve protective labor legislation: "Now that the new constitution has been adopted, the work of this convention will be especially important, as it will have to adjust itself to new conditions, and the legislative demands of organized labor will not be made in the fear that some court will stand over the law and wipe it out of existence."[88] Labor leaders were particularly energized and optimistic about the prospect of passing labor legislation because of the extensive support that labor's amendments received when they were ratified. The *Toledo Union Leader* explained: "The fact that nearly every labor amendment received over 100,000 majority is best evidence that the people of Ohio are ready and willing to give labor such legislation as may be needed for its protection and welfare."[89] At the convention itself, speakers raised the explicit idea of using all of this voting strength to threaten legislators into acting on labor's demands. For example, one speaker stated: "Public sentiment can be so aroused as to force punishment of the party that fails or refuses to comply with its express contract."[90] In the legislative session that followed, Ohio's workmen's compensation law was extended and an eight-hour law for public works was established. The legislature passed further safety regulations for both mines and railroads. The state's existing lien laws were repealed and replaced, and the legislature required that employers institute a semi-monthly payday. Mercantile establishments were required to report on the hours and wages of their female employees and the ten-hour day for women extended to mercantile establishments. In addition, the legislature created an industrial commission created to collect labor statistics and enforce the states' existing laws.[91]

As Ohio's experience demonstrates, constitutional amendments did not mark the end of labor organizations' efforts to secure regulation. Instead, labor organizations viewed these amendments as a step on the road to establishing legislation. After constitutional provisions were incorporated into constitutions, labor organizations resumed their pursuit of legislative action. They behaved this way in new states as well as existing ones. For instance, an observer from Arizona noted, "the coming campaign for the constitutional convention is expected to demonstrate that the political power of the working class is becoming one that will have to be considered in the affairs

[88] "For the O.F. of L.," *Toledo Union Leader*, Toledo, September 6, 1912, 1.

[89] "On to Canton, Urges O.F. of L." *Toledo Union Leader*, Toledo, September 27, 1912, 1.

[90] Ohio State Federation of Labor, "Proceedings of the Twenty-Ninth Annual Convention of Ohio State Federation of Labor," Canton, October 14–19, 1912, 15.

[91] American Association for Labor Legislation, "Topical Index by States," *American Labor Legislation Review* 3, no. 3 (1913): 460–61.

of the territory or state hereafter."[92] After the passage of a labor-friendly constitution, the Arizona State Federation of Labor had twenty different labor bills introduced in the new state's first legislative session. Arizona's labor organizations felt convinced that they had been ignored by the territorial legislature and intended to follow their successes at the constitutional convention with legislative action. One labor newspaper explained: "considering the fact that this is the first legislature and that labor in the 'territory' got short shrift at the hands of the politicians and federal judges . . . The men of labor had more to do with securing the 'new constitution' than any other class in the territory and now they do not propose to neglect their opportunities."[93] The years following the passage of the Arizona constitution did in fact mark a high point for labor influence in legislative politics and witnessed the passage of many protective labor laws.[94] Constitutional change was thus only a part, and only occasionally a primary part, of labor organization's overall strategy. When opportunities presented themselves to pursue constitutional change, or court decisions made such changes seem necessary, constitutional rights made it onto the agenda of labor organizations, but constitutional change was always (at least in part) a means to some other end. One of those ends was to force reluctant, and even corrupt, legislatures to pass protective labor laws.

MOVEMENT BUILDING

By giving labor a place in the visible institutions of government, constitutional labor rights may also have appealed to labor organizations because of their potential value for what Michael McCann has termed "movement building." In his study of the way that rights claims empower their bearers, McCann notes that rights may facilitate the process of "raising citizen expectations regarding political change, activating potential constituents, building group alliances, and organizing resources for tactical action."[95] For instance, the Arizona territory's proposed constitution, which included the popular recall of state judges, was so radical that Taft threatened to veto it, denying Arizona statehood. Yet, some believed that labor's constitutional victories would be such a powerful organizing tool that, even in the face of a presidential veto, workers would rally around the constitution. In fact, the Miners' Magazine declared that Taft's veto would actually strengthen labor's position: "Plutocracy may kill a constitution that de-

---

[92] "Political Notes from Arizona," Miners' Magazine, Denver, July 7, 1910, 11–12.

[93] "That Constitutional Convention," Toledo Union Leader, Toledo, May 3, 1912, 2.

[94] James W. Byrkit, Forging the Copper Collar: Arizona's Labor Management War of 1901–1921 (Tucson: University of Arizona Press, 1982), 52.

[95] McCann, Rights at Work: Pay Equity Reform and the Politics of Legal Mobilization, 11.

mands liberty for the masses of the people, but assassinating the constitution . . . will only inspire men and women to stand more firmly on their feet
to demand that the people must be heard on the organic law which governs
the people of a state."[96]

A speaker at the Colorado Federation of Labor also touted the mobiliz-
ing potential of the eight-hour amendment to the Colorado Constitution.
He explained, "I believe that the adoption of the eight-hour amendment will
do more toward thoroughly organizing Colorado in all lines than all the
other agencies that could be introduced or all the eloquence possible to be
let loose from organizers."[97] In fact, labor organizers did point to the constitution's eight-hour amendment when justifying the labor strikes that followed its passage.

When the Colorado legislature remained reluctant to pass a meaningful
eight-hour law even after the creation of a constitutional mandate,[98] labor
leaders, particularly "Big Bill" Haywood of the Western Federation of Miners (WFM), pointed to the legislature's recalcitrance in the face of even an
explicit constitutional obligation as evidence that mining companies, rather
than the electorate, controlled the legislature. One journalist wrote, "Rarely
has there been in this country a more brazen conscienceless defeat of the will
of the people."[99] In 1903, only weeks after the legislature adjourned without
passing an eight-hour law, the WFM organized a strike at two smelters in
the Denver area. An infamous labor struggle known as "the battle of Cripple
Creek" followed. By mid-autumn, labor stoppages and violent conflicts between strikers and employers had spread across much of the state. These
mining strikes, organized in large part around the right to an eight-hour
workday, rocked Colorado with their duration, scale, and violence. Several
years later, President Roosevelt would write, "The [Governor's] failure to
insist that the legislature should obey the will of the people and pass the
eight hour law . . . was in my judgment unpardonable."[100] Thus, it seems clear
that the existence of a constitutional right helped to legitimate labor's claims
about the corruption of the state's political institutions and served as a ban-
ner which labor leaders used to rally miners.

Even in the absence of statewide strikes, labor advocates and publications
described the role of state constitutions as that of broadcasting the demands
of labor through a highly visible public institution. The *Miners' Magazine*'s
description of the state constitution as "the political mandate of the people"

[96] "That Constitution," *Miners Magazine*, Denver, January 5, 1911, 7.
[97] Colorado State Federation of Labor, "Report of Proceedings of the Seventh Annual Convention" (Trinidad, CO, June 9–13, 1902).
[98] Although the legislature passed a law regulating hours of work, this new statute lacked
penalties for violating the law.
[99] Cited in J. Anthony Lukas, *Big Trouble: A Murder in a Small Western Town Sets Off a
Struggle for the Soul of America* (New York: Simon & Schuster, 1997), 220.
[100] Cited in ibid., 368.

exemplifies this view. In fact, labor publications often described constitutions as the voice of the people, unmediated by legislatures and unmolested by courts. For example, one labor newspaper compared the delegates to the Oklahoma constitutional convention to the members of the Oklahoma legislature, calling the constitutional convention delegates the "real representatives of the people."[101] Similarly, when the New York Federation of Labor presented its slate of demands for the new constitution, it explained: "[our slate of labor proposals] constitutes a Bill of Rights. We earnestly petition that it be made part of the new state constitution . . . it represents the hopes and aspirations of the wage-earners for better living and working conditions in the future."[102] While labor publications and organizers almost always described labor-friendly state constitutions as broadcasting the voice of the people, they also took pains to credit the particular unionists and politicians who facilitated the drafting of labor provisions and to list the parts of the state in which labor's agenda received strong support, thereby emphasizing the vitality of their movement and the efficacy of its leaders.

CONCLUSION

Constitutions establish and order all of a state's other formal political institutions. Consequently, labor organizations used constitutional rights to tell state legislatures what they had to do while simultaneously telling courts what they could not do. Thus, attention to the origins of constitutional labor rights demonstrates that constitutional change is not always motivated by the desire to entrench the status quo or to judicialize conflicts. In fact, for the proponents of protective labor provisions, one of the primary goals was actually to prevent the judiciary from making labor policies. Like common school reformers before them, labor organizations also worked to include positive rights in state constitutions because they hoped to motivate reluctant legislatures to pass protective legislation, and like the "friends of education," the advocates of protective labor legislation were very unhappy with the status quo. Both movements turned to constitutions in their pursuit of political change. Their efforts resulted in constitutional mandates for government intervention and protection.

Not only do state constitutions impose explicit mandates on government to educate citizens; state constitutions also contain mandates for intervention in an area of domestic life in which America is supposed to be exceptionally wedded to Lockean liberalism: labor relations. Furthermore, these

---

[101] "Oklahoma Shows the Way: Government by Injunction Abolished—Michigan Should Follow Suit," *Michigan Union Advocate*, Detroit, November 1, 1907, 1.

[102] New York State Federation of Labor, "Document No. 17: Memorial of the New York State Federation of Labor," in *Documents of the Constitutional Convention of the State of New York 1915* (Albany: J. B. Lyon Company, 1915).

rights to protective and interventionist government were added to constitutions during the Gilded Age and Lochner Era, the very periods in which American constitutional law is often described as having been wholly devoted to the service of classical liberalism and laissez-faire capitalism. To be sure, during this period, many elements of both state and federal constitutions were interpreted as restraints on government and protections from an overly intrusive state. As we have seen, however, state constitutions also contained countervailing constitutional rights, positive rights.

Although many of these mandates are highly detailed policy instructions, we should nonetheless recognize them as constitutional rights. Rather than establishing explicit limitations on government action and intervention, labor rights mandated an active state role in protecting laborers. We can recognize labor rights as positive not only because their text seems to so clearly mandate active intervention and protection from the labor market, but also because their champions in labor movements, academic circles, and constitutional conventions consistently contrasted these new labor provisions with the existing negative rights that already mandated governmental restraint in order to protect private property. Laborers with little property to protect insisted that constitutions should also include the protections most meaningful to them. Thus, they pursued rights that could protect them from the dangers created by labor markets and employers. New industrial conditions, they insisted, required an abandonment of laissez-faire capitalism. Accordingly, they argued that constitutions should require governments to extend themselves in order to protect laborers' leisure, their health, and their lives.

The campaign to create positive labor rights was widespread, long-lived, and often successful. Since state governments were primarily responsible for the labor policies that existed at the time, laborers and their advocates drafted new mandates for intervention by state governments and fought to include these rights in state constitutions. As we have seen, individual state legislatures did not establish labor policies in a vacuum, and campaigns for constitutional change in one state were always conducted with reference to others. Although reformers may have sought changes to state-level law, their concerns extended well beyond the borders of their own states to the condition of the country more generally. Individual states' policies were routinely discussed in the context of national trends,[103] and when reformers wanted to demonstrate success at instituting a policy, they commonly counted the states that had individually instituted the kind

[103] Elizabeth Clemens has described reformers' tendencies to practice "comparative politics" when making American social policies. As Clemens notes, the danger in studying "state politics" is that it is easy to forget that "state-level moments have national consequences." Clemens, *The People's Lobby: Organizational Innovation and the Rise of Interest Group Politics in the United States, 1890–1925,* 68–73.

of law they were seeking and/or the number of state courts that had upheld such a law.[104] State constitutional change was similarly part of the nationwide effort at reform. The advocates of state-level rights advised and
copied one another, working together to change the national legal environment. Surely, this nationwide movement and the explicit positive rights it
succeeded in creating should inform our characterization of the American
rights tradition.

[104] For example, *The Garment Worker* reported that "the voters of Wyoming adopted the
constitutional amendment which provides for workmen's compensation . . . this maintains the
proportion of one-half of the states accepting this principle, and equalizes the loss sustained last
month by the Kentucky Court of Appeals when it held that the compensation act of the state
was unconstitutional." See "Wyoming in Line," *The Garment Worker*, New York, January 8,
1915, 6.

CHAPTER 7

Environmental Protection

POSITIVE CONSTITUTIONAL RIGHTS IN THE LATE
TWENTIETH CENTURY

The text of this conservation bill of rights manifests the
principle that a citizen has a right to natural beauty and an
unspoiled environment—a right as basic to human dignity
and the public welfare as freedom of speech and due process
of law. Further, it declares that protection of natural
resources is a duty of government.
Audubon, 1968[1]

The education rights in state constitutions establish that even before the
Civil War, American constitutions contained positive rights. The labor
rights in state constitutions demonstrate that Americans have ratified positive constitutional rights even in a realm of social and economic life that is
often said to be dominated by classical liberalism. Environmental rights are
instructive neither because they are very old nor because they address an
area of American life in which we might least expect to find positive rights,
but because they emerged at a time when we would least expect environmentalists (or any activists) to have cared about the content of state constitutions. I have argued that education and labor rights ended up in state
constitutions, rather than their federal counterpart, in part because states
(and not the federal government) were primarily responsible for shaping
education and labor policy during the periods in which these rights were
created.[2] Before the New Deal, reformers focused their efforts on state constitutions because state governments were the ones that would implement
the reforms they championed. However, as the twentieth century wore on,
the federal government addressed itself more actively to a wider and wider

---

[1] "A Conservation Bill of Rights for Your State Constitution," *Audubon*, New York, vol. 70,
no. 1, Jan/Feb, 1968.
[2] In fact, after the New Deal, when the fights over unionization and labor regulation shifted
from a state-level question to a federal one, the stream of new protective labor provisions
added to state constitutions more or less dried up.

array of social problems. Today, few salient political problems are still solely or even primarily state concerns. It seems quite possible that, as the federal government assumed greater responsibility for the country's social and economic policy, state constitutions would have become increasingly irrelevant to reformers. Consequently, by the 1960s, we might expect to see an end to the positive-rights tradition within state constitutional law. But we do not. Even in the period of the most extensive expansion of federal rights and responsibilities in America's history, we still see movements to add positive rights to state constitutions.

In the midst of high levels of national activity to address a wide variety of social issues, activists continued to try to add positive rights to state constitutions. Despite the creation of several landmark environmental statutes at the federal level during the 1960s and '70s and the creation of an administrative agency devoted to national environmental regulation, environmental activists continued to organize within their states, and as one of their efforts at policy change, they advocated the insertion of positive rights to environmental protection into their state constitutions. During the 1960s and 1970s, therefore, state constitutions came to include broad rights to environmental health and protection. My argument here is not that state-level rights were at the center of the environmental movement during this period, but that environmentalists did not choose to pursue these rights only at the federal level. Instead, states' constitutional conventions, environmental organizations, and even legislatures continued to alter state constitutions by adding mandates for protective and interventionist government. The creation of environmental rights near the end of the twentieth century demonstrates that America's positive-rights tradition did not end with the New Deal. Instead, even during the "rights revolution" when so much attention was focused on the meaning of America's federal Constitution, activists and social movements continued to organize at the state level and continued to add positive rights to state constitutions.

As we will see, the proponents of environmental bills of rights made very similar claims about the need for positive rights to those that educational and labor reformers advanced in earlier decades. Like their predecessors in the quest for social rights, these activists argued that existing, negative rights were not enough to provide meaningful protection. The most urgent dangers, they insisted, no longer stemmed primarily from tyrannical government. Therefore, they wanted a new kind of right, one that would guarantee government's active intervention to protect them from other sorts of dangers.

By the 1960s and '70s, state constitutions already contained many detailed provisions related to the natural environment. These provisions were added to state constitutions throughout the late-nineteenth and twentieth centuries, and some certainly constituted mandates on government. Like the education and labor rights discussed in the previous chapters, these rights provisions often took the form of narrow, specific instructions to legislatures, obligating state governments to undertake the responsible management of the natural resources that the state controlled through its ownership of public lands. In dry Western states, constitutions contained detailed policies governing the use of fresh water sources. This chapter does not trace this long history of constitutional rights related to the natural environment. It focuses instead on the emergence (during the 1960s and 1970s) of broad constitutional declarations that the state must maintain a healthy or healthful natural environment. These sweeping mandates were often known as environmental bills of rights, and as we will see, environmental activists (both within and outside of legislatures) generally drafted these provisions not merely to require the responsible management of particular state-owned lands or resources, but also to mandate that legislatures combat problems of pollution and environmental degradation throughout their states. Like the narrower mandates described in previous chapters, these environmental bills of rights were a product of their particular political context and reflect the policy concerns and political tactics of their champions at the time of their drafting.

In this chapter, I first describe the ways in which environmental organizations worked to create environmental rights and the new constitutional rights that they generated through their efforts. Then I ask why these groups pursued the creation of state-level rights at a time when the federal government was already devoted to addressing environmental concerns. After explaining why environmental activists bothered with state politics during the 1960s and 1970s, I ask what strategic advantages they saw in constitutional rights, and argue that the primary appeal of constitutional rights for environmental organizations was the hope that these rights would facilitate public interest litigation to effect policy change. Environmental organizations also hoped that environmental rights would make their efforts at legislative lobbying more effective and would help organize their broader social movement. After discussing each of these motivations for constitutional change, I briefly address the place of these environmental bills of rights within the larger tradition of environmental rights in state constitutions. The unusual breadth of the modern rights to environmental protection was a product of their framers' intent to enable litigation. As environmentalists lost faith in the promise of litigation, however, they began to draft narrower provisions, reminiscent of the positive rights developed in the nineteenth century. Despite their changing form, however, environmental rights are in their essentials very much like the positive rights that came before.

Environmental Activism and State Constitutions

The 1960s and '70s witnessed an unprecedented explosion in federal environmental regulation. During these decades, Congress passed the National Environmental Protection Act as well as a series of "Clean Air," "Clean

Water," and "Endangered Species" acts. The federal Environmental Protection Agency was founded in 1970, and in the same year, United States Senator Gaylord Nelson organized the first Earth Day as a national "teach-in" about the need for environmental protection. In his 1970 State of the Union address, President Nixon declared that clean air, clean water, and open spaces should be the birthright of every American citizen, and announced "the [pollution control] program I shall propose to Congress will be the most comprehensive and costly program in this field in America's history."[3] By 1970, the federal government had officially committed itself to environmental protection.

Yet even during this period of heightened national attention to environmental issues, environmental organizations still lobbied to include rights to environmental protection in their state constitutions. For instance, Montana's League of Conservation Voters circulated a questionnaire to all of the candidates in elections for the state's 1971 constitutional convention, asking candidates to declare their position on the inclusion of a particular slate of environmental rights.[4] One delegate to the state's constitutional convention even reminded the convention, "For what it's worth, I pledged to the Montana League of Conservation Voters that I would support an environment proposal that they suggested and set forth. I think most of you did too."[5] Similarly, the Montana Conservation Council determined that it needed to devote energy to "electing the right people" to the convention, and then planned to "educate" whichever delegates were actually elected. Its Board of Directors also agreed on the necessity of raising the money to hire a full-time "lawyer-lobbyist" to attend the constitutional convention on their behalf. Through these measures, it hoped to serve a "watchdog function" that would allow it to "guard against environmental inroads by industry, business, et al."[6] in the process of drafting the state's new constitution.

Many environmental organizations also sent their own experts to testify before the appropriate committees at their states' constitutional conventions, often drafting suggested provisions for the conventions to consider. For instance, the Conservation Council of Hawaii (CCH), an affiliate of the National Wildlife Federation, proposed the addition of environmental rights to the state constitution and then testified before the constitutional convention. In its newsletter, the CCH explained, "The purpose [of its efforts] was to get early input into the convention and stimulate delegates to submit proposals of interest to us." The CCH also drafted its own suggested provi-

---

[3] "Transcript of the President's State of the Union Message to Joint Session of Congress," *New York Times*, New York, January 23, 1970, 22.

[4] Montana Constitutional Convention of 1971–2: 1229.

[5] Ibid., 1222.

[6] Montana Conservation Council, Minutes, Board of Directors meeting Oct. 2, 1971, Helena, Montana, pp. 2–3. In Montana Conservation Council Records, K. Ross Toole Archives, Mansfield Library, The University of Montana–Missoula. Montana Conservation Council Records, Collection 189, Series III, Box 6, Folder 19.

sion, which it distributed to the convention's 102 delegates.[7] Similarly, the Illinois Planning and Conservation League offered itself to Illinois's constitutional convention as a "technical resource" for testimony on behalf of the environmental rights provision.[8]

Between 1964 and 1978, fourteen state constitutions addressed the state's role in environmental protection (see table 7.1). While many state constitutions addressed natural resource policies both before the 1960s and after the 1970s, all of the broad conservation provisions in state constitutions (often dubbed "environmental bills of rights") were added between 1964 and 1978. I have allowed the timing of these constitutional additions to determine the period on which this chapter is focused. These distinctive provisions about environmental protection took several different forms, and the constitutions that addressed environmental protection often did so using multiple approaches. Six constitutions explicitly declared the existence of citizens' rights or the state's duty. For instance, the Illinois Constitution declares, "Each person has the right to a healthful environment," and the Rhode Island Constitution says that it is the state's duty "to provide for the conservation of the air, land, water, plant, animal, mineral and other natural resources of the state." Another type of constitutional provision related to environmental protection is the legislative mandate. These provisions simply declare that the legislature will take a particular type of action. For instance, the New Mexico Constitution states, "The legislature shall provide for control of pollution and control of despoilment of the air, water and other natural resources of this state." Nine constitutions contain this type of provision. Finally, state constitutions also came to include provisions explaining or establishing the state's commitment to conservation or environmental protection. These provisions typically begin, "It shall be the policy of the state to conserve and protect its natural resources." Ten state constitutions included one of these declarations about the policy of the state. Table 7.1, constructed primarily from the NBER State Constitutions Project (Wallis), shows all of the states that added broad statements about environmental protection and which types of provisions they included.

As we can see from table 7.1, the movement to add constitutional mandates for environmental protection was not limited to a single region of the country, nor was any geographic region particularly prominent in this movement. However, the states that addressed environmental protection using only one type of provision were South Carolina, Virginia, and North Carolina. These three Southeastern states included only what is arguably the weakest type of provision about environmental protection. The other eleven states that addressed environmental protection did so with a combination of provisions, at least one of which was either a clear legislative mandate or the explicit statement of constitutional right or state duty. Thus, one could plau-

---

[7] "CCH And The Con Con." *Conservation Council for Hawaii Newsletter*, Honolulu, 1978.
[8] "Environmental Lobby Seeks Rights Bill," *Chicago Tribune*, Chicago, April 26, 1970, S16.

TABLE 7.1. Environmental Provisions Added to State
Constitutions between 1960 and 1980

Year	State	Policy Statement	Legislative Mandate	Explicit Right/ State Duty
1963	**MI**	X	X	
1968	**FL**	X	X	
1969	NY	X	X	
1970	RI		X	X
1970	**IL**	X		X
1971	NM	X	X	
1971	SC	X		
1971	PA		X	X
1971	VA	X		
1972	MA	X		X
1973	**MT**		X	X
1973	NC	X		
1974	LA	X	X	
1978	**HI**		X	X

States that wrote environmental provisions into new constitutions appear
in bold.

sibly argue that constitutional rights to environmental protection were
weakest in the Southeast. There is some regional variation in the strength of
constitutional guarantees to environmental protection. However, the political campaigns for state constitutional change were clearly not restricted by
geographic region, and some states that lack a robust constitutional mandate for environmental protection were nonetheless the sites of failed efforts
to create these rights. It is challenging to generate a comprehensive list of
failed attempts at constitutional change, but during the late 1960s and
1970s, unsuccessful attempts to add environmental rights to state constitutions seem to have taken place in at least the following states: Maryland,
Arkansas, Texas, Alaska, and North Dakota.

The data also make it clear that movements for environmental rights
were not dependent upon larger constitutional revision processes. In other
words, these rights were not added to constitutions only when the entire
document was already in the midst of upheaval, but were also added as independent, freestanding amendments. Of the states that included broad environmental provisions in their state constitution, legislatures in many states
initiated the passage of these provisions as independent amendments to their
existing constitutions (see table 7.1). State legislatures' willingness to amend

their constitutions suggests that environmental rights were not merely after-thoughts, shoehorned into constitutions during unrelated moments of major revision, but the product of popular concerns about salient issues. The legislatures in Rhode Island, New Mexico, Pennsylvania, Massachusetts, and North Carolina all included environmental protections as amendments to their existing constitutions. The Rhode Island legislature even passed its environmental amendment after a similar provision had been rejected by the state's earlier constitutional convention. North Carolina's provision also passed with strong legislative support.[9] The first Earth Day seems to have motivated several state legislatures. For instance, the *Christian Science Monitor* reported that "indication of wide-scale public concern has made the issue [of environmental protection] a politician's delight. . . . the Massachusetts State Legislature approved 262–0 an amendment to the State Constitution to make an unpolluted environment a constitutional right."[10] Pennsylvania's legislature also passed its proposal to add environmental rights to its constitution on Earth Day.[11] It is clear from these freestanding amendments that environmentalists both within and outside state legislatures pursued the creation of constitutional rights not only when they could "piggyback" on existing processes of constitutional reform, but also as a means of capitalizing on popular concern about the environment.

Although some of these environmental rights did originate with independent legislative proposals, nine of the fourteen states that added broad conservation provisions did so as part of large-scale projects of constitutional revision. Michigan, Florida, Illinois, Montana, Louisiana, and Hawaii all added these provisions during constitutional conventions. South Carolina and Virginia added these amendments upon the suggestion of constitutional revision commissions, which were engaged in reviews of the states' entire constitutions. New York's "conservation bill of rights" was technically passed as an independent amendment, but was actually drafted by an earlier constitutional convention and included in a proposed constitution that was never ratified. Thus, the majority of broad statements about environmental protection were added to state constitutions as part of larger revision processes.

While they were clearly not necessary to generate a constitutional amendment to a healthy environment, state constitutional conventions or revision commissions may have been important in prompting activists to pursue environmental rights because, unlike the issues of education and labor (over

[9] "Rhode Island Renews Charter-Reform Drive," *Christian Science Monitor*, Boston, July 35, 1968, 13, and "Bowles Introduces Environment Bill," *Times-News*, Hendersonville, NC, February 3, 1971, 12.

[10] Trudy Rubin, "Ahead: the Job of Cleaning Up a Planet," *Christian Science Monitor*, Boston, April 24, 1970, 1.

[11] Matthew Thor Kirsch, "Upholding the Public Trust in State Constitutions," *Duke Law Journal* 46, no. 5 (1997): 1169.

which the federal government had little authority at the time that reformers sought constitutional rights), the environmental activists of the 1960s and 1970s might very reasonably have sought national policy changes through federal channels. As we have seen, during this period, the federal government was already engaged in the field of environmental regulation. State politics, therefore, was only one avenue through which activists could address environmental concerns. Because environmentalists saw many possible avenues for their pursuit of policy change, they may have been willing to devote resources to state-level changes primarily when the prior existence of a revision process (like a constitutional convention or revision commission) created an opportunity for influence that was difficult to ignore. Of course, environmentalists need not have devoted any resources to the creation of state-level rights or even to state politics. Since environmental protection was understood to be a national problem, and the federal government was engaged in addressing it, it does seem somewhat puzzling that, during the 1960s and 1970s, we see any environmental activism in the states. The next section of this chapter explains why activists pursued state-level rights in the midst of so much federal activity.

WHY STATES?

With so much environmental action at the national level, why did environmental activists bother with state constitutions? I offer five different, though related, answers to this question. First, while broad rights to environmental protection were new in the 1960s and 1970s, state constitutions had long addressed the management of states' natural resources and the protection of the public's health. Thus, when states reconsidered their constitutions at times of heightened alarm about the preservation of a healthy natural environment, constitutional drafters simply expanded older provisions to address newer concerns. Second, just as state governments and state constitutions had for some time addressed environmental issues, environmentalists had long been organized at the state level. These state-level groups had a particular interest in shaping the policies of their own states. Third, even after the federal government turned its attention to the preservation of the natural environment, state governments remained active on these issues as well. Thus, state-level environmentalists continued their attempts to influence emerging state policies. In addition, in their attempts to change constitutions, environmental organizations consulted with and copied from one another, working state by state to engineer a response to environmental problems that would transcend state boundaries even as it operated through state law. Finally, environmental activists were not forced to choose between either federal or state-level lobbying. Instead, the environmental movement pursued many avenues to reform, seeking a federal constitutional right at the same time that its members crafted and lobbied on behalf of state-level rights. The following section addresses each of these explanations for state-level activism more fully.

In order to understand the reasons that activists pursued constitutional change at the state level, it is first important to remember that, well before the environmental movement of the 1960s, states had long been active in areas related to environmental management and public health. As far back as the nineteenth century, many states had established government agencies devoted to the management of natural resources, like fish, game, water, and forests. Similarly, the maintenance of public health was understood be such a central duty of state and local governments in the nineteenth century that it was seen as a fundamental justification for the state's police powers.[12] By the second half of the nineteenth century, state constitutions began to require explicitly that the legislature establish state boards of health, public hospitals, and asylums.[13] Thus, one answer to the question about why state constitutions ended up with environmental rights even during the 1960s and '70s is that state constitutions had already been used to address maintenance of the public health and natural resources for quite some time.

In the 1960s and 1970s, when environmentalists worked to add broad rights to a healthy environment to state constitutions, many explained their goals as the mere expansion of a role that states had long played in protecting the public's health. For instance, Hawaii's explicit right to environmental protection grew in part from its older constitutional mandates on public health. Hawaii's original constitution, ratified in 1950, included an article devoted to public health, and subsequent discussions of this provision continually referenced the role of the natural environment in preserving the health of the public.[14] In its preparatory study for the convention of 1978, the state's legislative reference bureau noted the persistent concern for environmental protection as a component of public health. Consequently, the authors of this report suggested the possibility of adding an explicit environmental amendment to the public health provision.[15]

---

[12] Novak, *The People's Welfare: Law and Regulation in Nineteenth-Century America.*

[13] For instance, South Carolina's constitution of 1896 stated, "It shall be the duty of the General Assembly to create Boards of Health wherever they may be necessary, giving to them power and authority to make such regulations as shall protect the health of the community and abate nuisances." Article 8 § 10.

[14] Its first section was phrased as a mandate on the state to "protect," and even "promote," the public's health. The next three sections of the public health article clarified that the state legislature was authorized to act in the care of handicapped persons, and slum clearance. Its fifth section stated, "the State shall have power to conserve and develop its natural beauty, objects and places of historic or cultural interest, sightliness and physical good order, and for that purpose private property shall be subject to reasonable regulation."

[15] Lois Yoon, "Article VIII: Public Health and Welfare," in *Hawaii Constitutional Convention Studies,* ed. Legislative Reference Bureau (Honolulu, 1978).

Like protection of the public's health, state governments had been involved in the management of natural resources since the nineteenth century, and nineteenth-century constitutions reflected this governmental function as well. Many of these natural resource provisions addressed the management of state-owned timber lands, specifically the state's obligation to protect those lands from forest fires and other forms of devaluation.[16] Another kind of environmental provision added to state constitutions during the Gilded Age related to the ownership and distribution of water in arid Western states. Constitutions addressed the issue of water rights with varying degrees of specificity; however, as Amy Bridges explains in her study of Western state constitutions: "the single constant was the critical role of state government in the management of water. It was never proposed in any of the [constitutional] conventions that the market, left to its own devices, would deliver water to all who needed it."[17] Thus, Western state constitutions outlined an active, interventionist role for government in the management of environmental resources almost one hundred years before the birth of the modern environmental movement.

Constitutional conventions in several states identified the new rights to clean air and water, or to clean and healthy environments as extensions of the older provisions about the management of state-owned lands and waters. For example, several delegates to New York's constitutional convention described the state's new environmental bill of rights as continuing the great tradition of the state's forever wild clause. One delegate argued for the environmental bill of rights, declaring, "The 1894 Constitutional Convention has been given a noted place in history because it brought forth the first constitutional protection on our state of the Forest Preserve. . . . I am confident this proposition will take its place beside the Forest Preserve Provision . . . as a highwater mark in this state of the conservation of natural resources."[18] Another delegate echoed this sentiment. He lauded the conservation bill of rights for "going beyond the 'forever wild' provisions." The new environmental article would not only preserve specific areas of state-owned wilderness where citizens might vacation, he explained, but would expand its protection, creating guarantees "about the quality of life,

[16] The focus of many earlier instances of environmental law, particularly those related to forestland, was on the profitable management of the resources actually owned by the state. Thus, most of the constitutional forestry provisions were intended to mandate state action only with reference to state-owned land. See Richard J. Lazarus, *The Making of Environmental Law* (Chicago: University of Chicago Press, 2004), 50. By contrast, the environmental provisions of the late twentieth century were explicitly intended to mandate government intervention in the use of private as well as publicly owned land.

[17] Bridges, "Managing the Periphery in the Gilded Age: Writing Constitutions for the Western States," 47.

[18] New York State Constitutional Convention, *Constitutional Convention Proceedings* (Albany 1967), 939.

about distribution of natural resources where the people live. We can all be proud of this proposition because it addresses itself to quality of life where people live and not just where they may visit."[19] Thus, one answer to the question about why rights to environmental health appear in state constitutions is that these provisions grew out of related commitments that were already there.

Another explanation for the existence of state-level environmental rights is the existence of environmental groups that were organized at the state level. Not only had state governments long been active in the field of environmental protection, but environmental organizations had long been organized in order to influence states' environmental policies. Even nationally organized groups, such as the Audubon Society, the Sierra Club, and the National Wildlife Fund organized (and indeed continue to maintain) active state chapters, which concerned themselves not only with their organizations' national agendas, but also with conservation problems specific to their states. These groups continued to pursue state-level action on environmental issues throughout the late twentieth century. As we might imagine, groups organized at the state level to influence state government supported changes to constitutions that could bolster their existing achievements and facilitate their future work within their states. As the Michigan United Conservation Clubs explained to the state's constitutional convention, "We would like to see language in the constitution which will protect the gains that have been made to date, and provide for the continuation and extension of these gains."[20]

Even when the federal government took up the charge of environmental protection, state governments continued their efforts at environmental management and protection. Therefore, state governments remained relevant

[19] Ibid., 945. In Virginia, environmental activists also identified the new environmental provision as an extension of the existing constitutional protections for natural resources. Since 1902, the Virginia Constitution had prohibited the state from either selling or leasing the tidal lands which contained its oyster beds. In his proposal to add environmental rights to the state constitution, one prominent activist argued: "The people of Virginia have already set a precedent for constitutional protection of public resources in Section 175 of the present Constitution . . . The effect of Section 175 has been to place on the legislature, and other public agencies under its jurisdiction, a high degree of responsibility commensurate with the irreplaceable nature of the oyster beds . . . The amendment proposed here would give all natural resources in the public domain the same degree of constitutional protection now afforded to the oyster beds of the state. Ted Pankowski, Co-Chairman Parks, Recreation & Libraries Committee—Fairfax County Federation of Citizens Association, "A Proposal to Revise the Virginia Constitution to provide a constitutional restriction against arbitrary management or disposition of natural resources in the public domain." In Papers of A. E. Dick Howard for the Virginia Commission for Constitutional Revision 1969–71, Box 4, Conservation, Bill of Rights, General (1968–69), Special Collections, University of Virginia Law Library, pp. 2–3.

[20] "Report of the Special Constitutional Convention Committee: The Views of Michigan United Conservation Clubs," February 28, 1962, p. 2. In the Katherine Moore Cushman Papers, Bentley Historical Library, University of Michigan, Michigan Constitutional Convention of 1961–2 (folder), Box 2.

targets for those seeking changes in environmental policy. During the 1960s and '70s, many state governments independently responded to public interest in environmental protection in much the same way that the federal government did, with increased attention and policymaking. In 1973, the deputy commissioner of the New York State Department of Environmental Conservation reported that, in response to increased public interest in environmental protection, "most states have taken a hard look at their conservation and environmental agencies to determine how well equipped they are to respond to the public's continuing concern that natural resources and the environment are major items of the agenda of unfinished public business."[21] Many states reorganized their bureaucracies, creating a single state agency that was responsible for the protection of the state's environment and natural resources.[22] Like Congress, state legislatures passed laws independently regulating the protection of endangered species, pesticide control, power plant siting, and vehicle emissions.[23] Thus, even at a time of intensive federal activity, state governments provided additional sources of environmental regulation. In addition, the federal environmental regulations created during the 1960s and 1970s were often designed to be implemented at the state level by state governments.[24] Given all of this activity at the level of state government, it is hardly surprising that environmental activists sought to influence state policy.

Different states did face environmental issues that were really quite different from one another. Environmentalists in some states worked to protect coastlines and coastal ecosystems, while others were concerned with the purity of their freshwater lakes and rivers. Others worked to decrease smog from polluting factories, while environmentalists in different states battled mining industries to protect mountain ranges and open spaces. In addition, different states had reached differing levels of industrial development, and thus required different amounts of remediation and cleanup. However, as we saw in both the labor and education cases, activists and constitutional framers consistently viewed their states' particular needs in the context of national problems.

Even as they addressed their own states' particular concerns, the proponents of environmental rights communicated across states, sharing ideas for constitutional change. For instance, one report for the Michigan constitutional convention's committee on local government began with a list of the state's unique natural resources and listed the problems that Michigan specifically might face or already faced with respect to those natural resources.

[21] W. Mason Lawrence, "Equipping State Government to Meet Resource Needs," in *Transactions of the Thirty-Eighth North American Wildlife and Natural Resources Conference* (Washington, DC: Wildlife Management Institute, 1973), 496–7.

[22] Ibid., 497.

[23] Ibid., 500–501.

[24] J. Clarence Davies and Jan Mazurek, *Pollution Control in the United States: Evaluating the System* (Washington, DC: Resources for the Future, 1998), 40.

The report went on to note, "as it is pointed out in the Alaska constitutional studies, state constitutional provisions on natural resources reflect the needs of the economy of individual states."[25] Although the convention's report began with an assertion that state constitutions reflected the needs of individual states, it went on to declare its aspiration to set an example for other states: "the Michigan Constitutional Convention, taking its inspiration from the Alaska Convention, 'has the opportunity of breaking new ground' (to quote the Alaska Studies), in the field of constitutional land and water policies for the older, industrial states with their late 20th century problems."[26] This belief that Michigan might set an example for other states reflected the extremely common practice of studying the fundamental laws of other states during the constitutional drafting process.

Just as we saw with education and labor, activists who understood problems as national in scope still worked to forge nationwide policies through the coordination of state governments and state constitutional mandates. Though environmental organizations naturally cited the threats to their own states, these movements for constitutional change were no more idiosyncratic or isolated than the labor or education movements to add rights to state constitutions, and perhaps even less so. Even as they lobbied state legislatures and constitutional conventions, environmental organizations were self-consciously participating in the nationwide environmental movement. As they sought to influence the shape of their own constitutions, they kept abreast of, and often imitated, the constitutional developments of other states. Thus, activists working across many different states and regions often made the same kinds of demands for constitutional change, and far-flung constitutional conventions adopted the same basic types of provisions. Constitutional convention debates and the interest groups that lobbied them often described the environmental rights in the constitutions of other states, and argued that their state constitution should adopt similar rights.[27] One delegate to the Montana Constitutional Convention even called the Attorney General of Illinois to discuss that state's experience with its relatively new environmental rights provision.[28]

[25] "Preliminary Report to the Committee on Local Government" (undated) in the Katherine Moore Cushman Papers, Bentley Historical Library, University of Michigan, Michigan Constitutional Convention of 1961–2 (folder), Box 2; emphasis in original.

[26] "Preliminary Report to the Committee on Local Government" (undated), p. 4. In the Katherine Moore Cushman Papers, Bentley Historical Library, University of Michigan, Michigan Constitutional Convention of 1961–2 (folder), Box 2.

[27] See for example Franklin L. Kury, *Natural Resources and the Public Estate: A Biography of Article I, Section 27 of the Pennsylvania Constitution, Written by Franklin L. Kury for the Maurice K. Goddard Chair Program* (Reed Smith Shaw & McClay, 1985), appendix 3; Illinois Constitutional Convention, Record of Proceedings: Sixth Illinois Constitutional Convention. December 8, 1969–September 3, 1970 (Springfield, IL: John W. Lewis, 1970), 3002; Montana Constitutional Convention of 1971–2, 1204–18.

[28] Montana Constitutional Convention of 1971–2, 1218.

Although the Michigan constitutional convention believed its new constitution would serve as a nationwide example, New York's provision actually seems to have been the primary reference point for many advocates of constitutional rights to environmental protection. For example, Franklin L. Kury, the author of Pennsylvania's constitutional provision, who served in the state house of representatives and shepherded it through the legislature, wrote that he "first got the idea for the amendment in 1968 from reading an article in the *New York Times* on New York State's then proposed environmental amendment."[29] Fitzgerald Bemiss, a Virginia state senator and environmental leader who testified before the state's constitutional revision commission, received a letter from a professor of chemistry at the College of William and Mary. The letter's author stated that he had come across an item [in *Audubon* magazine][30] which included a copy of the proposed New York State constitution's "environmental bill of rights," and suggested that "if time has not run out for such proposals, someone might try to have such a conservation bill of rights included in the proposed Virginia constitution."[31]

The newsletters of environmental organizations helped to facilitate the sharing of environmental rights across states. For instance, the *Audubon* article cited above quoted the text of New York's amendment at length, and it too recommended that other states adapt New York's provision for use in their own constitutions: "New York conservationists plan to strive for the adoption of this bill of rights as an amendment to the existing state constitution. It could, by deletion of a phrase which has pertinence only in New York, be fitted into the constitution of any state. We recommend it." Similarly, a periodical published by the Missouri Department of Conservation asked, "Do the citizens of a state have certain 'inalienable rights' to the perpetuation and use and enjoyment of natural resources, as they do certain basic human rights?" It continued, "Some conservationists think so, and are pressing for inclusion of a 'bill of rights' in state constitutions that would outline the responsibility of the state to protect the environment and corresponding rights of the people to the protection of their natural and historic heritage." This article also provided the text of New York's provision, explaining, "we cite an amendment unanimously approved by New York State's constitutional convention . . . it does contain ideas worth thinking

[29] Kury, *Natural Resources and the Public Estate: A Biography of Article I, Section 27 of the Pennsylvania Constitution, Written by Franklin L. Kury for the Maurice K. Goddard Chair Program* 4.

[30] "A Conservation Bill of Rights for Your State Constitution," *Audubon*, vol. 70, no. 1, Jan/Feb 1968. This publication was the magazine of the National Audubon Society.

[31] Letter from Alfred R. Armstrong to Fitzgerald Bemiss, Nov. 19, 1969. Found in Special Collections, University of Virginia Law Library, The Papers Of A. E. Dick Howard For The Virginia Commission For Constitutional Revision, Box 4, 1968–1968; Conservation Bill of Rights. General. Emphasis in original.

about for Missouri."[32] Thanks to this sharing of ideas across states, activists could work toward nationwide reform even as they lobbied to change state constitutions. At the same time that environmental activists pushed for new congressional legislation and federal regulations, state-level organizations attempted to secure coordinated state action.

Finally, activists did not need to choose between working at the state level and working at the federal level. Environmentalists did not argue that states should be the only governmental entities working to protect the natural environment or that state constitutions should be the only ones to contain environmental rights. On the contrary, at the same time that environmentalists were working to amend state constitutions, members of the movement were also seeking similar changes to the federal Constitution. In fact, there were a handful of sustained and fairly high-profile attempts to add environmental rights to the text of the federal Constitution through the formal amendment process, and environmental activists and public interest lawyers also asked the federal judiciary to interpret the existing constitutional text to include environmental rights. Environmentalists waged this campaign for federal constitutional change at the same time they pushed state legislatures and constitutional conventions to create state-level constitutional rights.

Unlike the campaigns for environmental rights at the state level, none of the attempts at federal constitutional change ever came particularly close to succeeding.[33] Litigation proved just as unsuccessful in establishing federal constitutional rights to environmental health and protection. In *Tanner v. Armco Steel Corp.*, a federal district court rejected the argument that the Ninth Amendment should be construed to embrace environmental rights. Its opinion stated unequivocally that the Ninth Amendment through its "penumbra or otherwise embodies no legally assertable right to a healthful environment."[34] In *Environmental Defense Fund v. Hoerner Waldorf*, a federal judge did express the conviction that health, and even environmental health, do seem to be protected by Fifth and Fourteenth Amendments. However, the judge also ruled that these provisions of the federal Constitution only protect people from government and its actions, not from the actions of private individuals. Consequently, he dismissed the Environmental Defense Fund's (EDF's) claims against the Hoerner Waldorf Paper Mill because the EDF did not claim that any governmental actions had violated the Constitution's protection of a healthy environment.[35] As we know, this question about whether a right protects its bearers only from government is one of the cen-

[32] "Conservation Bill of Rights," *The Conservationist: Missouri Department of Conservation*, October 1968, vol. 29, no, 10, page 1.

[33] Carole Gallagher, "The Movement to Create an Environmental Bill of Rights: From Earth Day, 1970 to the Present," *Fordham Environmental Law Journal* 9, no. 1 (1997): 120–9; Robert McLaren, "Environmental Protection Based on State Constitutional Law: A Call for Reinterpretation," *University of Hawaii Law Review* 12, no. 1 (1990): 124–5.

[34] *Tanner v. Armaco Steel Corp.*, 340 F. Supp. 532 (1972).

[35] *Environmental Defense Fund v. Hoerner Waldorf*, 1 Environ. Rep. 1640 (1970).

tral ways in which negative rights are distinguished from positive ones. In its assertion that the U.S. Constitution offers protection only from the threat of intrusive governmental action but not the action of third parties or market forces, this opinion adopted a squarely negative-rights understanding of due process, and consequently suggested that the federal courts were unlikely to find positive environmental rights in the federal Constitution.

The failure of positive environmental rights at the federal level may also help to explain why environmental activists pursued state-level constitutional rights, but its timing suggests that failure at the national level cannot account for a good deal of state-level activism. Even before the early 1970s, when these federal cases were decided, several states had already placed mandates for environmental protection in their constitutions (see table 7.1), and in several other states, legislatures and constitutional conventions had already begun to consider taking similar steps. State constitutions were not simply a second choice for activists who had failed at the national level, but were appealing venues in their own right.

Environmental Provisions as Positive Rights

The debates of constitutional conventions and the personal papers of their delegates, scholarly articles, the newsletters and internal records of the environmental organizations, as well as newspaper accounts of their involvement all shed light on the origins of constitutional rights to environmental protection. These sources provide compelling evidence that we ought to consider the environmental provisions in question to be positive rights. Like labor organizations at the turn of the nineteenth century, the proponents of environmental rights insisted that a negative-rights regime was no longer adequate to provide protection from the most immediate and meaningful dangers in people's lives. Constitutional rights had already been successful in creating a safe and healthy political environment, they argued, and the natural environment required comparable protection. Franklin Kury, the author of the environmental rights amendment to Pennsylvania's constitution, explained it this way:

> When the Constitution writers of the 18th century did their work, there was no apparent need to be concerned about the natural environment. Their concern was the political environment. The result was that our national and state constitutions provided explicit and strong protection for our political environment, but were silent—absolutely silent—concerning the natural environment.[36]

[36] Kury, *Natural Resources and the Public Estate: A Biography of Article I, Section 27 of the Pennsylvania Constitution, Written by Franklin L. Kury for the Maurice K. Goddard Chair Program 1.*

This silence he argued, had allowed special interests (coal companies, railroads, and the steel industry, for example) to take over the state legislature and had brought the state nearly to the point of environmental catastrophe. Thus, Kury insisted, it was clear that protections for political freedoms alone had become insufficient, and that Pennsylvania could no longer afford to have its fundamental law remain inadequate with respect to natural resources.

Many other proponents of environmental rights drew a similar parallel between political and environmental safeguards. For instance, when one delegate to Maryland's Constitutional Convention of 1967 argued that social and economic rights, like the right to environmental protection, had no place in a constitution, another responded: "I believe that these concerns reflect our most deep-seated needs, just as in the 18th and 19th century, political requirements did." He continued by asserting that existing constitutional rights meant very little in the absence of a healthy and beautiful environment. Thus, he asked, "what good is the ballot without bread and without the joy of living?"[37]

In New York, one delegate to the state's constitutional convention of the same year echoed the sentiment that environmental rights were as relevant and fundamental as traditional political protections, saying, "In these days when the earth may be overcome by garbage, the cloud indistinguishable from smog, and the sky itself only a blue memory unless we somehow turn our genius to the environment, a basic statement of the protection of natural resources is truly a bill of rights."[38] Another described his view of an environmental "bill of rights" as an extension of existing constitutional protections: "I regard it as something that is basically fundamental, as a necessary extension to the due process clause, due process requires that every citizen of the state must have the right to protection of those resources which alone can make life worthwhile in an age of increasing mechanism."[39]

In this new context, one in which increased technological development threatened "the joy of living" and even posed a threat to human health and life itself, proponents of environmental rights argued that these new rights were necessary to supplement the old. In the Illinois constitutional convention of 1970, one delegate said, "The right to life has been constitutionally protected against other threats; it now needs protection against the continued deterioration of the environment."[40] And in the Montana Constitutional Convention of 1972, one delegate explained that constitutions could no

[37] Maryland Constitutional Convention of 1967, *Proceedings and Debates of the 1967 Constitutional Convention*, 104, 753.

[38] New York State Constitutional Convention, *Constitutional Convention Proceedings*, 948.

[39] Ibid., 941.

[40] Illinois Constitutional Convention, *Record of Proceedings: Sixth Illinois Constitutional Convention*. December 8, 1969–September 3, 1970: 249.

longer continue to protect traditional property rights alone. He said, "I think the issue is . . . whether or not we wish to sustain property rights in our Constitution for its term or whether we want to enlarge human rights in our Constitution by this amendment."[41] Environmental activists argued for constitutions that would not simply shield private property or political liberties, but also protect people's lives and their health.

These environmental arguments paralleled the claims of the labor activists who argued for the necessity of positive constitutional rights. As the *Atlantic Monthly* explained it in 1906, the existing law guaranteed the "right to do any unforbidden thing," but at a time when so many were being materially harmed, crippled, and even killed by unsafe working conditions, grueling hours, and pitifully low wages, these old, negative rights were totally inadequate to successfully safeguard the happiness, health, and even the lives of their bearers.[42] Industrialized society, he continued, required a different kind of law.

Like the proponents of positive labor rights, environmentalists argued that changing technologies rendered the existing constitutional rights insufficient, and typically argued that air and water pollution in particular posed new, urgent, and dire threats to society. For instance, the Michigan Conservation Council described the degradation of Michigan's natural environment to the state's constitutional convention of 1961–62, and made this prediction: "We believe . . . that this society will disintegrate when these [natural] resources diminish to low levels. We believe that every individual concerned with the use of these resources has rights involved in their use."[43] Eugene Sloane, an expert on air pollution, testified before one of the committees of the Michigan constitutional convention, stating, "There is a direct relationship between air pollution and the health of the people. A steady exposure of polluted air robs one of his health." Mary Lee Leahy, who spearheaded the movement to add environmental rights to the Illinois Constitution, centered her campaign for election to the state's constitutional convention around the need to address pollution, and attributed her successful election to a period of particularly severe air pollution over Chicago.[44]

In order to determine whether the new constitutional provisions environmentalists proposed should be considered positive rights, it is necessary to ask three questions: (1) Are these provisions even rights at all? (2) Are these provisions telling government to refrain from intervention in social and eco-

[41] Montana Constitutional Convention of 1971–2, 1265.

[42] Alger, "Some Equivocal Rights of Labor."

[43] "Report of the Special Constitutional Convention Committee: The Views of Michigan United Conservation Clubs." February 28, 1962. In the Katherine Moore Cushman Papers, Bentley Historical Library, University of Michigan, Michigan Constitutional Convention of 1961–2 (folder), Box 2.

[44] Mark DePue, *Interview with Mary Leahy* (Springfield, IL: Conducted for the Abraham Lincoln Presidential Library, 2008), 54.

nomic life or encouraging government to intervene? (3) Do these rights protect their bearers only from government itself, or do they also require the state to provide protection from non-governmental threats?

First, should we consider these environmental provisions rights? For purposes of this book, I have considered constitutional rights those provisions that can serve as the basis for demands (rather than simply requests) on government. Thus, I have characterized provisions as rights not only when they contain the word "rights," but also when they contain explicit mandates to government or create an obligation on government to act in a particular way. It is clear that the advocates of the environmental provisions in state constitutions understood the provisions they drafted and championed to embody just this sort of mandate.

In Michigan, the first state to include a broadly worded provision about the protection of the state's natural environment, the constitutional convention engaged in a lengthy debate about the nature of the environmental provision. All of the delegates involved agreed that one purpose of the provision was simply to ensure that the state constitution could not be used to prevent the legislature from passing protective regulations. However, there was some disagreement about whether the provision also created mandates on the legislature. One delegate believed that it did not, explaining that the constitution's statement on the environment would draw legislative attention to environmental problems, but should leave the legislature free to act or not act as it saw fit. Even though the provision stated, "The legislature shall provide for the protection of the air, water and other natural resources of the state from pollution, impairment and destruction," this delegate nevertheless claimed that it did not create an obligation. He argued, "the legislature retains, in fact, full discretion to act or not to act as it wishes, but the responsibility of the legislature for evolving public policy in these matters is emphatically emphasized."[45]

Other delegates expressed the opinion that the environmental provision did more than simply emphasize the legislature's responsibility, and argued that the statement "the legislature shall" must certainly place new mandates on the legislature. For example, one delegate (actually an opponent of the right) opposed the provision precisely because he believed it would create an obligation on the legislature. He explained that by stating that the legislature "shall" provide for the protection of natural resources, the provision clearly mandated government action.[46] Several supporters of the provision agreed with this assessment, and argued that the mandatory character of the provision was a desirable and even necessary feature. One exclaimed, for instance, "[this provision] does institute the obligation of conservation in the interest of the people and I therefore urge its support." He explained that

[45] State of Michigan Constitutional Convention, Official Record: Proceedings (Lansing 1961), 2602.
[46] Ibid., 2610.

it was not enough simply to remove barriers to legislative action and hope for the best, arguing that "a positive rather than a merely defensive posture in regard to matters of conservation is of the utmost importance to guarantee that this type of mass exploitation and spoilage shall not again occur."[47]

Six years later, the delegates to New York's constitutional convention evinced a much firmer agreement that the phrase "the legislature shall . . ." constituted a mandate for government. Consequently, although New York's provision does not use the term "right," the delegates who drafted it and the organizations that supported it consistently described it as a "a conservation bill of rights."[48] For instance, one delegate to the constitutional convention stated, "If we adopt the Conservation Bill of Rights, we have defined the role of the state in the practice of Conservation . . . in essence we have mandated upon the state the duty of protection the inalienable rights of its citizens."[49] This idea of a mandate became widely agreed upon by the proponents of future environmental provisions. For instance, a delegate to the Maryland Constitutional Convention described the environmental provision he championed as "an attempt on behalf of the conservationists who appeared before us, and I say again, intensely, immensely interested in this, that the General Assembly no longer have the option of what they might do; but that they shall be required to act; it is a directive to do so."[50] A contemporaneous review of environmental rights in state constitutions similarly concluded that "most recent environmental provisions in state constitutions (e.g., Illinois, Montana, New Mexico, Massachusetts) *command* legislatures to pass supplemental legislation . . . Thus, the language is mandatory rather than permissive."[51] Ultimately, five states included the term "right" in their constitutional provisions, and Rhode Island's constitution established an explicit governmental duty to protect the environment (see table 7.1). Five other state constitutions combined a declaration of the state's policy on environmental protection with a statement beginning "the legislature shall." These provisions do seem to have been drafted as mandates or obligations on government. Therefore, we should certainly consider them rights.

In order to classify these provisions as positive rights, we must ask whether state constitutional rights to a healthy environment were designed to require that government restrain itself or to mandate active government intervention in social and economic life. Most advocates of explicit environ-

[47] Ibid., 2604.

[48] Although the constitution drafted by this convention was rejected by the state's voters, its environmental provision was so popular that the state legislature proposed it as a free-standing constitutional amendment.

[49] New York State Constitutional Convention, *Constitutional Convention Proceedings*, 940.

[50] Maryland Constitutional Convention of 1967, *Proceedings and Debates of the 1967 Constitutional Convention*, 104, 757.

[51] Richard J. Tobin, "Some Observations on the Use of State Constitutions to Protect the Environment," *Environmental Affairs* 3, no. 3 (1974): 481–2.

mental rights were quite clear that they hoped these constitutional rights would force government into action. As we have already seen from the arguments of convention delegates, these environmental provisions were not only mandates on government, but they were mandates for legislatures to take (and not to refrain) from action. Thus, the article that reviewed states' environmental provisions not only described them as "commands" to legislatures, but as commands "to pass supplemental legislation."[52] Similarly, the delegate to the Maryland Constitutional Convention who described his proposed provision as a "directive" also specified "the General Assembly [will] no longer have the option of what they might do . . . they shall be required to act."[53] Clearly, then, these rights were not understood as restraints on government, but as mandates for an involved, interventionist state. In fact, most of the proponents of these rights described them in similar terms.

When delegate Mary Lee Leahy introduced the idea of an environmental rights article to Illinois's constitutional convention, she explained that the right was necessary in part because "government action has been erratic in the past, and although right now it is a hot political issue . . . There's no guarantee that government will keep on acting."[54] Similarly, Franklin L. Kury, the author of Pennsylvania's provision guaranteeing the right to a healthy environment, explained that he thought the right was so significant because it obligated Pennsylvania's legislature to take an active role in protecting the environment. He explained, "From now on, state government [will] be the trustee of our natural resources for future generations, rather than a silent accomplice to their exploitation. Thus, I believe, for all time to come, the power of government [will] be used to protect and preserve our environment."[55] According to Kury, then, the right to a healthy environment was clearly designed to combat government's inaction, not to stay its hand. Through its inaction, or silence, the state's government had allied itself with the forces of environmental ruin. Therefore, the virtue of the constitutional right to environmental protection was that it would no longer allow government to passively acquiesce in the destruction of the natural environment. Instead, it would force government into the role of trustee, a role that would require the state actively to protect and preserve the environment and by extension, those living within it. One law review article about Pennsylvania's provision even described it by saying, "The first sentence creates (or affirms) a positive constitutional right in individual citizens."[56] Yet even

[52] Ibid.

[53] Maryland Constitutional Convention of 1967, *Proceedings and Debates of the 1967 Constitutional Convention*, 104, 757.

[54] Illinois Constitutional Convention, *Record of Proceedings: Sixth Illinois Constitutional Convention*. December 8, 1969–September 3, 1970: 2991.

[55] Franklin L. Kury, "Pennsylvania's Environmental Amendment," Pennsylvania Land Trust Association, http://conserveland.org/policy/envirorights.

[56] Robert Broughton, "Proposed Pennsylvania Declaration of Environmental Rights, Analysis of Hb 958," *Pennsylvania Bar Association Quarterly* 41, no. 4 (1970): 422.

when their proponents did not use the term "positive rights," the advocates of these environmental provisions were explicit about their goals to create mandates for active governmental intervention. For instance, one delegate to Montana's Constitutional Convention explained the purpose of Montana's environmental provision this way: "What we did is mandate the legislature to take immediate, forceful action. What they did isn't enough. We want more."[57]

New York's Conservation Bill of Rights, which, as we have seen, served as a template and inspiration for many other states, also seems to have been conceived as a mandate for active intervention in order to improve the cleanliness and health of the environment. One delegate to the constitutional convention explained:

> Conservation means preservation; but it also means enhancement. . . . The Conservation Bill of Rights is in its broad scope, an environmental bill of rights. It includes creation as well as conservation; promotion as well as protection; revision as well as retention . . . in essence we have mandated upon the state the duty of protecting the inalienable rights of its citizens.[58]

On this reading, New York's environmental rights provision requires government action not only to maintain the existing condition of the environment to improve upon the condition of the environment through active intervention.

Many proponents of positive rights expressed the sense that public regulations were necessary to combat powerful and destructive private interests. For instance, the papers of one of the delegates to the Michigan constitutional convention contain a document labeled "Air Pollution," which stated, "Residents of industrial areas are becoming increasingly aware that the phrase 'free as air' is no longer true. To keep air pure and clean now requires expensive controls."[59] In part as a consequence of this expense, many stressed the need for the state to regulate private actors in order to ensure the public's safety. Thus, the delegate's memo on air pollution continues, "there is a conflict here between public and private interest, between the people who need to live and work in unpolluted air and the industrial interests." The final report of the Michigan convention's subcommittee on natural resources also explained that the state no longer needed to encourage the fruitful exploitation of its environment, but to halt this exploitation by some in the interests of preserving the natural world for the good of the whole: "Today

[57] Montana Constitutional Convention of 1971–2: 1223.

[58] New York State Constitutional Convention, *Constitutional Convention Proceedings*, 940.

[59] "Air Pollution" Oct. 30th (no year). In the Katherine Moore Cushman Papers, Bentley Historical Library, University of Michigan, Michigan Constitutional Convention of 1961–2 (folder), Box 2.

the plentiful minerals, forests, waters, fish, wildlife and open land of 1908 and 1850 are in ever shorter supply . . . Our problem, then, is not . . . how to put to use vast resources, but how to conserve what we have left in the public interest."[60] A contemporaneous law review article about environmental rights echoed this conviction that government must regulate private action in the public interest, explaining, "Environmental problems essentially are conflicts between members of society in the use of land, air, and water."[61] It went on to cite an influential ecologist, Garrett Hardin, who argued that rational self-interest will lead people to exploit communal resources even if everyone involved realizes that this behavior will ultimately destroy those resources: "as Garrett Hardin has written, 'Freedom in a commons brings ruin to all.'" The article concluded "It is, therefore, the vital function of law adequately to regulate the use of air, water, and land in the interest of mutual survival."[62] Like labor activists, who argued that government must intervene to protect society (or at least to protect society's laborers) and educational activists, who argued that the state had a moral responsibility to protect children from growing up in ignorance and poverty, environmental advocates argued that freedom, unaccompanied by protective regulation, would have enormously destructive consequences. Clearly, the authors and proponents of these provisions did not view them as a means of restraining government, but as a mandate to government to interfere in and hinder degradation of the environment. In this respect, these environmental provisions must be categorized as positive rights.

The second question one must ask to distinguish a positive from a negative right is whether the right protects its bearer from government only, or whether it obligates government to protect its bearers from other dangers as well.[63] Here again, the environmental rights in state constitutions should be

---

[60] "Final Report of the Special Subcommittee on Natural Resources of the Committee on Local Government," November 14, 1961, page 3. In the Katherine Moore Cushman Papers, Bentley Historical Library, University of Michigan, Michigan Constitutional Convention of 1961–2 (folder), Box 2.

[61] Rutherford H. Platt, "Toward Constitutional Recognition of the Environment," *American Bar Association Journal* 56 (November 1970): 1061.

[62] Ibid.

[63] Before answering this question, it is important to note that environmental rights are unusual in that it is not entirely clear who their bearers are. Do plants and non-human animals have constitutional rights, or are these rights only intended to protect people from the consequences of environmental degradation? The wording of many of the constitutional provisions alone makes their focus on human rights quite clear. Many state that "each person" or "every individual" has a right to a clean or healthful or decent environment or to enjoy the scenic beauty of the state. Many discussions of these rights, and some constitutional provisions themselves, also emphasize the state's role in protecting the environment for the benefit of future generations. See, for example, Montana Constitutional Convention of 1971–2: 2607; Illinois Constitutional Convention, *Record of Proceedings: Sixth Illinois Constitutional Convention*, December 8, 1969–September 3, 1970: 2996 and 3017; State of Michigan Constitutional Convention, *Official Record: Proceedings*: 2607. In Maryland, a convention delegate explained

characterized as positive. As we have seen, almost all of the arguments in favor of environmental rights focused on protecting people from the prospect of living in an environment that was dangerous to their health or too despoiled for them to use or enjoy. On this reading, the unhealthy or unappealing environment (or perhaps the entities responsible for destroying the environment) was the threat against which environmental rights were created to offer protection. It is certainly conceivable that government could be directly responsible for causing the environmental damage against which a constitutional right might protect people. However, these environmental provisions were enacted with the additional aim of protecting people from air and water pollution, and from the private actors (particularly corporate actors) that contributed to it.

The champions of positive rights consistently described these rights as guarantees of protection from polluters and corporations bent on environmental destruction. For instance, in a 1966 hearing before the Michigan state legislature, one member of the group Citizens for Clean Air stated, "my rights are being constantly violated by my neighbor—a paper mill."[64] In support of a constitutional provision that would give citizens standing to sue to enforce their right to a clean environment, one delegate to Montana's constitutional convention explained that in order to vindicate his constitutional right to a healthful environment, "I can envision going into court to prove that . . . the sulphur that's being emitted from the steam plant in Billings . . . I can prove that that's not healthful."[65] He offered a similar assessment critique of mining companies in the state's Beartooth mountain range. After praising the beauty of the mountains, he said:

> We've got five mining companies that want to go in there, and they want to take those mountains, they want to rip them wide open. They want to dig a pit 5 miles long and 3 miles wide. And once they've dug that pit and taken that soil and that land out of there and polluted the rivers down below it, it's not going to be there anymore, and you can't put it back . . . well, it's time for us to decide who's running the state of Montana—the people who elected us here or the companies.[66]

Clearly, this delegate did not conceive of the constitutional provision as a means of protection from a tyrannical or dangerous government alone, but

---

that their provision "exists fundamentally for man; the conservation of resources, the enhancement of natural beauty, the purification of our air, is for man's benefit. It is not for the birds and bees." Maryland Constitutional Convention of 1967, *Proceedings and Debates of the 1967 Constitutional Convention*, 104: 753. The majority of state constitutions' environmental provisions, as in the case of Maryland's proposed provision, do seem to have been geared toward the protection of human beings, with environmental protection as a means to that end.

[64] Quoted in Dave Dempsey, *Ruin & Recovery: Michigan's Rise as a Conservation Leader* (Ann Arbor: University of Michigan Press, 2001), 157.

[65] Montana Constitutional Convention of 1971–2: 1206.

[66] Ibid., 1227.

also, and indeed primarily, as a protection from private corporations that planned to exploit the state's natural environment.

Other states' conventions also described the hope that environmental rights could protect citizens from polluting corporations. For instance, one delegate to Illinois's constitutional convention said, "If giving the individual citizen the right of standing in court so that he can effectively sue a polluter or a destroyer of the environment . . . if it reduces or controls pollution, I feel that I can support it."[67] This consistent reference to polluters and pollution and the many assertions that state regulation was necessary to combat these problems demonstrate that environmental rights were most frequently designed to protect people, not from an overbearing and intrusive state, but from dangers like pollution and the private actors that created it.

It seems clear that the environmental mandates in state constitutions exhibit both of the defining features of positive rights. These provisions were not designed only to restrain government or to protect people from its tyranny, but to mandate more active government involvement in order to protect people from life in a despoiled environment and from those who would despoil it. What should we think, however, about the environmental provisions that did not include explicit mandates? Can we characterize these provisions as positive rights also?

The three constitutions that contain only policy statements about the importance of conservation (rather than mandates on government) seem the least like legal rights. Since they do not explicitly command the state to do (or not do) something, it is difficult to see how they could justify a demand on government. In the case of Virginia, at least, conservation groups urged the state legislature to add stronger, clearer mandates to its constitution. Virginia's environmental organizations testified before their state's legislature to urge it to adopt more robust constitutional rights than the constitutional revision commission had proposed. Several also provided their own suggested phrasing. The Izaak Walton League declared, "It is our conviction that sections 1 and 2 should be strongly reinforced to assure that the natural land, water and air resources of the state will be managed for the benefit of the people of the state,"[68] and the Atlantic Chapter of the Sierra Club called the convention's proposed policy statement "unacceptable," declaring it "completely inadequate for furthering conservation in Virginia." They too suggested specific and more explicit mandates for action by the

[67] Illinois Constitutional Convention, *Record of Proceedings: Sixth Illinois Constitutional Convention*, December 8, 1969–September 3, 1970: 3017.

[68] "Statement of the Virginia Division, Izaak Walton League of America, With Respect to Article XI of the Proposed Revisions to the Virginia State Constitution, Before the Committee for General Laws, Richmond, Virginia March 4, 1969," p. 1 (of 1), 1969. Found in Special Collections, University of Virginia Law Library, The Papers Of A. E. Dick Howard For The Virginia Commission For Constitutional Revision, Special Session of the State Legislature, Art. XI–Conservation, Box 26, March–April 1969.

state's General Assembly.[69] However, these clear legislative mandates were never actually included in the state's constitution. Thus, we may be reluctant to characterize this constitutional policy statement and those like it as full-fledged rights.

Despite their lack of a clear mandate on government, these mere policy statements do seem to promote government intervention, and do not ask government merely to restrain itself in order to protect citizens from a tyrannical or overreaching state. Like positive rights, they lay out (although less forcefully than do explicit mandates) a governmental responsibility to protect the environment. The degree of action that these provisions require of government is extremely ambiguous, but these provisions certainly do not appear to be limitations on government's scope or authority. For instance, the Virginia Constitution reads, "To the end that the people have clean air, pure water, and the use and enjoyment for recreation of adequate public lands, waters, and other natural resources, it shall be the policy of the Commonwealth to conserve, develop, and utilize its natural resources . . . Further, it shall be the Commonwealth's policy to protect its atmosphere, lands, and waters from pollution, impairment, or destruction, for the benefit, enjoyment, and general welfare of the people of the Commonwealth." Although this statement is not accompanied by explicit instructions for legislative action, we might well conclude that a state policy to "conserve, develop, utilize," and "protect" its natural resources would require active intervention on the part of the legislature. Thus, while we might not regard them as full-fledged rights, these policy statements about environmental protection do resemble positive rights far more than negative ones. However, a closer examination of the political context in Virginia highlights some of the complexities inherent in distinguishing positive from negative rights.

The environmental organizations that lobbied for a constitutional provision in Virginia did want to mandate active governmental intervention. However, they also wanted to force the state to refrain from other kinds of action. In particular, they did not want the state to continue disposing of the lands in its possession in ways that would be environmentally destructive. Shortly before the state's new constitution was drafted, Virginia environmentalists fought a heated battle over the legislature's decision to sell a piece of state-owned land, known as Hunting Creek, to a private party. They strenuously opposed this diminution of the state's green and open space. Thus, environmental organizations not only wanted government to offer more protection from polluting industries; they were also determined to create constitutional checks on the legislature's power so that it could not continue to sell its undeveloped lands to private developers. In explaining the

---

[69] "Chapter Finds Proposed Conservation Article in Constitution Revision Is Unacceptable" Found in Special Collections, University of Virginia Law Library, The Papers of A. E. Dick Howard for the Virginia Commission for Constitutional Revision, Special Session of the State Legislature, Art. XI–Conservation, Box 26, March–April 1969.

need for a constitutional amendment, a prominent environmental activist explained, "Parks, submerged lands, mineral deposits, forest preserves and other public holdings can be sold, leased, managed or otherwise disposed of by the General Assembly without any restrictions . . . [Currently,] the people of Virginia, . . . have no constitutional control over the exercise of this power."[70] With respect to public lands, it seems that constitutional control was desirable in order to impose restrictions on the legislature, so that it would be forced to refrain from disposing of lands in an irresponsible way. Of course, when the state stops giving away public lands, it simultaneously begins conserving them. Thus, in this case, it does not seem possible to draw a meaningful distinction between government action and government restraint.

The collapse of the dichotomy between governmental action and restraint might seem to pose a problem for one of the central distinctions between positive and negative rights. After all, one of the primary criticisms of the distinction between the two classes of rights is that government is, in the most meaningful sense, always active—that state action and restraint are really two sides of the same coin. However, it is important to notice that this challenge to the distinction between positive and negative rights only applies in the cases of state-owned lands. Governmental action and inaction are only indistinguishable in this case because the state is also the land-owner. In cases where pollution from private industry is the problem or cases in which the disposal of privately owned land is creating the environmental hazard, the distinction between government action and inaction is quite clear. Government can either intervene through regulations that prohibit the creation of environmental hazards, actively extending itself to protect the environment or refrain from intervention, passively allowing environmental degradation.

Only when it owns land can government participate in conservation simply by doing nothing at all. As we have already seen, it is clear that many of the advocates of these provisions were thinking not only of state-owned lands, but also of resources like air and water. Thus, as the proponents of these rights understood it, environmental protection required that states not only refrain from degrading the wild lands and open spaces they actually owned, but also that they interpose themselves between private polluters and the environment. Thus, while government action and inaction may, at a very high level of abstraction, be indistinguishable from one another, it is clear that the proponents of environmental rights did distinguish between

[70] Ted Pankowski, Co-Chairman Parks, Recreation & Libraraies Committee—Fairfax County Federation of Citizens Association, "A Proposal to Revise the Virginia Constitution to provide a constitutional restriction against arbitrary management or disposition of natural resources in the public domain." In Papers of A. E. Dick Howard for the Virginia Commission for Constitutional Revision 1969–71, Box 4, Conservation, Bill of Rights, General (1968–69), Special Collections, University of Virginia Law Library.

these different kinds of rights, and crafted rights in order to restrain certain kinds of government action while simultaneously promoting the development of an active regulatory regime to protect the environment. Furthermore, they designed these rights not only to protect citizens from any environmental damage that state government might cause to publicly owned land, but also to force government to guard against the environmental degradation caused by private industry. Some identified these rights using the term "positive rights" but, as we have seen, even those who did not use this language nonetheless used the logic of positive rights.

ENABLING LITIGATION

Since positive rights are, by definition, designed to mandate active governmental intervention, it seems somewhat strange that the activists promoting their intervention would devote resources to constitutional design. If environmental organizations wanted their state legislatures to pass regulatory statutes, why didn't they simply lobby legislatures to pass those statutes? What advantages, in other words, did environmental activists hope to obtain through the use of constitutional politics? The primary reason that environmental activists of the 1960s and 1970s created state constitutional rights was to enable public interest litigation on behalf of environmental protection.

The conventional explanation for the emergence of new constitutional rights tells us that groups create rights in order to get into court, where sympathetic judges can promote their policy agendas.[71] While this court-centered explanation was not a very good fit for the origins of education or labor rights, it does seem to do a better job of explaining why environmental organizations pursued constitutional change. Indeed, most proponents of environmental rights shared the conviction that constitutional provisions would be beneficial primarily because they could serve as the basis for litigation. In the wake of the Civil Rights movement, many believed that the environmental movement could make dramatic strides through public interest law. For instance, Joseph Sax, a law professor at the University of Michigan, wrote a widely influential book about environmental rights, which the delegates to several different constitutional conventions referenced.[72] In it, Sax argued that the environmental movement should pursue its policy aims in court. Through litigation, he explained, "the individual citizen or community group can obtain a hearing on equal terms with the highly organized

[71] Hirschl, *Towards Juristocracy: The Origins and Consequences of the New Constitutionalism.*

[72] See for example Montana Constitutional Convention of 1971–2: 1225; James T. Shon, "Article X: Conservation and Development of Resources," in *Hawaii Constitutional Convention Studies*, ed. Legislative Reference Bureau (Honolulu, 1978), 36.

and experienced interests that have learned so skillfully to manipulate legislative and administrative institutions."[73] Sax urged environmentalists to pursue litigation and to claim environmental rights in court.

Sax was not the only environmentalist arguing that the future of the environmental movement lay in courts. In the late 1960s and early 1970s, environmental litigation seemed to hold a great deal of promise. One environmental activist noted that "Many environmentalists see the courts as the only hope to stop polluters."[74] Victor Yanaconne, one of the early proponents of public interest litigation on behalf of the environment, gave a speech before the National Audubon Society at its 1967 annual convention. He told the environmental activists gathered there, "The time has come for you who are committed to the preservation of our environment to . . . enter the courtroom to protect our natural resources . . . It is time to assert your basic rights as citizens . . . Today, while there is still time, you must knock on the door of courthouses throughout this nation."[75] One law professor (who was himself somewhat more reserved in his endorsement of environmental litigation) explained the political context that had created environmentalists' tremendous faith in courts: "In other fields, [litigation has] seemed remarkably effective. Millions of children have had their right to equal treatment vindicated in the courts. Millions of impoverished persons have had their welfare benefits increased. Millions have been given a greater voice in electing their legislators. Why not do the same things in environmental law?"[76] Thus, the major rulings of the Warren Court seem to have suggested to environmentalists that judiciaries would also support their movement and vindicate the rights they understood as fundamental.

Many believed that judicial interpretations of constitutional law would expand to include environmental rights, and some argued that federal and state constitutions already contained implicit environmental rights. Environmental lawyers asserted that if people could not be deprived of their lives without due process of law, then surely they could not be deprived of a livable natural environment. Environmental advocates also located environmental rights in the Ninth Amendment of the U.S. Constitution, which states, "the enumeration in the Constitution of certain rights, shall not be

[73] Joseph L. Sax, Defending the Environment; a Strategy for Citizen Action (New York: Knopf, 1971), xviii. Sax himself was doubtful about the wisdom of constitutionalizing these rights. He believed that constitutional rights, unlike statutes, would give courts ultimate authority over the scope and meaning of environmental rights and that this situation would pose a threat to the environmental movements and its aims.

[74] John S. Winder, Jr., "Citizen Groups, the Law and the Environment," Utah Law Review 1970, no. 3 (1970): 405.

[75] Cited in Victor John Yannacone, Jr., "The Environment and the Law," Forum 9, no. 5 (1974): 797.

[76] Thomas Lynch and Jan S. Stevens, "Environmental Law—the Uncertain Trumpet," University of San Francisco Law Review 5, no. 1 (1970): 17.

construed to deny or disparage others retained by the people." They found particularly heartening a 1965 ruling, in which the Supreme Court overturned a Connecticut statute making it illegal to use or sell contraceptives on the grounds that the statute violated these unenumerated constitutional rights.[77] Environmental activists reasoned that "if the Ninth Amendment afford[ed] even partial support for the right to receive birth control data," it must certainly protect the right to a decent environment.[78] This idea was grounded in the belief that the constitution should, and indeed would, evolve with society to meet its ever-changing needs. Given this view of constitutional adjudication, it seemed entirely possible that courts would include environmental rights in the growing panoply of constitutional protections. As one law review article explained:

> When the courts fully recognize that there is a constitutionally protected right to breathe clean air, drink clean water, eat uncontaminated food, and have wilderness areas preserved, they will also have to recognize that the state or federal government having dominion or control over air, water, food, or other valuable resources, has obligations imposed on it by a public trust to guard against environmental insults . . . the failure to carry out the obligations of the trust amounts to a breach of constitutionally protected rights.[79]

Through litigation, environmentalists hoped to ease the scales from judges' eyes and to usher in a new era, in which courts would recognize implicit constitutional rights to environmental protection.

At the same time that environmental activists argued that American constitutions, particularly the federal Constitution, already contained implicit environmental rights, they saw little harm in making those rights explicit. Reasoning that a textual basis would make it even easier for judges to support their agenda, environmentalists pursued textual changes to leave no room for doubt about the existence of constitutional environmental rights. One environmental activist explained it this way: "Some who have less faith in the speed or vitality of our living Constitution, suggest more immediate articulations of our environmental rights." Thus, he explained, "Legislative proposals to amend the Federal as well as many state constitutions by adding such an 'environmental bill of rights' have been introduced with increas-

---

[77] *Griswold v. Connecticut*, 381 U.S. 479 (1965).

[78] E. E. Roberts, "The Right to a Decent Environment: Progress Along a Constitutional Avenue," in *Law and the Environment*, ed. Malcolm F. Baldwin and James K. Page (New York: Walker, 1970), 163.

[79] Bernard S. Cohen, "The Constitution, the Public Trust Doctrine, and the Environment," *Utah Law Review* 1970, no. 3 (1970): 392.

ing frequency."[80] These textual expressions of environmental rights were intended to further the litigation campaigns that many viewed as the future of environmentalism.

The environmental rights in state constitutions were created for the primary purpose of facilitating the public interest lawsuits about which the environmental movement was so optimistic. Again and again, the champions of these rights explained that they were necessary to enable environmental litigation. For instance, a delegate to the Montana Constitutional Convention declared, "I feel . . . that the real heart of this proposal is the last sentence, which calls for the right to sue."[81] The *Washington Post* described a proposal to amend the Maryland constitution this way: "The amendment is considered significant by environmental groups because it would assure that individuals and groups can sue polluters."[82] Similarly, the *Chicago Tribune* reported that the General Government committee of Illinois's constitutional convention fought a move to revise the provision to explicitly deny citizens the ability to sue polluters. The *Tribune* explained, "Committee members fought the move on the grounds the right of individuals to sue is 'the heart of the new article.'"[83] The *Christian Science Monitor* reported that Rhode Island's environmental rights had a similar purpose: "Its backers say it would provide constitutional support for legal action in conservation matters,"[84] and the *Anchorage Daily News* repeated this sentiment with reference to Alaska's proposed environmental amendment to the state constitution: "Proponents of the legislation said its underlying intent was to give individuals standing to stop public or private polluters through courts."[85] Clearly, environmentalists pursued the creation of new constitutional rights in order to move environmental conflicts into courts.

This is not to say that it was impossible to involve courts in questions of environmental policy before constitutional rights existed on the subject. In fact, the well-established common law doctrine of private nuisance had long allowed private parties to sue people or corporations for hindering their use or enjoyment of their own property. Even where no environmental regulations existed at either the statutory or constitutional levels, therefore, it was nonetheless possible to take individual polluters to court by claiming that they created a private nuisance. However, the doctrine of private nuisance was developed to protect individual property owners from the direct threats

[80] John S. Winder, Jr., "Environmental Rights for the Environmental Polity," *Suffolk University Law Review* 5, no. 3 (1971): 834.

[81] Montana Constitutional Convention of 1971–2: 1231.

[82] "Right to Clean Air Backed," *Washington Post*, Washington, DC, March 16, 1972, B4.

[83] Edith Herman, "Con-Con Acts on Pollution: Civil Suits Permitted Against Violators," *Chicago Tribune*, Chicago, July 23, 1970, 4.

[84] "Rhode Island Renews Charter-Reform Drive," *Christian Science Monitor*, Boston, July 35, 1968, 13.

[85] John Greely, "House Adopts Bill on Environmental Rights," *Anchorage Daily News*, Anchorage, March 4, 1976, 1.

that neighboring property owners might cause to the use or enjoyment of that property through unreasonable use of their own land. As a consequence, it was very difficult for publicly interested environmentalists to demonstrate their standing to sue polluters.

Environmental activists certainly attempted to litigate using the nuisance doctrine, but they consistently complained about courts' reluctance to grant then standing or to rule against a polluting corporation or factory in a nuisance suit. For instance, in the journal of the Western Pennsylvania Conservancy, environmental lawyer Robert Broughton explained the difficulties with winning nuisance suits: "Even if the harm is serious enough to be a private nuisance, the courts traditionally tend to favor productive economic interests over environmental or aesthetic interests."[86] In a law review article about state constitutional provisions, a staff member at the center for the study of environmental policy at Pennsylvania State University offered a similar assessment, complaining that "the traditional legal view [is] that pollution is often an inevitable consequence of economic and industrial progress."[87] This view rendered nuisance suits on behalf of environmental protection an uphill battle. Furthermore, environmentalists did not simply want to defend the claims of individual property holders to the enjoyment of their private property rights. They were interested in combating harms to the public at large, harms caused by the pollution of their states' air and water, or the destruction of their wild spaces.

A common law doctrine of public nuisance also existed, but in order for a private individual to sue under the doctrine of public nuisance, he or she had to demonstrate that he or she had suffered a harm that could be distinguished from harms suffered by the general public.[88] As one delegate told his fellow members of the Illinois Constitutional Convention, if they felt that their water was polluted and unhealthy, the state's new environmental rights provision would alter their legal status, allowing any of them to sue to correct the problem. He explained, under the new provision, "[you] would not be subject to the defense to which you are presently subject . . . that you can show no special damage or no damage different than that suffered by your next door neighbor. Presently, that is what prevents you from having standing."[89] It was extremely difficult to meet the standing requirements of the public nuisance doctrine, while the private nuisance doctrine remained an uneasy fit with the goals of the environmental movement.

[86] Robert Broughton, "Constitutional Amendment Covers Environment," *Water Land and Life* 12, no. 2 (1970): 8.

[87] Tobin, "Some Observations on the Use of State Constitutions to Protect the Environment," 482.

[88] Steven Ferrey, *Environmental Law: Examples & Explanations*, 5th ed. (New York: Aspen Publishers, 2010), 25.

[89] Illinois Constitutional Convention, *Record of Proceedings: Sixth Illinois Constitutional Convention*, December 8, 1969–September 3, 1970: 2996.

It would have been possible to address the limitations of nuisance doctrine through statutory law alone. In fact, Michigan's legislature passed a law for exactly this purpose.[90] However, the proponents of constitutional rights to environmental protection certainly hoped the existence of textual, constitutional environmental rights would also alter judges' calculations in nuisance suits. Broughton, for instance, predicted that Pennsylvania's constitutional amendment would "become the nucleus of an enlargement of the common law action of private nuisance," and described his conviction that the constitutional provision could "substantially change the weight given to various factors when a court, in deciding whether to enjoin particular acts, balances the benefits and burdens of granting an injunction [to protect the environment]."[91] Tobin expressed similar hopes, writing: "since environmental provisions mandate consideration of environmental factors . . . when state courts apply their traditional balancing of interests, they must now include environmental concerns in the scales. Thus, constitutional provisions may tip the scales in favor of environmental protection at the expense of unrestrained industrial development."[92]

Although the champions of environmental rights were optimistic about the effects of these laws in nuisance suits, the advocates of these rights typically had more ambitious goals than simply extending nuisance doctrine. Nuisance law grew out of property law, and threats posed by neighbors to the enjoyment of one's own property, but the proponents of rights to environmental rights wanted to challenge the assumption that the environment could be adequately protected based on traditional protections for individuals' private property. For instance, one delegate to the Montana Constitutional Convention said, "There was a talk about can you, you know, go and sue when I haven't been affected? I think that's the point." He went on to explain that the point of these new environmental rights was to establish that everyone was affected by environmental problems, and thus everyone should have standing to seek to remedy them in court. He explained:

> Environment is different than anything else because we are all affected. It's different than any other type of litigation, and we know this now better than we have ever known it before . . . we're all in it together and survival is something that we'll do or don't do together, and so it is different than any other type of litigation we've known in the past because we are all affected.[93]

---

[90] Joseph L. Sax and Joseph F. DiMento, "Environmental Citizen Suits: Three Years' Experience under the Michigan Environmental Protection Act," *Ecology Law Quarterly* 4, no. 1 (1974).

[91] Broughton, "Constitutional Amendment Covers Environment," 8.

[92] Tobin, "Some Observations on the Use of State Constitutions to Protect the Environment," 482.

[93] Montana Constitutional Convention of 1971–2: 1260.

Because nuisance law was developed to combat threats to particular property owners, it no longer applied effectively to the kinds of environmental dangers that threatened the existence of entire societies. As Steven Ferrey has explained, "Nuisance actions are a case-by-case one-shot attempt to cure a particular problem. Nuisance law does not provide an ongoing construct to supervise discharges to the ambient air and water supply."[94] Thus, while environmentalists hoped that constitutional changes would render their nuisance suits easier to win, few believed that nuisance doctrine alone could be a sufficient vehicle for the emerging field of public interest litigation on behalf of environmental protection. One incidental advantage of a constitutional right to environmental protection was that it might make nuisance suits easier to win, but the champions of positive environmental rights typically wanted to expand environmental lawsuits beyond the confines of nuisance doctrine.

The other common law doctrine under which environmentalists attempted to litigate before the adoption of constitutional rights to environmental protection was the public trust doctrine, which established that certain public resources were held in trust by government for benefit of the people. Under public trust doctrine, their role as trustee prevented state governments from alienating the resources they held in trust and prohibited them from impairing the public's right to use those resources.[95] While the public trust doctrine does seem like a far better complement to the goals of the environmental movement, it too proved an imperfect vehicle. From the perspective of those seeking broad political changes, the primary problem with the public trust doctrine was that it had developed only with reference to submerged lands, shorelines, and navigable waters. In addition, the doctrine of public trust originated as a means of protecting the public's access to fishing grounds and shipping channels. Thus, it was not at all obvious that the public trust doctrine applied to the states' forests, wildlife, or air quality. Furthermore, even in the case of waters clearly covered by the public trust doctrine, it was not clear that this doctrine required the state to make sure that its waters were healthy for bathing and drinking or that their ecosystems remained intact, especially when those goals conflicted with the traditionally protected, commercial uses of these waterways.[96]

One way to view the addition of environmental rights to state constitutions is as a means to expand the public trust doctrine beyond fishing grounds and shorelines and to make environmental preservation a paramount goal of the state in its capacity as trustee. Several state constitutions used the phrase "public trust" directly in their conservation provisions. Rhode Island's provision even added the legislative duty to provide for the

---

[94] Ferrey, *Environmental Law: Examples & Explanations*, 25.
[95] Gregor I. McGregor, *Environmental Law and Enforcement* (Boston: CRC Press, 1994).
[96] Jack H. Archer, *The Public Trust Doctrine and the Management of America's Coasts* (Amherst: University of Massachusetts Press, 1994).

conservation of natural resources to the state's historical provision guaranteeing the preservation of "public fishery rights and privileges of shore." Hawaii's constitution also declared that "all public resources are held in trust by the state for the benefit of the people." By creating a public trust to all of their states' natural resources, and by specifying the state's responsibility to preserve and protect them, environmental activists hoped to ensure that standing to invoke the public doctrine would no longer be restricted to individuals that had been denied access to fishing grounds or public shorelines, but expanded to all who felt that the state was failing to manage and conserve public resources for their benefit.[97] Under an expanded doctrine of public trust, environmentalists could wage the kind of large-scale, reform-oriented litigation campaigns that seemed to hold so much promise.

Because the major appeal of textual rights to environmental protection was that they could enable public interest litigation by private environmental organizations, their proponents sometimes described these provisions as vehicles for the creation of "private attorneys general." These new attorneys general could (through their own, privately funded lawsuits) simply assist state governments in enforcing the laws they were already trying to enforce. For instance, a delegate to the Illinois constitutional convention explained, "Government action simply may not be enough in the next ten or twenty years to handle this problem, and [government agencies will] be glad to see individuals doing some of this work."[98] The Montana Constitutional Convention also discussed the idea that, if it were easier for environmentalists to demonstrate standing to sue, they could enforce existing environmental regulations alongside of well-meaning, public agencies. For instance, when a delegate to the Montana Constitutional Convention objected to the addition of an environmental right, arguing that the state already had agencies enforcing environmental law, an advocate of environmental rights acknowledged that his opponent was "absolutely right when he [said] that we have good agencies that try to enforce these rights." However, he continued, "The trouble is that sometimes the good agencies get thwarted. The trouble is that sometimes the good agencies get lazy or turn out to be not-so-good agencies."[99] Whether or not environmental agencies were doing their jobs, many hoped that, by making it possible for regular citizens to litigate, they could allow private actors to increase the state's capacity to enforce its environmental regulations.

Of course, constitutional law is not the only way to create private attorneys general. As we saw with nuisance law, statutes themselves may establish broad standing to sue for purposes of their enforcement. Thus, it was certainly possible to pass environmental statutes that created private attor-

[97] Kirsch, "Upholding the Public Trust in State Constitutions."

[98] Illinois Constitutional Convention, *Record of Proceedings: Sixth Illinois Constitutional Convention*, December 8, 1969–September 3, 1970: 3000.

[99] Montana Constitutional Convention of 1971–2: 1265.

neys general without recourse to constitutional rights. If environmental activists were only interested in endowing citizens with standing to sue under
existing statutes, constitutional activism would not have been necessary to
achieve this end. However, constitutional rights were generally understood
to offer additional strategic benefits.

One reason constitutions were considered superior to mere statutes was
that judicial decisions grounded in statutory law alone could be overturned
by legislatures. By contrast, decisions that enforced constitutions could not
be overruled by the simple majority vote of a legislature. A report to Hawaii's constitutional convention of 1978 explained it this way: "There is
greater authority with a constitutional provision, as opposed to a legislative
act. As the well-known legal scholar Joseph Sax has said, 'a court enforcing
a statutory right (even though it may have the same wording as a constitutional provision) can always be overruled by subsequent legislation'."[100] The
study went on to explain that polluting industries possessed significant legislative influence, and thus posed a continual threat to any legislation that
allowed environmentalists to sue them. It repeated Sax's assessment that
courts were less susceptible than legislatures to pressure from polluters.
Thus, it concluded, citizens' standing to sue was more safely guaranteed
through a constitutional amendment than a statute.

Constitutional rights to a healthy environment were not only designed to
safeguard the existence of private attorneys general from unfriendly legislatures; they were also intended to allow for other, even farther-reaching,
forms of litigation. The private attorneys general model envisions environmental organizations as supplements to the public mechanisms for the enforcement of existing laws. After all, attorneys general (public or private)
work on behalf of the state. Many advocates of constitutional rights to a
healthy environment, however, did not view their role in this way. The problem, according to some, was not simply that governmental agencies had
difficulty enforcing the existing regulations, but also that state legislatures
and agencies had failed to establish sufficient regulation in the first place.
Thus, the proponents of constitutional rights hoped that this new kind of
right would allow citizens not only to enforce the environmental regulations
that legislatures had already passed, but also, through courts, to establish
new and more stringent regulations.

The most ambitious proponents of environmental rights hoped that constitutional rights to a healthy environment would allow environmental interest groups to move beyond lawsuits against individual polluters and even
beyond the enforcement of existing law. Rather than restricting their activities to the enforcement of current statutes, they hoped that citizens who
possessed the constitutional right to a clean or healthful environment would
be able to sue state legislatures and agencies to demand the passage of new,

---

[100] Shon, "Article X: Conservation and Development of Resources," 36.

stronger regulations and more stringent enforcement. Positive rights to environmental protection could thereby help citizens demand (in court) that their governments do more to protect the environment than they had ever even intended to do. For instance, the Massachusetts Forest and Park Association explained that a constitutional amendment guaranteeing environmental rights "would make it easier for a citizen to go into court and bring suit . . . against an agency which is responsible for controlling pollution and which perhaps isn't carrying out its responsibilities."[101] Similarly, one Montana delegate explained to the constitutional convention, "The present problems we have with our environment are the product of the inability or unwillingness of legislatures to recognize environmental problems and to take proper corrective action."[102] Consequently, the delegate concluded that the provision granting private actors standing to sue was "of critical importance" to solving the state's environmental problems. The idea behind these constitutional changes was not only to aid in state's effort to regulate polluters, but also to ensure that legislatures did not get the last word on the subject of environmental protection. By enabling this kind of litigation, the proponents of environmental rights hoped to force legislatures into more aggressive protection of the environment than they had thus far attempted. This ability to overcome legislative inactivity or recalcitrance is something that a statute, even one that grants private citizens standing to sue, cannot accomplish.

Mary Leahy, the primary sponsor of Illinois's environmental rights provision, also explained the necessity of establishing citizens' standing to sue with reference to the possibility of suing the state. It would not be necessary to sue in cases in which government was doing an adequate job, she explained. However, she noted, government does not always do an adequate job of protecting the environment. In cases of insufficient government action, citizens' rights to a clean and healthy environment would be violated. The proponents of positive environmental rights in Illinois believed that they could solve this problem by placing the right to a clean and healthful environment directly in the constitution, and by ensuring that citizens could sue to enforce it. Leahy told the constitutional convention: "I see this section . . . as forcing government to do the job it ought to be doing, yet providing the individual with a remedy if his right is invaded."[103] Environmental activists, armed with the constitutional right to a healthy environment, would be able to enforce their rights not only against private polluters, but also against the state itself.

---

[101] "Citizen Right to Sue Polluters Seen As Major Conservation Issue," *Forest & Park News* 35, no. 1, Boston, Winter 1971, 1.

[102] Montana Constitutional Convention of 1971–2: 1229.

[103] Illinois Constitutional Convention, *Record of Proceedings: Sixth Illinois Constitutional Convention.* December 8, 1969–September 3, 1970: 2991.

While the possibility that constitutional rights would allow environmentalists to sue the state for failing to protect the environment struck some contemporaneous observers as unlikely,[104] the political context of the 1960s and 1970s made it seem at least plausible that courts would enforce constitutional rights against inactive legislatures. The Warren Court had very famously challenged the policies of state legislatures, interpreting broad constitutional rights to mandate concrete and dramatic changes in state policy, and it seemed possible that state supreme courts could adopt a similar stance with respect to environmental rights. Elroy Boyer, the delegate who presented the proposal for an environmental provision to the Maryland constitutional convention, argued that courts would indeed be willing to enforce this new constitutional right against inactive legislatures. He explained, "if the constitutional provision is passed and the General Assembly is put on notice that they shall by law provide for enhancement, improvement and protection of natural resources, and if, following that, they refuse or neglect to do so, certainly the court by mandamus could direct them to act."[105] When another delegate questioned the likelihood of such an outcome, Boyer pointed to the judicial mandates that had already required the reapportionment of state legislatures.[106] Just as the courts had required reapportionment to vindicate citizens' voting rights, he suggested, they could similarly declare that legislative inaction had violated citizens' constitutional right to a clean environment and specify the type of action that the legislature must take to protect that right. As we have already seen, the broader "rights revolution," of which these reapportionment rulings were a part, had buttressed the view (especially among those on the political left) that constitutional rights should expand through judicial interpretation to keep pace with social change, and that this kind of "living" constitution was necessary and desirable. In this intellectual and political context, the belief that courts would enforce positive environmental rights against legislatures did not appear particularly quixotic. Courts appeared both capable of demanding and willing to demand dramatic changes, particularly to state law.

The proponents of environmental rights hoped that, if they could move environmental conflicts more squarely into courts, judges would assist them in forcing legislatures and state agencies to take a more aggressive, regulatory stance. Environmental interest groups created constitutional rights in order to get into courts. Entrenchment theories tell us that people create rights in order to judicialize conflicts. Thus far, the origins of environmental rights fit neatly with the conventional account of where rights come from. However, like both labor organizations and education activists, environmentalists wanted to create new rights not because they wanted to entrench

[104] Broughton, "Constitutional Amendment Covers Environment."
[105] Maryland Constitutional Convention of 1967, *Proceedings and Debates of the 1967 Constitutional Convention*, 104: 736.
[106] Ibid., 738.

the status quo against future legislatures (as entrenchment theories predict), but because they were dissatisfied with the status quo and were, themselves, attempting to change it. They hoped that they could use litigation to achieve that change.

FORCING THE LEGISLATURE'S HAND

Even in the absence of judicial enforcement, some believed that by placing mandates in constitutions, they could strengthen environmentalists' position when lobbying legislatures. For instance, although law professor and environmental activist Robert Broughton was skeptical about the capacity of environmental rights to sustain successful lawsuits against the state, he nonetheless believed that Pennsylvania's constitutional guarantee would facilitate environmental protection. A constitutional mandate, he explained, would increase the legitimacy and electoral appeal of environmental demands on the legislature. "The existence of a constitutional mandate can materially strengthen political efforts to deal with all forms of governmental inaction." Broughton argued that explicit constitutional instructions to the legislature would have this effect because "Legislatures, public officials, and citizens all seem to take constitutional mandates seriously." As a result, he concluded that "political pressure applied in the context of a constitutional command is likely to be more effective than political pressure applied in its absence."[107]

This argument about the enhanced power of legislative appeals made in the presence of a constitutional mandate will likely sound familiar. The advocates of both labor and education rights imagined that the "enforcement" of these rights would occur in large part through their continued (and constitutionally justified) demands on the legislature. One delegate to the Maryland constitutional convention actually drew this parallel between the state's historic declaration that the legislature must establish common schools and the environmental provision then under consideration. He explained that the education provision in Maryland's constitution of 1845 created a statewide recognition that Maryland was committed to public education. He acknowledged that the state did not establish a statewide school system for another twenty years after the constitutional change, but asserted that:

> immediately after this exhortatory statement [was added to the constitution] in 1845, the public schools of Baltimore . . . received great impetus, as did the public county schools. There were no enforcements that you could depend upon. The same kind of question is asked today as to the meaning of this [environmental] statement. What good was it to say that the legislature ought to encourage the diffusion of knowledge back

---

[107] Broughton, "Constitutional Amendment Covers Environment."

in 1845; the truth of the matter is that the public schools of the State of Maryland received their great impetus under this exhortatory directional statement.[108]

The argument here was that constitutional rights would place moral as well as legal obligations on legislatures, and that those moral obligations would be recognized both by those in office and those who could vote them out. Even when there were no serious threats of judicial enforcement, therefore, advocates of environmental rights believed it would be harder for legislatures to ignore their demands if those demands were rooted in explicit constitutional rights. Ultimately (as the chairman of the Maryland constitutional convention explained), where judges did not enforce these rights, citizens would do it at the ballot box.[109]

It should come as no surprise, therefore, that environmental activists continued to pursue legislative lobbying after the creation of new constitutional rights. Even before the state's environmental rights provision had been formally ratified, for instance, the Illinois Planning and Conservation League formulated plans to maintain their influence in the state's legislature. According to the *Chicago Tribune*, the League planned to hold a policy conference to "spell out [a] specific strategy for pressuring the legislature," and the League's eight sections planned to use the summer before this policy conference to conduct research and formulate recommendations. The League made all of these preparations with the proximate goal of positioning itself as an advisor to the legislature as it tackled environmental issues, and the ultimate goal of pushing the legislature to enact new laws.[110] The Montana Conservation Council (MCC) developed a similar plan to follow the enactment of a constitutional right with continued legislative lobbying. In 1971, well before the state's constitutional right to environmental protection had been ratified, the board of directors held a meeting at which they considered (among other questions) what they would do after its ratification. The meeting minutes include the heading: "Preparation for Future," under which they record the MCC's plan to lobby the state legislature after the adoption of the new constitution, and to push it to adopt active legislation on behalf of environmental protection.[111] It is clear, therefore, that these organizations

[108] Maryland Constitutional Convention of 1967, *Proceedings and Debates of the 1967 Constitutional Convention*, 104: 752.

[109] Ibid., 741.

[110] "Environmental Lobby Seeks Rights Bill," *Chicago Tribune*, Chicago, April 26, 1970, S16.

[111] Montana Conservation Council, Minutes, Board of Directors meeting Oct. 2, 1971, Helena, 3. In Montana Conservation Council Records, K. Ross Toole Archives, Mansfield Library, The University of Montana–Missoula. Montana Conservation Council Records, Collection 189, Series III, Box 6, Folder 19. The meeting minutes actually said: "A. The lobby as continuing educational/adversary force in environmental issues in Montana. B. The 1973 Legislature, C. Working for passage of positive proposals at final adoption of Constitution by the people."

understood that a constitutional amendment on its own was unlikely to change the political landscape and that they saw constitutional rights not as ends in themselves, but as tools that could facilitate their ongoing efforts to achieve policy change.

MOVEMENT BUILDING

One final reason that environmental organizations worked to add explicit positive rights to constitutions was to facilitate the growth of the environmental movement within their states. In Maryland, one delegate to the constitutional convention explained that "Representatives from many organizations dealing with conservation have indicated that this [environmental rights provision] will stimulate and help integrate their efforts."[112] It is clear that the proponents of environmental provisions in other states had a similar goal in mind. The champions of environmental provisions consistently stated that constitutional amendments would contribute to a general awareness of the environmental movement's ascendance, and signal a widespread acceptance of its principles. For instance, one explanation of the proposed environmental article in Virginia's constitution stated: "The proposed conservation article . . . should operate as part of the climate of state and private initiative to deal with such increasingly important problems."[113] A delegate to the New York constitutional convention also described the potential for a constitutional mandate to facilitate the creation of a general climate of environmental awareness and concern. He declared, "this proposal is badly needed at this time because it dramatizes and lays stress on the need for the conservation of our natural resources." He went on to assert that all of the state's environmental agencies and existing regulations had thus far been insufficient to bring about significant change, and argued that it was "only through the recognition of ecology that we will come to find out the true importance of natural resources to the good of mankind himself."[114] This defense of environmental rights draws an implicit contrast between the capacity of statutes and that of constitutions to focus popular attention on a social problem, and suggests that constitutional statements are louder and more likely to focus the public's attention.

Constitutional provisions could also justify the claim that the residents of a state had declared environmental protection to be an issue of fundamental

---

[112] Maryland Constitutional Convention of 1967, Proceedings *and Debates of the 1967 Constitutional Convention*, 104: 759.

[113] "Article XI: Conservation," November 25, 1968, Draft of Commentary–Conservation: Article XI, From the Papers of A. E. Dick Howard for the Virginia Commission for Constitutional Revision 1969–71, Box 19, Special Collections, University of Virginia Law Library.

[114] New York State Constitutional Convention, *Constitutional Convention Proceedings*: 946–7.

importance. In fact, constitutional changes, even when they originated in legislatures, were often described as the embodiment of the popular will and of the people's concern for the environment. For instance, the author and legislative sponsor of Pennsylvania's environmental rights provision described the significance of the constitutional provision this way: "Like a sleeping giant, the people of Pennsylvania were suddenly aroused and, acting through the legislature, moved with great force to undo the wrongs of a century of exploitation."[115] This formulation implied that constitutional rights evidenced long-term, public commitments to a particular goal or value. Thus, Kury even went on to declare that "the message to all was loud, clear and irreversible—Pennsylvania's period of environmental exploitation was gone forever."[116] Constitutional rights were described as heralds of a new era of environmental protection, and at the threshold of that era, environmental organizations claimed primacy for their political projects.

In addition to claiming that the ratification of environmental rights signaled the arrival of sweeping social changes, interest groups could use constitutional provisions to demonstrate their own, particular prowess. To this end, the organizations that successfully lobbied for the adoption of environmental rights often claimed credit for having altered the state's highest law.[117] Recognizing the potential to demonstrate its value and efficacy in this way, the Massachusetts Forest and Park Association (MFPA) determined to adopt a leadership role in the lobbying effort to insert environmental rights into the Massachusetts constitution. The MFPA's Executive Committee meeting minutes reflect this ambition. For instance, the minutes from November 1971 report: "It was voted that the Association undertake a special project to lead the support for voter endorsement in November, 1972, of the 'Environmental Bill of Rights' amendment to the State Constitution." Not only did the MFPA plan to lead the campaign for constitutional change, it also determined to alert the state's other environmental organizations that it would be leader.[118]

---

[115] Kury, *Natural Resources and the Public Estate: A Biography of Article I, Section 27 of the Pennsylvania Constitution, Written by Franklin L. Kury for the Maurice K. Goddard Chair Program 2.*

[116] Ibid., 2.

[117] For example, the Conservation Council for Hawaii declared in its newsletter, "Con Con Efforts Rewarded," and explained that "changes [to the existing constitution] suggested in our opening-day document, which was distributed to all delegates, and in subsequent testimony, frequently coincided with elements of adopted amendments." *Conservation Council for Hawaii Newsletter*, Honolulu, 1978.

[118] The organization's meeting minutes explain: "The Executive Director will write to other groups telling them of the project and the Association's expected leadership role." Executive Committee of the Massachusetts Forest and Park Association, Minutes, Boston, November 29, 1971. In the Records of the Massachusetts Forest and Park Association, Massachusetts Historical Society, Executive Committee minutes, Carton 2.

The MFPA decided to lead the effort at constitutional reform at a time when its position among the state's other environmental organizations had become a bit precarious. Internal memos reveal that the MFPA was having trouble acquiring new members.[119] Internal communications noted the state's Audubon society chapter was "far ahead in public recognition," and that the MFPA's Executive Committee had engaged in "a lengthy discussion" about how to remedy the problem. The attached report went on to explain the relative success of the Audubon Society in its "ability to get its case clearly before the public," and concluded, "Much opportunity remains for the MFPA in both areas—public understanding and public participation . . . we have not reached the public effectively enough."[120] Thus, after declaring itself leader of the movement for constitutional change, the MFPA was quick to claim credit for the successful adoption of the state's new environmental rights provision. For example, the MFPA newsletter declared: "After a long and involved fight led by the Massachusetts Forest and Park Association, legislative arm of the conservation movement, the voters of the commonwealth have won the right to have a say on their right to clean air and water, freedom from excessive and unnecessary noise, and the natural, scenic, historic, and esthetic qualities of their environment."[121]

The fact that environmental organizations claimed credit for constitutional changes in their own newsletters suggests that they used constitutional victories not only to make a point to legislatures, but to reach their own members as well. It is certainly possible to claim credit for a legislative victory, and many organizations did claim credit for the passage of regulatory statutes as well. However, it seems quite possible that constitutional statements of environmental organizations' central policy goals would be particularly potent symbols of political power and of the centrality of their agendas to public life. Thus, environmental groups not only sought constitutional changes to facilitate litigation and to buttress their legislative lobbying efforts, but also as a tool in their movement building efforts.

Constitutional provisions could support efforts at movement building not only through their symbolic power, but also through their ability to enable litigation. Many proponents of positive rights believed that the litigation of sympathetic test cases would not only achieve direct policy change, but also facilitate political organizing. For instance, the executive director of

---

[119] On September 16, 1971, the executive committee discussed changing the organization's name to appeal to a broader public. On October 21, 1971, it resolved to contact other like-minded organizations within the state, and to ask these organizations to urge their members to join the MFPA as well. Records of the Massachusetts Forest and Park Association, Massachusetts Historical Society, Executive Committee minutes, Carton 2.

[120] Executive Committee of the Massachusetts Forest and Park Association, Minutes, Boston, November 29, 1971. In the Records of the Massachusetts Forest and Park Association, Massachusetts Historical Society, Executive Committee minutes, Carton 2.

[121] "Bill of Rights on 1972 Ballot: Citizens to Vote on Clean Air and Water," *Forest & Park News* 25, no. 2, Boston, Spring 1971, 1.

the Washington Coalition for Clean Air explained that litigation could serve two purposes simultaneously: "More important than the slow but steady growth of environmental case law is the public awareness created by such lawsuits. Many times, for example, the public interest comes under closer scrutiny in judicial proceedings due to the combative nature of such proceedings."[122] Environmental activist Victor Yanconne echoed this sentiment, explaining that even when environmentalists lost in court, legal action could help the movement to "focus public attention and disseminate information about intolerable conditions."[123] As the studies of public interest litigation in other contexts has demonstrated, reformers often pursue litigation to help them dramatize their claims, while providing a highly visible platform on which to play out those dramas.[124] Thus, environmental rights were appealing not only because they would make it easier to change policy through courts, but also because the litigation they enabled might make it easier to change public opinion.

CONCLUSION: ENVIRONMENTAL PROTECTION AND THE POSITIVE-RIGHTS TRADITION

The environmental rights crafted during the 1960s and 1970s look somewhat different from many of the positive rights I have discussed in previous chapters. In the areas of education and labor, a few state constitutions do include broad statements of rights or sweeping legislative mandates. In general, however, the positive rights created to mandate governmental action on education and labor issues were written in much narrower terms than the broad rights to a clean and healthy environment on which this chapter is focused. Even the nineteenth-century mandates to establish common school systems are arguably more specific than provisions guaranteeing the right to clean air and water. As we have seen, the environmental movement's faith in the progressive potential of judicial interpretation helps to explain why these positive rights are particularly sweeping. The 1960s and 1970s witnessed the rapid proliferation of rights claims, and a faith (on the part of the political left) in the logic and language of rights. In the wake of the Civil Rights movement and in the middle of the women's rights movement and welfare rights movement, it seemed possible that citizens would rally around

---

[122] Winder, "Environmental Rights for the Environmental Polity," 842.

[123] Lee Flor, "Legal Units Formed By Conservationists to Fight Pollution," *Evening Star*, Washington, DC, September 15, 1969.

[124] Douglas Nejaime, "Winning through Losing," *Iowa Law Review* (2011); McCann, *Rights at Work: Pay Equity Reform and the Politics of Legal Mobilization*; Thomas M. Keck, "Beyond Backlash: Assessing the Impact of Judicial Decisions on LGBT Rights," *Law & Society Review* 43, no. 1 (2009); Emily Zackin, "Popular Constitutionalism's Hard When You're Not Very Popular: Why the ACLU Turned to Courts," *Law & Society Review* 42, no. 2 (2008).

broad and ambitious rights claims, and that legislators could be made to listen to these movements or to the courts, which would support them. Thus, the breadth of the constitutional provisions that emerged in this period was, in part, a testament to environmentalists' optimism about the potential growth of their movement and the ability of constitutional provisions to grow and expand with changing understandings and social needs.

Proponents of environmental rights alluded to the process through which judges had elaborated the meaning of federal constitutional rights, and expressed their belief that state-level environmental rights would give rise to the same types of evolving constructions. For example, Mary Leahy explained, "We do define in the report what we mean by healthful environment, but ultimately, it would be the courts in the same way that the courts have decided over the years what the terms 'due process' and 'equal protection' mean."[125] Similarly, in urging voters to approve Massachusetts's environmental rights amendment, the executive director of the MFPA said, "I think the measure has ramifications far beyond what people right now are thinking about."[126] It is hard to imagine a member of the labor or common school movement making such a prediction. As we have seen, nineteenth- and early-twentieth-century activists attempted to craft clear, detailed, and specific instructions in the hopes that legislatures and courts could be made to follow them. The activists of the 1960s and '70s, by contrast, wanted to leave room for the meaning of their new rights to grow and develop over time, perhaps even beyond their own, original conceptions. Their sweeping mandates for environmental protection reflected their belief that the language and politics of rights would allow for the continued evolution and efficacy of their movements.

As the political context changed, however, and constitutional litigation appeared significantly less promising, state constitutional provisions for environmental protection shifted back toward more traditional statements of detailed legislative mandates. Judicial doctrine did not develop in the way that the champions of positive rights had hoped. Several courts have made declarations about the importance of environmental protection and the need for courts to enforce the environmental rights in state constitutions. The Montana Supreme Court has even declared the right to a clean and healthy environment to be a fundamental right.[127] However, few state courts

---

[125] Illinois Constitutional Convention, *Record of Proceedings: Sixth Illinois Constitutional Convention.* December 8, 1969–September 3, 1970: 3000.

[126] "Vote Yes on Referendum 5," *Forest & Park News* 36, no. 3, Massachusetts Forest & Park Association, Boston, Fall 1972, 2.

[127] Citing the constitutional right to a clean and healthy environment, the Montana Environmental Information Center (MEIC) challenged the constitutionality of a state statute, which exempted a particular mining activity (pumping water from test wells into infiltration galleries, which in turn, fed into rivers) from environmental review by the state's Department of Environmental Quality. In its 1999 ruling, the state supreme court agreed with MEIC that this exemption violated citizens' constitutional right to environmental protection and ruled that the legislature could not exempt test well pumping from environmental review. More significantly, the

have provided a particularly robust defense for environmental rights. Instead, their rulings have tended to declare that rights to environmental protection must be balanced against other aims of state policy. Thus, courts
have generally established low standards for the fulfillment of state legislatures' constitutional obligations to protect the environment.[128] In addition,
some state courts have ruled that the environmental rights in state constitutions are not self-executing, which means that legislative action is required
before individuals can assert a judicially enforceable claim.[129]

In general, state courts' rulings have limited the value of environmental
rights as foundations for the sweeping public interest lawsuits that their
proponents originally envisioned. In a fairly typical statement of disappointment, one law professor declared that courts had betrayed the trust of the
American people:

> Faced with the prospect of continuing environmental degradation,
> people across America concluded that the time has come to take mat-
> ters out of the hands of elected officials. They chose to elevate envi-
> ronmental protection to constitutional status where, they hoped,
> these values would be beyond the political milieu, and where they
> would receive the highest protection. Citizens counted on the judi-
> ciary to guarantee these environmental values. But state courts have
> let America down.[130]

State judiciaries have not used the environmental rights in state constitutions to support the aims of the environmental movement or fulfill the hopes
of their advocates.

As it became clear that the judiciary would not develop a robust doctrine
of environmental protection based on state constitutional rights, the movement to create "environmental bills of rights" faded. Although proposals to
add broad statements of environmental rights to state constitutions continued throughout the rest of the twentieth century,[131] sweeping rights to a clean

---

court also established that the MEIC had standing to sue preemptively, even before it could
possibly demonstrate an injury in fact or an actual violation of its rights. Finally, the court declared that the right to environmental protection was a fundamental constitutional right and,
as a result, ruled that all legislative activities that implicated the right to a clean and healthful
environment would be subject to strict judicial scrutiny. In other words, courts would now
consider state actions that threatened the health or cleanliness of the environment to be unconstitutional unless they served a compelling state interest and were narrowly tailored to achieve
that interest.

[128] Barton H. Thompson, "Constitutionalizing the Environment: The History and Future of
Montana's Environmental Provisions," *Montana Law Review* 64, no. 1 (2003): 158–9.

[129] Mary Ellen Cusack, "Comment: Judicial Interpretation of State Constitutional Rights to
a Healthful Environment," *Boston College Environmental Affairs Law Review* 20, no. 1
(1993): 182–6.

[130] McLaren, "Environmental Protection Based on State Constitutional Law: A Call for
Reinterpretation," 151–2.

[131] The Colorado legislature considered adding a broad statement of environmental rights
to the state constitution in 2000. See Steven K. Paulson, "Senator Introduces Clean Environ-

and healthy environment were not added to state constitutions after 1978. Instead, the broad provisions characteristic of the 1960s and 1970s were succeeded by more detailed policies that would not be as subject to judicial interpretation and were far less likely to require judicial enforcement.[132]

The development of the Florida constitution exemplifies this trend in constitutional protection of the environment. Since 1968, the Florida constitution has contained a statement that it is the policy of the state to conserve its natural resources, along with a mandate that the legislature must pass laws for the abatement of air and water pollution. In 1978, the state's constitutional revision commission recommended language to add an explicit "right" to a clean environment to the state's constitution, but voters rejected the entire slate of recommendations from the commission, including the environmental right. However, in 1994, Florida's voters did ratify an environmental amendment to the state's constitution. This amendment, which was placed on the ballot through the initiative and referendum process, was quite different from a broad statement of environmental rights. Dubbed by its proponents the "Save Our Sealife" amendment, it banned the use of particular kinds of environmentally destructive, commercial fishing nets.

The proponents of the Save Our Sealife amendment argued both that the nets in question were devastating Florida's marine ecosystem and that the state government had been totally unresponsive to this environmental catastrophe. A letter to the editor of the *Orlando Sentinel* put it this way: "This issue is on the ballot because Governor Lawton Chiles and the Cabinet officers bowed to the pressure of the commercial fishing lobbyists time after time and failed to prevent the drastic declines of Florida's fish populations."[133] The president of the Florida Wildlife Federation also declared: "We've attempted to work within the existing system . . . We sought regulatory changes. These have been systematically and consistently opposed."[134] Because they could not achieve change within the system, the Save Our Sealife coalition attempted to change that system by changing the constitution that established it. These interest groups were able to overcome legislative recalcitrance by using the initiative and referendum process to write their preferred policy directly into the state's highest law. Consequently, the editorial page of Fort Lauderdale's *Sun Sentinel* praised the constitutional net ban as a model of democratic policymaking: "It shows the citizen initiative process

---

ment Resolution," Associated Press Newswires, March 22, 2000. It has also been proposed that Oregon adopt a similar amendment. Anil Karia, "A Right to a Clean and Healthy Environment: A Proposed Amendment to Oregon's Constitution," *University of Baltimore Journal of Environmental Law* 14, no. 1 (2006).

[132] See for example Fernando Pinguelo, "Laboratory of Ideas: One State's Successful Attempt to Constitutionally Ensure a Healthier Environment," *Buffalo Environmental Law Journal* 4, no. 2 (1997): 274.

[133] Jim Gray, "Money Isn't the Only Issue of the Net-Ban Amendment," *Orlando Sentinel*, Orlando, October 19, 1994, A16.

[134] Associated Press, "Net Ban Backers Turning to Voters," *Lakeland Ledger*, Lakeland, November 29, 1992, B.

of amending the Constitution at its best, as a check and balance on unresponsive government. Rightly angered at inaction by state officials, a grassroots group of marine scientists, environmentalists and sports fishermen . . . collected half a million voter signatures" to place this constitutional amendment on the ballot.[135]

Two years later, environmental activists once again tried to use the constitution to make detailed environmental policy, this time about pollution in the Everglades. Angered that state legislature had not properly funded its Everglades restoration program, environmental organizations attempted to secure the necessary funding through the creation of three, related constitutional amendments. Since sugar production was responsible for the lion's share of pollution in the Everglades, the first proposed amendment imposed a fee on sugar production, the second explicitly established the principle that the polluters of the Everglades would become "primarily responsible" for the cost of Everglades restoration, and the third created a trust fund into which the proceeds of the new sugar fee would be placed, and whose contents would only be available for Everglades cleanup."[136] The debate over these amendments was hard-fought and highly publicized, and the political campaigns that preceded the vote on these amendments proved to be the costliest in the state's history.[137] Just as with the ban on fishing nets, proponents of the Everglades amendments argued that a constitutional amendment was necessary to overcome legislative recalcitrance. The *Palm Beach Post* reported that it was "traditional political resistance that prompted Save Our Everglades to go directly to the voters instead of to lawmakers, who environmentalists say are under the spell of the sugar interests."[138] Florida's subsequent environmental provisions continued this pattern of constitutionalizing detailed policy instructions to the legislature.[139]

[135] "Amendment 3: Floridians Should Vote `Yes' For Limits On Net Fishing," *Sun Sentinel*, Fort Lauderdale, October 26, 1994, 14A.

[136] David Olinger, "Florida Constitutional Amendments Amendments 4, 5 And 6 Series: Know Your Candidates; The 96 Race," *St. Petersburg Times*, St. Petersburg, October 30, 1996, 8G.

[137] "Orlando-based Save Our Everglades spent more than $10 million in support of Amendments 4, 5 and 6. The sugar-cane industry, made up of about 130 growers but dominated by U.S. Sugar and Flo-Sun Inc., spent more than $18 million to oppose the amendments." Jeff Kunerth, "Voters Not Sweet On 1-Cent Sugar Tax But Amendment 5, Requiring Polluters To Pay Cleanup Costs, Gave Everglades Supporters Something To Smile About," *Orlando Sentinel*, Orlando, November 6, 1996, A1. See also Larry Kaplow, "War Over Sugar Tax Costliest In History," *Palm Beach Post*, West Palm Beach, October 22, 1996, 1.A. Ultimately, state voters approved the trust fund and "polluters pays" amendments, but not the new fee on sugar production.

[138] Larry Kaplow and Lisa Shuchman, "Should State Tax Sugar? You'll Decide Supreme Court Says Penny-A-Pound Questions Can Go On Ballot," *Palm Beach Post*, West Palm Beach, September 25, 1996, 1A.

[139] In 1998, the Florida voters ratified another conservation amendment. The Constitutional Revision Commission considered adding broad rights language with reference to the environment, but the committee ultimately decided against this course. Instead, they expanded the legislative mandate from just the abatement of air and water pollution to a requirement that

This use of constitutions will, by now, seem quite familiar from the other rights movements that this book describes. The labor and education movements also enshrined very specific mandates to legislatures in state constitutions. As with those movements, the proponents of the net ban and Everglades amendments pursued constitutional change because they were engaged in particular political battles that they were not winning under the existing constitution. In this respect, the constitutional ban on fishing nets is quite similar to the constitutional establishment of an eight-hour day or a workmen's compensation program. By changing the constitution, the advocates of these policies were able to circumvent reluctant legislatures, and to insist on the establishment of protective regulation. The proponents of these constitutional changes did not express the hope that courts would interpret these provisions to create an ever-widening regime of environmental protection, thus they did not leave room in the provisions for their meaning to evolve through judicial interpretation. On the contrary, because these policies were intended to force reluctant legislatures into action, they were very specific about the types of intervention they required of government.

New Jersey pursued a similar course with respect to constitutional protection of the environment. Its constitution has never contained a broad constitutional right to a clean or healthful environment. However, the New Jersey constitution contains a very clear mandate about government's obligation to address some of the state's most pressing environmental problems. In 1996, the constitution was amended to require that the state engage in the cleanup of hazardous waste, the improvement of underground storage tanks, and the maintenance of surface water quality. Like the original Everglades proposal in Florida, the New Jersey constitution went even further than merely to require cleanup. It also established and protected a source of funding for these initiatives by setting aside 4 percent of the revenue from the state's corporate business tax and specifying that money from this fund could not be used for any other purpose. A contemporaneous law review article explained why the primary sponsor of this amendment sought a constitutional provision, rather than a statute, to establish this policy: "Senator Bennett's experience taught him that a statute was not enough to prevent

---

the legislature enact adequate laws for the conservation of all natural resources. It also required the legislature to authorize bonds for the acquisition of environmentally sensitive lands for conservation purposes, required the protection of existing conservation lands and went further saying not only that the lands had to be managed for the benefit of their citizens but also that they could not be disposed of without a supermajority (2/3) vote of the board governing those lands, and created a new and independent agency with jurisdiction over wildlife and habitat. Reflecting on Florida's constitutional development with respect to the environment, one legal scholar argued, "The stark reality is that there are times when legislative bodies become permanently gridlocked or just plain refuse to do the will of the people. Constitutional amendments engendered by citizen initiative and periodic constitutional revisions provide a potential avenue to overcome non-responsive elected officials." John Tucker, "Constitutional Codification of an Environmental Ethic," *Florida Law Review* 52(2000): 325.

former Governors . . . from siphoning off the money when budgets got tight. Senator Bennett knew from this experience that this new measure needed to be very specific and as unchangeable as politically possible."[140] He explained that, unlike a statute, "'With a constitutional amendment, no games can be played.'"[141] This is a classic explanation for the pursuit of constitutional change. The advantage of a constitutional provision was that it could shelter the cleanup funds, and by extension, the policy aims they supported, from state legislatures and governors. A similar amendment was added to the Minnesota constitution in 1990, funding the state's environment and natural resources trust fund by dedicating 40 percent of the state's lottery proceeds to the fund.[142] These constitutional trust funds for the environment are quite similar to the common school funds that were created through nineteenth-century constitutions. Like common school reformers, environmental activists also pursued the creation of detailed constitutional mandates regarding these funds because they recognized that legislatures and governors could not be trusted to manage them wisely or even to spend them for their designated purposes.

It will come as no surprise that this more detailed type of environmental provision has been widely criticized by constitutional scholars. Because of their detail, they have been dismissed as mundane and derided as improper intrusions into constitutional law.[143] Yet, rather than view these detailed legislative mandates as a new and distressing degradation of constitutional law, or as an abandonment of a majestic rights tradition, we should instead see them as a return to a much older form of constitution making, particularly in the field of positive rights. As we have seen in the cases of education and labor, dissatisfied parties wanted the positive rights they drafted to be detailed enough to ensure that their instructions were so clear that it would be difficult to deviate from them. Because they did not intend to use these rights as the basis for expansive litigation or evolving claims to increasing heights of governmental action, many activists believed that breadth and ambiguity would only allow their opponents to flout or manipulate positive rights. Thus, environmentalists came to see legislative mandates' specificity as a

[140] Pinguelo, "Laboratory of Ideas: One State's Successful Attempt to Constitutionally Ensure a Healthier Environment."

[141] Ibid.

[142] Dean Rebuffoni, "Voters Back Environmental Amendment by Huge Margin," *Star-Tribune Newspaper of the Twin Cities* Minneapolis–St. Paul, November 8, 1990, 11A. As we have seen with many other constitutional amendments, after its successful passage, proponents of this amendment used their success to make a point to the legislature about the electoral salience of their agendas. For instance, one Twin Cities conservationist said, "Elected officials have again been shown that the public is very concerned about the state of our environment." Rebuffoni, ibid.

[143] See, for example, Ryan Maloney, "Smoking Laws, High-Speed Trains, and Fishing Nets a State Constitution Does Not Make: Florida's Desperate Need for a Statutory Citizens Initiative," *University of Florida Journal of Law & Public Policy* 14, no. 1 (2002).

strength, rather than as a signal that their content was not sufficiently important to warrant a place in the fundamental law.[144]

In their essential features, these narrow environmental rights are identical to their broader predecessors. They require the state to protect citizens from threats that do not stem primary, or most proximately, from the state itself. Furthermore, they mandate government intervention and regulation to provide this protection. It is these features that render even these narrow provisions positive rights. From this perspective, the sweeping statements of principle, which so many observers have deemed to be more appropriate for constitutions, appear to be aberrations, at least in the American context. Positive constitutional rights in the United States have tended to look like specific instructions. Yet they originated for the same fundamental purpose as their broader, and therefore more recognizable, counterparts. While some were intended as vehicles to turn courts off and others as vehicles to enable litigation, all were crafted to mandate government intervention to protect vulnerable citizens.

The sweeping environmental rights added to state constitutions in the mid- to late twentieth century demonstrate that neither positive rights nor state constitutions became obsolete after the New Deal. The specific environmental mandates that followed them continued in the same tradition of requiring protective governmental regulation and cleanup. This way of using constitutions was limited by neither geographic region nor historical period. Again and again, throughout American history, social movements and reformers have turned to United States' constitutions to insist that government adopt a more active, more interventionist stance. These movements have had different expectations about how their mandates would be enforced, and different political challenges have driven each to seek constitutional changes. However, across varying issues and over more than a century, reformers have made strikingly similar arguments about the need for new constitutional rights. As they argued on behalf of education rights, labor rights, and rights to environmental protections, activists have insisted that citizens needed protection and help from their state governments, and that these needs were too fundamental to give legislatures any choice about whether or not to act. It is these central claims that unite these movements for constitutional change into a single positive-rights tradition.

---

[144] For example, New Jersey's environmental amendment has been praised precisely because it seemed to require little or no judicial interpretation. Pinguelo, "Laboratory of Ideas: One State's Successful Attempt to Constitutionally Ensure a Healthier Environment."

Conclusion

This book began by introducing the widespread idea that American's rights are different from everyone else's, and that the U.S. Constitution testifies to the exceptionally anti-statist nature of Americans' political commitments. As we have seen, this assessment of American rights and political culture cannot withstand the serious study of state constitutions. Indeed, when we include state constitutions in our view of American constitutionalism, many successful movements for positive constitutional rights become immediately apparent. These positive rights were by no means as widely embraced or strongly enforced in America as they might have been. However, the lengthy and enduring American practice of writing and amending state constitutions to include mandates for protective, welfarist governance demonstrates that the American rights tradition is more complicated and less libertarian than many have argued. Like the fundamental laws of countries all over the world, American constitutions contain rights to protection *by*, and not merely *from*, government.

The particular controversies that have shaped state constitutions (whether to mandate the construction of escapement shafts in mines or provide detailed instructions about the management of school funds, for instance) might seem trivial and mundane at first blush. However, the proponents of these policies were quite clear that big principles were at stake in their struggles. American campaigns for positive rights have varied across states and over time, but each has worked for a more expansive government, one that would protect people from threats other than a tyrannical state, and often from the dangers associated with unfettered capitalism. Whether activists wanted the state to offer protection from the environmental degradation caused by unregulated industrial practices, the lack of educational opportunity available to children of the poor, or the dehumanizing conditions established by labor markets, all wanted government to intervene on behalf of those in danger. Through constitutional conventions and/or referenda, reformers added mandates to their state constitutions, demanding that government intervene in social and economic life. These efforts to secure governments' protection created positive constitutional rights.

In the context of American politics, constitutional change has often appeared to offer tactical advantages that other kinds of politics alone could not. Thus, this study of state constitutional development not only revises the prevailing interpretation of American political culture, but also enhances our understanding of the strategic calculations that can give rise to constitutional change. Scholars of constitutionalism, and of rights in particular, have sometimes claimed that constitutional drafting and change should occur through some form of higher lawmaking, distinct from the ordinary, interest-based bargaining through which legislatures make statutes.[1] However, the champions of positive rights understood their efforts both as a form of higher lawmaking and as a means to further their legislative agendas. Thus, this analysis of positive-rights movements suggests that constitutions are different from statutes not because they transcend the struggles of ordinary politics, but because they play a different role in resolving those struggles.

While there are certainly important differences between statutory and constitutional politics (even at the state level), the differences are not those of ordinary versus higher politics. Instead, the differences between state constitutions and statutes lie in their different institutional capacities. One well-understood advantage of constitutional politics (over statutory politics alone) is that when a policy has been added directly to a constitution, courts can nullify any legislative attempts to tinker with that policy. Thus, by ushering courts into particular policy battles, constitutions can render policies more stable over time by entrenching them against the wishes of changing legislative majorities.[2] State-level activists certainly understood and attempted to exploit this property of constitutional politics. However, they also articulated other (less documented) advantages that a constitutional strategy held over statutory change alone. For instance, even the environmental movement, which used constitutions to facilitate litigation, was not hoping to entrench the status quo, but to achieve policy reform through public interest lawsuits. In addition, just as constitutions can be used to switch courts on, ushering them into particular policy battles, constitutional provisions (unlike statutes) can also be used to switch courts off, excluding courts from specific fights.[3]

The strategic appeal of constitutional provisions was not limited to constitutions' effect on the judiciary. In fact, many of the movements that shaped state constitutions were motivated largely by calculations that had little to do with courts. For example, constitutional provisions struck political organizers as valuable and highly visible banners for their cause. Not only did

---

[1] Gardner, "The Failed Discourse of State Constitutionalism."

[2] Hirschl, *Towards Juristocracy: The Origins and Consequences of the New Constitutionalism*; Howard Gillman, "Party Politics in Constitutional Change: The Political Origins of Liberal Judicial Activism," in *The Supreme Court and American Political Development*, ed. Ronald Kahn and Kenneth Ira Kersch (Lawrence: University Press of Kansas, 2006).

[3] As chapter 5 argues, Labor organizations in particular found that they could prevent courts from declaring protective labor regulation unconstitutional by placing those regulations directly in constitutions.

movement leaders believe that citizens would rally around the constitutional provisions they drafted, they also hoped that successful constitutional change would demonstrate their movement's electoral strength to the states' legislatures. Thus, when it was difficult to get legislation through state legislatures, reform-oriented organizations used constitutions to speak directly to those legislatures, writing explicit mandates for action into constitutions, while simultaneously demonstrating the political power of their supporters.

The Exclusionary Side to Positive Rights

The movements to add positive rights to state constitutions are noteworthy in part because they are examples of popular constitutionalism. In characterizing these popular campaigns for positive constitutional rights, I have emphasized their redistributive and equality-promoting features. The organizations and reformers that sought these positive rights wanted the state to intervene in the market and to provide protection (often to very vulnerable people) from the potentially crippling consequences of laissez-faire liberalism. There is certainly normative appeal in this idea of the people, themselves, determining the meaning of their own fundamental law, and shaping that law into a shield against the dangers associated with capitalism and poverty.

However, it would be a mistake to imagine that the movements behind the inclusion of positive rights were interested in providing universal protection from the dangers they decried. Even as popular movements worked to establish protective state policies, they were often animated by a desire to limit the state's protection to members of their own racial and religious groups. Indeed, many popular movements have simply sought to expel other racial and religious groups from their states or to establish their permanent subjugation. Just as campaigns for positive constitutional rights were often part of larger political projects on behalf of protective governance, so too were they part of larger political projects to exclude particular groups of people from the state's protection and often to physically exclude those people from the state itself. In addition to their genuinely redistributive features, therefore, the state-level positive rights described in this book have often been associated with exclusion and bigotry.

This dynamic was particularly apparent in the campaigns of Western labor organizations around the turn of the nineteenth century. At the same time that they worked to constitutionalize protections for some laborers, many labor organizations also fought to entirely exclude non-white laborers from their states. As part of this exclusionary project, they supported constitutional amendments that would require the legislature to bar non-white, alien laborers from working in the state (at least on publicly funded projects). These exclusionary motives may seem to be at odds with the rhetoric and even the logic of positive rights. It seems hypocritical to insist on the state's moral duty to offer active protection to labor while at the same time requiring that the state cut a large segment of its laborers off from any way to earn a living. However, the anti-immigrant provisions that labor championed are clearly also positive rights (as I have defined them); they represent the attempts of organized labor to require the state to intervene in the labor market in order to protect them from poverty and unemployment. On this reading, these anti-immigrant provisions were not simply an unfortunate deviation from the equality-promoting agenda of labor organizations at the turn of the nineteenth century, but were instead entirely consistent with their desire to protect and empower their own members through mandates for state intervention.

The most famous and successful campaign to this effect was staged by California's Workingmen's Party in 1879. The Workingmen's Party emphasized the need for stronger and better-enforced legislation to secure an eight-hour workday. The demand for state enforcement of the eight-hour day was a central plank of the party's platform, one that its leaders repeated again and again both before and during the constitutional convention. In their own organization's convention, the Workingmen's Party passed a resolution stating: "Eight hours is a sufficient day's work for any man, and the law should make it so."[4] Despite this universal-sounding rhetoric, however, the Workingmen's Party was very clear about which workers should receive governmental protection.

In California, the issue of the eight-hour day was clearly understood as an objection to the presence Chinese laborers, who were known to work long hours for excruciatingly little pay.[5] The Workingmen's Party asserted that Chinese labor was far too cheap and was driving down the price of native labor and depriving the state's many unemployed white laborers of much-needed work. The anti-Chinese sentiment was not merely a racist undertone in the Workingmen's Party's rhetoric, but lay at the very core of its mission. The party's slogan "The Chinese Must Go" left little room for ambiguity about its central goals. In fact, some historians have claimed that the entire purpose of the constitutional convention of 1879 was to give the increasingly popular Workingmen's Party the legal tools to purge the state of Chinese laborers.[6] The labor-friendly constitutional convention did, in fact, draft an entire constitutional article devoted to Chinese exclusion.[7] It began, "The presence of foreigners ineligible to become citizens of the United States

---

[4] Lucile Eaves, *A History of California Labor Legislation: With an Introductory Sketch of the San Francisco Labor Movement*, vol. 2, University of California Publications in Economics (Berkeley: The University Press, 1910), 215.

[5] Jean Pfaelzer, *Driven Out: The Forgotten War against Chinese Americans*, 1st ed. (New York: Random House, 2007), 74.

[6] Ibid., 145.

[7] See California Constitution of 1879, Article XIX.

is declared to be dangerous to the well-being of the State, and the Legislature shall discourage their immigration by all the means within its power." The article went on to mandate that the legislature empower cities and towns to remove the Chinese from their limits and establish legislation to prevent any further Chinese immigration into the state.

Although California may have had the most visible and extreme laborers' movement to expel non-citizen and non-white workers, labor movements in other Western states also used constitutions to demand that their governments eliminate or reduce the practice of hiring non-native labor. In Arizona, the Western Federation of Miners (WFM) devoted its energies to the exclusion of Mexican laborers from the state's mines and even its borders. After mining companies succeeded in breaking Colorado's mining strikes with the use of strikebreakers from Mexico in 1904, union organizers often directed their efforts in the Arizona territory to the exclusion of laborers from Mexico.[8] Although Mexican workers had successfully organized, and had even staged a large-scale mining strike in the Arizona territory, many union leaders still described the employment of Mexican labor as the single greatest threat to the well-being of Arizona's labor unions. Believing that alien laborers from Mexico would be too difficult to organize, the Western Federation of Miners generally focused its organizing efforts on higher paid Anglo-American workers, and frequently used a platform of anti-Mexican labor to gain their support.[9] To this end, WFM leaders emphasized the specter of millions of non-unionized laborers just across the border, ready to pour into mining towns and take over jobs in the event of a strike.[10] Unsurprisingly, the growing sentiment against laborers from Mexico tended to shape white miners' views on Mexican American miners, whom they often lumped into the class of cheap laborers that threatened their own economic position.[11]

It was white miners, organized around a policy of Mexican exclusion, who set about attempting to shape Arizona's first constitution. Their organizations had a great deal of success in influencing Arizona's constitution, inserting provisions into the state's organic law that created an eight-hour workday, a mandatory state program for workmen's compensation, and required the state to outlaw blacklisting. At the same time that Arizona's labor organizations tried to use the state's new constitution to mandate that the legislature establish protective policies like the eight-hour day and workmen's compensation program, however, they also tried to use the constitution to demand the elimination of Mexican labor. Organizations at the town and county levels sent petitions to the constitutional convention urg-

[8] Joseph Park, "The History of Mexican Labor in Arizona During the Territorial Period" (PhD Diss., University of Arizona, 1961), 244.

[9] Ibid., 253.

[10] Thomas E. Sheridan, *Arizona: A History* (Tucson: University of Arizona Press, 1995), 176.

[11] Park, "The History of Mexican Labor in Arizona During the Territorial Period," 244–6.

ing the passage of anti-Mexican articles. One such petition proposed a quota system which would require employers to ensure that at least 80 percent of their labor force was comprised of American citizens.[12] The Democratic delegates to the convention even introduced an amendment (known as proposition 91) which required the legislature to prevent anyone who did not speak English from working in the state. The hope was that proposition 91 would force mining companies to eliminate thousands of Mexicans (and perhaps Mexican Americans) from their payrolls and open the jobs to native, unionized workers at higher salaries.[13] This measure was defeated not only by the representatives of mining interests, but also by the representatives of ranchers and farmers, who often employed casual Mexican labor. However, labor organizations did succeed in using the state's new constitution to exclude alien laborers from jobs in public works. Wyoming and Idaho added similar provisions to their constitutions, forbidding those who had not expressed the intention to become citizens from working on public works.[14]

One other strategy that labor employed to facilitate the exclusion of immigrant labor was banning alien landowning. These bans were not motivated purely by anti-immigrant sentiment, but were also seen as anti-corporate measures that would reduce the absentee landlordism of big corporations like railroads. However, bans on alien landholding were also designed to play an unmistakably exclusionary function. Like California's Workingmen's Party, the Knights of Labor in the Washington territory were strongly devoted to an anti-Chinese agenda, and in the years leading up to statehood, many of their prominent members conducted vigilante raids to try to drive Chinese laborers out of particular parts of the state. When the convention of 1889 assembled to draft the state's first constitution, labor interests in the convention adopted the slogan "America for Americans." Many resolutions from labor organizations were circulated during the convention in support of the ban on alien landowning. One commentator noted, "All the influence that organized labor in all of its departments could command was brought to bear on this question."[15] These bans on alien landowning were added to the constitutions of Oregon, Florida, California, and Oklahoma as well.

The labor movement was not unique in its desire to create protections exclusively for its own members, nor in its attempts to shape the social structure of the state through constitutional activism. The common school movement, which worked for the creation of uniform state systems of free, tax-supported schools, clearly fought for state protection and redistribution

[12] Ibid., 273.

[13] Ibid., 271.

[14] Since the Chinese Exclusion Act, passed in 1882, prohibited the Chinese nationals from attaining citizenship, this prohibition was clearly aimed at Chinese laborers.

[15] Lebbeus Knapp, "The Origin of the Constitution of the State of Washington," *Washington Historical Quarterly* 4, no. 4 (1913): 248.

on the one hand while, on the other, it crafted state constitutions to ensure that educational benefits accrued primarily to white children and Protestant communities. The earliest free schools in Northern states were almost always racially segregated, and were integrated only slowly over the first half of the nineteenth century.[16] In the antebellum South, where common schools were clearly established for the benefit of white children alone, common school activists sometimes even justified public schools as a necessary tool for the maintenance of slavery. For instance, common school activists and state superintendent of schools, Calvin Wiley, often described the great benefit of common schools as their ability to educate poor whites so that those whites would not blur the line between slaves and white citizens by associating too closely with black people or by exhibiting the kind of moral degeneracy that would undermine the legitimacy of a ruling white race.[17]

America's common school movement was also firmly committed to the exclusion of Catholicism from civic life. Throughout much of the nineteenth century, the common school curriculum included reading of the King James Bible and student recitation from the Book of Common Prayer. This curriculum may have developed largely as the unconscious product of compromises among the country's many Protestants sects. However, to Catholics, whose tradition included neither reading of the King James Bible nor the Book of Common Prayer, these practices appeared unmistakably sectarian.

In other cases, the Protestant norms embodied by common school curricula unambiguously reflected the conscious desire among common school advocates to cleanse the population of Catholic beliefs, which they characterized as dangerous and un-American. Common school education often included explicitly anti-Catholic teachings, and many common schools adopted textbooks that described social, political, and moral dangers associated with allegiance to the Pope. In fact, public school advocates frequently promoted their cause as a solution to the problem of Catholic immigration. The anti-Catholic writer Nicholas Murray opined, "We have a mill, of which the common school is the nether, and the Bible and its institutions the upper stone; into this mill let us cast the people of all countries and all forms of religion that come here, and they will come out in the grist Americans and Protestants."[18]

Protestant common school activists grew even more explicit and ferocious in their anti-Catholicism when Catholic leaders objected to the Protestant bias in the common school program. When American Catholics built

[16] Carl F. Kaestle, *Pillars of the Republic: Common Schools and American Society, 1780–1860,* ed. Eric Foner, 1st ed., American Century Series (New York: Hill and Wang, 1983).

[17] James L. Leloudis, *Schooling the New South: Pedagogy, Self, and Society in North Carolina, 1880–1920,* The Fred W. Morrison Series in Southern Studies (Chapel Hill: University of North Carolina Press, 1996).

[18] Tracy Fessenden, "The Nineteenth-Century Bible Wars and the Separation of Church and State," *Church History* 74, no. 4 (2005), quote appears on p. 789.

a parallel school system, they argued that if money from state school funds was given to Protestant, common schools, school fund monies should also be available to Catholic schools. They then requested support from their states' school funds or exemptions from their states' school taxes.[19] In response, many common school advocates began to describe Catholics as the enemies of common schooling. They fought ferociously to keep the common school fund from Catholic schools while simultaneously defending practices like bible reading in public school. Trading on this highly salient political issue, U.S. Senator James G. Blaine proposed an amendment to the federal Constitution banning any public support for sectarian schools. Though seemingly neutral on its face, this amendment was widely understood as an anti-Catholic measure. Although this amendment ultimately failed at the federal level, it was so popular that it was promptly incorporated into state constitutions across the country, and Congress began to require, through its enabling acts, that new states prohibit public funds from being used for "sectarian" schooling. Approximately two-thirds of the states' constitutions came to contain such a prohibition.[20] These widely adopted provisions were designed to ensure that the state's support would only benefit schools that would promote Protestant religious values and practices.

Like organized labor, the common school movement argued that the state had a responsibility to protect the vulnerable from the potentially dire consequences of life in a capitalist system, and used constitutions to mandate state intervention in the affairs of society. Without public education, they explained, children born to poor parents would be doomed to a life of poverty, toil, and ignorance. Despite their rhetoric about the moral imperative to establish universal and equality-promoting educational opportunities, however, mainstream common school reformers were not at all interested in casting the most inclusive possible net. Like labor advocates, common school activists wanted the state's intervention to benefit only members of their own religious and ethnic groups. Suggestions of dividing those benefits so that they could be distributed more broadly were met with outrage and then constitutional bans.

Even the campaign to preserve the Adirondack wilderness (described in chapter 2) followed a similar pattern. New York's notorious mention of ski trails in its state constitution was actually designed to modify the state constitution's "Forever Wild" provision, which protected the state's Adirondack forest. In arguing for this constitutional protection of forests, its proponents described (among other advantages) the benefits that the people of the state, especially the ever-growing masses of urban dwellers, would derive from the continued existence of preserved land. Some even called the protected for-

[19] Steven K. Green, "The Blaine Amendment Reconsidered," *American Journal of Legal History* 36, no. 1 (1992): 42–4.

[20] Steven K. Green, "Blaine Amendment," in *Encyclopedia of American Civil Liberties*, ed. Paul Finkelman (New York: Routledge, 2006).

estland "a people's park." One 1888 letter to the *New York Times* emphasized the fundamentally democratic nature of the proposal by comparing the proposed Adirondack park to the royal game preserves and parks in Europe: "it is an intelligent effort to give to the common people what has hitherto been the luxury of the rich and noble. Even as the Princes and gentry of other countries have their game preserves and magnificent parks, so the . . . Adirondack mountains are to be reserved for the health and enjoyment of the American masses."[21] The *Times* ran a similar argument a year later: "The rich must be taught that the people's park is a scheme for the people, and that whoever opposes it is working against the welfare of the masses, both in this generation and in future centuries."[22] Rhetoric like this might lead one to believe that the movement to preserve the Adirondack wilderness was primarily a populist one. However, the Adirondack Protection Association (APA), the most steadfast and uncompromising advocate for the preservation of the Adirondack wilderness, was composed of many of the country's wealthiest men. The APA was an extraordinary elite organization founded by magnates such as J. Pierpont Morgan, Alfred Vanderbilt, and William Rockefeller, and held its regular meetings on Wall Street.[23]

It is no coincidence that these men all shared a commitment to preserving this particular piece of wild forest. They not only summered in the Adirondacks, but also owned sizeable tracts of land abutting the state-owned forest.[24] Because of its illustrious vacationers, the Adirondacks quickly gained a reputation as a rich man's paradise where the wealthy and fashionable spent their summer months hunting and fishing on their privately owned estates. Thus, the APA members' commitment to preservation, free from the specter of logging or development, was not entirely disinterested. The scenic and monetary value of their privately owned property was dramatically enhanced by the existence of nearby protected forestland. As one historian has explained, the constitutional protection for Adirondack wilderness rendered the state "the perfect abutter: it laid no roads, blocked no views, erected no buildings, and committed resources to fire prevention and firefighting."[25] Consequently, many critics of the constitutional provision to protect the Adirondacks argued that the real purpose of this provision was to protect the forest for the benefit of a wealthy few, by preventing all others from using it.

Opponents of the "Forever Wild" provision charged that it protected the Adirondacks as a playground for the rich, while denying the people of the

[21] "The Adirondack Forests," *New York Times*, New York, May 2, 1888, 4.

[22] "The People's Park in the Adirondacks," *New York Times*, New York, August 21, 1889, 4.

[23] Graham and Graham, *The Adirondack Park: A Political History*, 147.

[24] Philip Terrie, *Contested Terrain: A New History of Nature and People in the Adirondacks* (Syracuse: Syracuse University Press, 1997).

[25] Louise Halper, "'A Rich Man's Paradise': Constitutional Preservation of New York State's Adirondack Forest, a Centenary Consideration," *Ecology Law Quarterly* 19, no. 2 (1992): 226.

state the economic benefits that would flow from industrial development. One commentator noted that the private landowners had all logged their own lands for profit, but sought to prevent the state from reaping any economic benefit from its adjacent forest. He argued that the wealthy had already developed their pieces of forestland, yet employed high-sounding, patriotic rhetoric to protect and preserve only the trees that belonged to the public. He declared, "Our reply to [these landowners] is that just as soon as we have arrived where they have arrived we will be willing to join their patriotic band." The *Times* ran this complaint under the subhead "Millionaire Owners Criticized . . . Accused of Denuding their own lands, but trying to bar others from the Adirondacks."[26] Wishing to use parts of the protected Adirondack forests for hydroelectric power, but meeting resistance from the APA, "[State] Senator Malby also referred to that organization as a body of millionaires who would protect the Adirondacks for themselves to the exclusion of everybody else."[27] And in 1915, when the state's next constitutional convention revisited the question of constitutional protection for the forest preserve, one delegate quoted a *New York Evening Mail* article which read: "The simple fact is that the Adirondack forests are not considered by our sapient legislators to be the property of the people, but of the 'rich' camp owners and club men who go up there to enjoy themselves in a luxuriant manner."[28]

Through their own behavior, the APA members themselves provided plenty of additional evidence that at least one of their goals in protecting the Adirondack forest was to exclude "undesirable" people from it. Not only did the APA's members reap particular personal benefit from the state's protection of the forest, they were also not terribly keen on increased tourism or on the appearance of less distinguished visitors to the region. They typically opposed the construction of roads or railroads that would have increased the accessibility of the region to working-class city dwellers, arguing that these additions to the forest would only open it up to loggers.[29] As tourism to the state forests increased with the increased availability of moderately priced automobiles, wealthy private landowners were quick to complain about the increased traffic.[30] Furthermore, the elite hunting clubs and magnates who owned land in the Adirondack forest built large fences around their own properties to keep game in and people out, and Rockefeller famously bought the smaller privately owned homes in the vicinity of his property so that he could remove their occupants.[31] The region's hunting

[26] "Preservation of Forests," *New York Times*, New York, April 3, 1902, 2.

[27] "Pass Forest Grab Bill," *New York Times*, New York, May 2, 1906, 1.

[28] New York Constitutional Convention, *Journal of the Constitutional Convention of the State of New York, 1915, Begun and Held at the Capitol in the City of Albany on Tuesday the Sixth Day of April* (Albany: J. B. Lyon Co., 1915), 370.

[29] "The Adirondack Invasion," *New York Times*, New York, May 28, 1891, 4.

[30] Terrie, *Contested Terrain: A New History of Nature and People in the Adirondacks*, 128–9.

[31] "Pass Forest Grab Bill," *New York Tribune*, New York, May 2, 1906, 1.

clubs barred access to anyone against whom their members might lodge "physical, moral, social, or racial objection,"[32] and resorts posted signs and placed advertisements warning Jews in particular that they were unwelcome. While members of the middle class visited the Catskills for vacation, high society millionaires summered in, and sought to protect, only the Adirondacks.[33]

The policy of wilderness protection, to which the "Forever Wild" provision belonged, was not only geared toward the exclusion of undesirable visitors to the region, but also had an enormous (and exclusionary) impact on the full-time residents of the Adirondack forests. The imposition of protective regulations on the forest made their traditional small-scale logging businesses illegal and severely restricted the subsistence hunting they had practiced for generations. At the same time that it destroyed their traditional economy, it created demands for new kinds of labor. Unable to continue their self-sufficient use of the forest, residents began to work as hunting guides for exclusive clubs and as domestic servants for their members. This transition bred a great deal of resentment among local residents, many of whom were eager to see the wilderness preserved, but felt that it had been preserved only for the exploitation of the very wealthy.[34] Their resentment reached such heights that local residents even murdered a large estate owner, and some began setting fire to the forests as a means of protest.[35] While constitutional protection for the Adirondacks was championed as a measure that would benefit all the people of the state, the movement for this constitutional protection, like those behind labor and education rights, was targeted at the protection of particular groups and the exclusion and subjugation of others.

Critics of the modern environmental movement have pointed out that its policy goals, while phrased in universal terms, are also often demonstrably exclusionary. For instance, zoning rules often protect the environment by excluding new residents of protected areas for the benefit of existing residents. Wildlife preservation and anti-development projects have been similarly characterized as protections for the aesthetic sensibilities of an elite few while denying local residents of protected (and sometimes economically depressed) areas jobs and economic benefits. Thus, while the supporters of environmental rights talked about the needs of all the people, critics of the environmental movement branded it a movement of the leisure class,[36] and even as state legislatures were adding environmental rights to their state constitutions to commemorate Earth Day, anti-poverty activists were ex-

---

[32] Terrie, *Contested Terrain: A New History of Nature and People in the Adirondacks*, 120.

[33] "Adirondacks for the Rich," *New York Times*, New York, April 6, 1904, 8.

[34] Karl Jacoby, "Class and Environmental History: Lessons from 'the War in the Adirondacks'," *Environmental History* 2, no. 3 (1997).

[35] Ibid.

[36] William Tucker, "Environmentalism and the Leisure Class," *Harper's* December (1977).

pressing concern about the consequences of conservation. The director of the national Welfare Rights Organization declared, "Many conservation programs will be paid for by the poor in the form of higher costs passed on to the consumer, which the poor can least afford."[37]

The environmental provisions added to state constitutions at the close of the twentieth century have been subject to many of the same critiques that were leveled against New York's Forever Wild provision at its beginning. For instance, Florida's constitutional ban on net fishing was widely accused of benefiting the wealthy sport fisherman and elite environmentalists at the cost of thousands of fishermen's jobs. One vocal opponent of the constitutional amendment, himself a fisherman, declared that the net ban was entirely about social class: "They're trying to annihilate us . . . These folks who want to ban the nets, they've got money, they're used to having their way, and they see us Crackers down here on the water and try to brush us aside."[38] It may well be possible to develop an environmental movement that does not pit environmental protections against working-class jobs. However, it is important to note that the positive rights described in this book, even the environmental rights created during the second half of the twentieth century, were often at least perceived as exclusive protections and exclusionary constitutional provisions.

AMERICAN CONSTITUTIONAL DEVELOPMENT
(BRINGING THE STATES BACK IN)

While these histories of positive rights may be unfamiliar, the exclusionary side of state-level politics can hardly be considered news. I have been writing about state-level rights, but states' rights (against the federal government) have earned themselves a very bad name. When states have defended their rights to govern the internal affairs of their polities against incursions by the federal government, they have almost always done so in order to continue their oppression of the African Americans within their borders.[39] It may be *theoretically* possible to distinguish arguments in favor of states' rights from defenses of racist policies.[40] In the context of American politics, however, assertions of states' sovereignty have been most pronounced in defense of racial subjugation. As a result, the studies of American constitutional devel-

[37] Trudy Rubin, "Ahead: the Job of Cleaning Up a Planet," *Christian Science Monitor*, Boston, April 24, 1970, 1.

[38] Jeff Klinkenberg, "Both Sides Of The Net," *St. Petersburg Times*, St. Petersburg, October 23, 1994, Floridian 1F.

[39] Michael J. Klarman, *From Jim Crow to Civil Rights: The Supreme Court and the Struggle for Racial Equality* (Oxford: Oxford University Press, 2004).

[40] Edward G. Carmines and James A. Stimson, *Issue Evolution: Race and the Transformation of American Politics* (Princeton, NJ: Princeton University Press, 1989).

opment that have included states have tended to describe this process as one of slow federal triumph over America's retrogressive states. States' own constitutions have, until recently, rarely featured in analyses of American constitutional development, and most studies of state constitutions have tended to focus predominantly on describing state-level developments.

Rather than considering the state and federal constitutional traditions in isolation from one another, or describing American constitutional development as a steady triumph of the federal Constitution over state practices, it may be more fruitful to explore the many, mutually influential connections between constitutional development at the state and federal levels.[41] After all, each time the boundary between state and federal authority has been a source of controversy, the resolution of that controversy has simultaneously shaped both state and federal constitutions. The state and federal constitutions have therefore developed together as a single system (albeit an overlapping and often disorderly one) of laws and institutions.[42]

As we have seen throughout this study, political movements have long understood the state and federal constitutions as two pieces of America's constitutional system. Indeed, through their attempts to achieve particular policy goals in whatever constitutional venue seemed most feasible, political reformers have often been responsible for the tandem development of state and federal constitutional law. Their successes (or failures) at one level of government often drove them to seek (or not seek) constitutional changes at the other. For instance, some interest groups have first attempted to bring about federal constitutional change, turning to state constitutions only when the federal option was foreclosed. Thus, in the 1960s and '70s, when

[41] The exchange of text and ideas is clearly one mechanism connecting state and federal constitutional development. Donald Lutz has convincingly demonstrated that the content of the U.S. Bill of Rights was drawn largely from rights already present in the eighteen state constitutions that existed when the federal constitution was drafted. Donald Lutz, "The State Constitutional Pedigree of the U.S. Bill of Rights," *Publius: The Journal of Federalism* 22, no. 2 (1992). In addition, it is certainly no coincidence that most state governments are structured very much like the central one. While state constitutional conventions made some conscious decisions to depart from the federal model, many state constitutions were nonetheless largely patterned upon it. On this point, see Dinan, *The American State Constitutional Tradition*.

[42] Lutz has begun to develop this argument as well. He contends that when the federal Constitution was written and adopted, "the existence of [the] states was a brute fact" of such importance that the Constitutions' drafters wrote its text with state governments and constitutions firmly in mind. Thus, he argues that the founding fathers left many gaps in the meaning and scope of the federal Constitution, gaps they assumed its interpreters would fill by consulting state constitutions. Consequently, he describes the federal Constitution as an "incomplete text." A complete (or at least more complete) text consists of both state and federal constitutions, as well (he argues) a the Declaration of Independence. Donald Lutz, "The United States Constitution as an Incomplete Text," *Annals of the American Academy of Political and Social Science* 46 (1988). On this reading, federal constitutional law should not be taken as complete system of constitutional order, but simply as an additional layer of fundamental law overlaid atop an already crowded landscape of state constitutions. It is possible to think about this project on positive rights as an extension of that view.

federal constitutional jurisprudence seemed to promise the Court would adopt an increasingly expansive interpretation of the penumbra of the Ninth Amendment and the Due Process and Equal Protection Clauses, education activists argued that the right to education was a fundamental constitutional right. When the Supreme Court rejected this argument, the public interest lawyers who crafted the federal constitutional strategy turned to state constitutions.[43] Those who wanted more redistributive systems of school financing began altering the meaning of state constitutions, both through formal, textual amendments and by seeking new judicial interpretations of existing education clauses. Thus, state constitutions changed as a result of a lack of change at the federal level.[44]

An even more obvious example of this connection between state and federal constitutional development is the fact that changes at the level of the federal Constitution often require changes to state constitutions, which operate within it. The constitutional changes of the Civil War and Civil Rights movement, for instance, highlight this vertical relationship. During Reconstruction, the federal Constitution was formally amended so that the federal government could exert new kinds of control over states' domestic politics. At the same time, state constitutions throughout the former Confederacy were rewritten to comport with federal demands and expectations. Almost a century later, when the federal government again attempted to end racial subjugation in the South, the desegregation decisions of the Warren Court not only gave new meaning to the Fourteenth Amendment of the federal Constitution, they also required a dramatic restructuring of state government and state constitutions. Federal rulings nullified the clauses in state constitutions that disenfranchised black voters, outlawed miscegenation, and mandated segregated schooling. In states that chose to resist federal efforts at desegregation, some white legislatures amended their state constitutions in an effort to circumvent federal dictates.[45] In each of these instances, state and federal constitutions developed together as part of a single system of governance. However, this hierarchical relationship is not the only way that state and federal constitutional development are connected.

---

[43] Berke, "Recent Adventures of State School Finance—Saga of Rocket Ships and Glider Planes."

[44] The "new judicial federalism" is a similar case of state constitutional change resulting from developments in federal constitutionalism. As the Burger Court moved away from the Warren Court's emphasis on civil liberties, Justice Brennan suggested that state constitutions might be able to offer stronger protections for civil liberties, and that the provisions shared by state and federal constitutions might mean something different (and more protective) when they appeared in state constitutions. William Brennan, "State Constitutions and the Protection of Individual Rights," *Harvard Law Review* 90, no. 3 (1977).

[45] See for example Matthew D. Lassiter and Andrew B. Lewis, *The Moderates' Dilemma: Massive Resistance to School Desegregation in Virginia* (Charlottesville: University Press of Virginia, 1998); Elizabeth Jacoway, "Jim Johnson of Arkansas: Segregationist Prototype," in *The Role of Ideas in the Civil Rights South*, ed. Anthony J. Badger and Ted Ownby (Jackson: University Press of Mississippi, 2002).

The state and federal constitutions have often operated as two complementary and parallel pieces of America's constitutional system. For much of American history, areas of state and federal authority were clearly distinguished from one another. State governments regulated different spheres of political life than the federal government, and as a result, state constitutions dealt with issue areas on which the federal Constitution was silent. As I have already argued, state constitutions explicitly addressed education and labor rights at a time when these areas were understood to be primarily state responsibilities. State constitutions also addressed government's responsibility to care for those who could not support themselves and those unable to pay their creditors. State constitutional law spoke on matters of public health, marital relationships, and farmers' welfare. Because these were considered appropriate matters for state government, it was state, and not federal, constitutions that addressed these topics.

When we study constitutional development at the federal level alone, it is all too easy to misunderstand the dramatic shifts that have occurred over the course of U.S. history in federal and state responsibilities. For instance, the New Deal settlement is often described as a discreet and fleeting "constitutional moment" in which the Supreme Court's Lochner Era jurisprudence became so unpopular that the entire American people considered and decided what their national Constitution ought to mean.[46] Yet as we have seen, this federal constitutional change was really the visible tip of a much larger iceberg. By including state constitutions in our analysis, we become aware of multiple (much older) battles over the meaning of due process rights and the scope of constitutional police powers in the states. In many respects, the informal constitutional amendment that signaled the Supreme Court's acceptance of the New Deal mirrored the formal amendments to state constitutions that labor organizations created throughout the Gilded Age and Progressive Era. Instead of an ephemeral "constitutional moment" during which popular pressure shaped a constitution, the New Deal settlement looks more like the final stage of a sustained popular campaign to alter the nation's constitutional law. In order to paint a fuller and more accurate picture of American constitutional development, we must attend not only to the existence of state constitutions, but to the central roles they have played.

AMERICAN UNEXCEPTIONALISM

State constitutions are an integral part of the American constitutional system, and positive rights are very much a part of state constitutions. However, these rights are not widely understood as a part of the federal Constitution, and there are surely important political differences between rights included only at the state level and those found in the national Constitution.

---

[46] Ackerman, *We the People: Transformations.*

We can only speculate about a counterfactual history in which the U.S. Constitution came to contain the kinds of explicit positive rights now found at the state level. Yet, the political outcome would likely have been at least somewhat, and potentially very, different. In other words, there may well have been dramatic consequences to the fact that America's positive rights appear only in state constitutions, and that some rights appear in only a handful of state constitutions. Thus, I am not arguing that state-level rights are identical to federal ones. My argument is far more modest. I am simply arguing that positive rights lie well within, rather than outside, the American constitutional tradition.

Tempting as it may be to imagine the Bill of Rights as a comprehensive list of Americans' most fundamental political commitments, it is nonetheless a big mistake. Constitutional texts are not records from which we can read the list of a polity's most fundamental values. Instead, constitutions reflect the pursuit of moral commitments within particular institutional environments. In other words, constitutions change in response to people's strategic calculations about how best to further their own political aims. Thus, constitutional texts simultaneously reflect both principled commitments and political struggles.

The positive-rights movements I have chronicled here demonstrate that the story of America's difference is primarily one of institutional opportunity, not political culture. To American reformers seeking rights to a more protective government, state constitutions have often appeared to be the most accessible and relevant constitutions. The federal structure of American governance meant that states (not the federal government) were widely responsible for regulating many areas of social and economic life, and the timing of their drafting and mechanisms for their revision rendered state constitutions far easier to shape and reshape than the federal document. To be sure, an America that more fully embraced positive rights might well have added those rights to its national constitution, either through formal amendment or judicial doctrine. However, the lack of explicit positive rights in the federal Constitution is a reflection of the structure of America's constitutional system, not of the absence of positive rights from American political life. Likewise, the existence of explicit positive rights in national constitutions all over the world is not good evidence that the citizens of these nations possess a differing set of political commitments from Americans, only that they encountered a different set of political openings when writing and revising their national constitutions.

We must reject the standard account of American constitutional exceptionalism, which holds that Americans' extreme suspicion of government power is evidenced by the exclusively negative character of the U.S. Constitution. In fact, U.S. history is replete with nationwide rights movements that demanded protection from the consequences of poverty and laissez-faire capitalism, and that succeeded in creating new, legally binding obligations on government. Scholars have widely overlooked or discounted these movements and their constitutional victories, much to the detriment of our understanding. It is important to correct this understanding, not to assert that the United States is just like the rest of the world or to dismiss the powerful influence of liberal ideology on American politics, but to paint a fuller, more sophisticated picture of American constitutional law.

Ideas about who we are shape who we can become. The belief that positive rights are outside the American constitutional tradition, and barred from inclusion by an enduring cultural boundary, might actually establish just this kind of boundary condition. By the same token, a richer understanding can liberate us from the cramped and deficient assumptions that still dominate discussions of American constitutionalism, creating new possibilities for both scholarship and politics.

BIBLIOGRAPHY

❖

Abraham, David. "Liberty without Equality: The Property-Rights Connection in a 'Negative Citizenship' Regime." *Law and Social Inquiry—Journal of the American Bar Foundation* 21, no. 1 (1996): 1–65.

Ackerman, Bruce A. *We the People: Transformations*. Cambridge, MA: Belknap Press of Harvard University Press, 1998.

Adams, John Clarke. *The Quest for Democratic Law: The Role of Parliament in the Legislative Process* New York: Crowell, 1970.

Alger, George W. "Some Equivocal Rights of Labor." *Atlantic Monthly*, 1906, 364–8.

Amar, Akhil Reed. "Republicanism and Minimal Entitlements: Of Safety Valves and the Safety Net." *George Mason University Law Review* 11, no. 2 (1988): 47–52.

———. *The Bill of Rights: Creation and Reconstruction*. New Haven: Yale University Press, 1998.

American Association for Labor Legislation. "Topical Index by States." *American Labor Legislation Review* 3, no. 3 (1913): 460–61.

Anderson, George. "General Discussion." *American Labor Legislation Review* 3, no. 1 (1913): 92–6.

Archer, Jack H. *The Public Trust Doctrine and the Management of America's Coasts*. Amherst: University of Massachusetts Press, 1994.

Bailyn, Bernard. *The Ideological Origins of the American Revolution*. Cambridge, MA: Belknap Press of Harvard University Press, 1967.

Balkin, Jack, and Sanford Levinson. "Understanding the Constitutional Revolution." *Virginia Law Review* 87, no. 6 (2001): 1045–1104.

Balogh, Brian. *A Government Out of Sight: The Mystery of National Authority in Nineteenth-Century America*. Cambridge: Cambridge University Press, 2009.

Bamberger, Michael A. *Reckless Legislation: How Lawmakers Ignore the Constitution*. New Brunswick, NJ: Rutgers University Press, 2000.

Barnett, Randy. "An Originalism for Nonoriginalists." *Loyola Law Review* 45, no. 4 (1999): 611–54.

Beadle, William Henry Harrison. *Source Materials in South Dakota History of Education: Three Important Contributions by General W. H. H. Beadle, Who Was the Champion of Public Schools During Territorial and Early Statehood Days*: s.n., 1884.

Beard, Charles Austin. *An Economic Interpretation of the Constitution of the United States*. New York: Macmillan Co., 1913.

Beatty, David M. *Human Rights and Judicial Review: A Comparative Perspective*. Norwell: Kluwer Academic Publishers, 1994.

Benjamin, Gerald, and Henrik N. Dullea. *Decision 1997: Constitutional Change in New York*. Albany, NY: Rockefeller Institute Press, 1997.

Bentley, Curt. "Constrained by the Liberal Tradition: Why the Supreme Court Has Not Found Positive Rights in the American Constitution." *Brigham Young University Law Review* 2007, no. 6 (2007): 1721–66.

Berke, J. S. "Recent Adventures of State School Finance—Saga of Rocket Ships and Glider Planes." *School Review* 82, no. 2 (1974): 183–206.

Berlin, Isaiah. "Two Concepts of Liberty." In *Four Essays on Liberty*, edited by Isaiah Berlin. Oxford: Oxford University Press, 1969. Essay originally published in 1958.

Besso, Michael. "Constitutional Amendment Procedures and the Informal Political Construction of Constitutions." *Journal of Politics* 67, no. 1 (2005): 69–87.

Bokkelen, L. Van. *Report of the State Superintendent of Public Instruction to the General Assembly of Maryland*. Annapolis, MD: Richard P. Bayly, Printer, 1865.

Brennan, William. "State Constitutions and the Protection of Individual Rights." *Harvard Law Review* 90, no. 3 (1977): 489–504.

Bridges, Amy. "Becoming American, the Working Classes of the United States before the Civil War." In *Working Class Formation: Patterns in Nineteenth Century United States and Europe*, edited by Aristide Zolberg and Ira Katznelson. Princeton, NJ: Princeton University Press, 1986.

———. "Managing the Periphery in the Gilded Age: Writing Constitutions for the Western States." *Studies in American Political Development* 22, no. 1 (2008): 32–58.

Broughton, Robert. "Constitutional Amendment Covers Environment." *Water Land and Life* 12, no. 2 (1970): 7–8.

———. "Proposed Pennsylvania Declaration of Environmental Rights, Analysis of Hb 958." *Pennsylvania Bar Association Quarterly* 41, no. 4 (1970): 421–38.

Bryant, Keith L., Jr. "Labor in Politics: The Oklahoma State Federation of Labor During the Age of Reform." *Labor History* 11, no. 3 (1970): 259–76.

Burrell, B. Jeannette, and R. H. Eckelberry. "The High-School Controversy in the Post-Civil-War Period: Times, Places, and Participants." *School Review* 42, no. 5 (1934): 333–45.

Byrkit, James W. *Forging the Copper Collar: Arizona's Labor Management War of 1901–1921*. Tucson: University of Arizona Press, 1982.

Carmines, Edward G., and James A. Stimson. *Issue Evolution: Race and the Transformation of American Politics*. Princeton, NJ: Princeton University Press, 1989.

Clark, Tom S. *The Limits of Judicial Independence, Political Economy of Institutions and Decisions*. New York: Cambridge University Press, 2010.

Clemens, Elisabeth Stephanie. *The People's Lobby: Organizational Innovation and the Rise of Interest Group Politics in the United States, 1890–1925*. Chicago: University of Chicago Press, 1997.

Cohen, Bernard S. "The Constitution, the Public Trust Doctrine, and the Environment." *Utah Law Review* 1970, no. 3 (1970): 388–94.

Colorado State Federation of Labor. "Report of Proceedings of the Seventh Annual Convention." Trinidad, CO, June 9–13, 1902.

Committee on Labor Legislation and the Constitutional Convention of New York State. *Constitutional Amendments Relating to Labor Legislation and Brief in Their Defense Submitted to the Constitutional Convention of New York State*. New York: American Association for Labor Legislation, 1915.

Connelley, William, and E. M. Coulter. *History of Kentucky*. Vol. 2. Chicago and New York: American Historical Society, 1922.

Cornwell, Elmer E., Jr., Jay S. Goodman, and Wayne R. Swanson. "State Constitutional Conventions: Delegates, Roll Calls, and Issues." *Midwest Journal of Political Science* 14, no. 1 (1970): 105–30.

Cremin, Lawrence A. *American Education: The National Experience 1783–1876*. New York: Harper & Row, 1980.

Cross, F. B. "The Error of Positive Rights." *UCLA Law Review* 48, no. 4 (2001): 857–924.

Cusack, Mary Ellen. "Comment: Judicial Interpretation of State Constitutional Rights to a Healthful Environment." *Boston College Environmental Affairs Law Review* 20, no. 1 (1993): 173–201.

Dahl, Robert. "Decision-Making in a Democracy: The Supreme Court as a National Policy-Maker." *Journal of Public Law* 6, no. 2 (1957): 279–95.

Davies, J. Clarence, and Jan Mazurek. *Pollution Control in the United States: Evaluating the System*. Washington, DC: Resources for the Future, 1998.

Dempsey, Dave. *Ruin & Recovery: Michigan's Rise as a Conservation Leader*. Ann Arbor: University of Michigan Press, 2001.

DePue, Mark. *Interview with Mary Leahy*. Springfield, IL: Conducted for the Abraham Lincoln Presidential Library, 2008.

Dinan, John J. "Framing a People's Government: State Constitution-Making in the Progressive Era." *Rutgers Law Journal* 30, no. 4 (1999): 933–86.

———. "'The Earth Belongs Always to the Living Generation': The Development of State Constitutional Amendment and Revision Procedures." *Review of Politics* 62, no. 4 (2000): 645–74.

———. *The American State Constitutional Tradition*. Lawrence: University Press of Kansas, 2006.

———. "Court-Constraining Amendments and the State Constitutional Tradition." *Rutgers Law Journal* 38, no. 4 (2007): 983–1040.

———. "The Meaning of State Constitutional Education Clauses: Evidence from the Constitutional Convention Debates." *Albany Law Review* 70, no. 3 (2007): 927–81.

Donaldson, Alfred L. *A History of the Adirondacks*. New York: Century Co., 1921.

Dworkin, R. M. *Taking Rights Seriously*. Cambridge MA: Harvard University Press, 1977.

Eastman, John C. "Reinterpreting the Education Clauses in State Constitutions." In *School Money Trials: The Legal Pursuit of Educational Adequacy*, edited by Martin R. West and Paul E. Peterson. Washington, DC: Brookings Institution Press, 2007.

Eaves, Lucile. *A History of California Labor Legislation: With an Introductory Sketch of the San Francisco Labor Movement*. Vol. 2, University of California Publications in Economics. Berkeley: The University Press, 1910.

Eby, Frederick. *The Development of Education in Texas*. New York: MacMillan Company, 1925.

Eisgruber, Christopher L. *Constitutional Self-Government*. Cambridge, MA: Harvard University Press, 2001.

Elster, Jon. *Ulysses and the Sirens: Studies in Rationality and Irrationality*. New York: Cambridge University Press, 1979.

———. *Ulysses Unbound: Studies in Rationality, Precommitment, and Constraints*. New York: Cambridge University Press, 2000.

Ely, John Hart. *Democracy and Distrust: A Theory of Judicial Review*. Cambridge, MA: Harvard University Press, 1980.

Enyeart, John P. "'The Exercise of the Intelligent Ballot': Rocky Mountain Workers, Urban Politics, and Shorter Hours, 1886–1911." *Labor: Studies in Working-Class History of the Americas* 1, no. 3 (2004): 45–69.

Epp, Charles R. *The Rights Revolution: Lawyers, Activists, and Supreme Courts in Comparative Perspective*. Chicago: University of Chicago Press, 1998.

Eskridge, William, and John Ferejohn. "Super-Statutes." *Duke Law Journal* 50, no. 5 (2001): 1215–76.

Fabre, Cécile. *Social Rights under the Constitution: Government and the Decent Life*. Oxford: Oxford University Press, 2000.

Ferrey, Steven. *Environmental Law: Examples & Explanations*. 5th ed. New York: Aspen Publishers, 2010.

Fessenden, Tracy. "The Nineteenth-Century Bible Wars and the Separation of Church and State." *Church History* 74, no. 4 (2005): 748–811.

Flint, Winston Allen. *The Progressive Movement in Vermont*. Washington, DC: American Council on Public Afairs, 1941.

Forbath, William E. *Law and the Shaping of the American Labor Movement*. Cambridge, MA: Harvard University Press, 1991.

Ford, Paul Leicester, ed. *The Works of Thomas Jefferson*. Vol. 6. New York, London: G. P. Putnam's Sons, 1904.

Frankfurter, Felix. "Legislation Affecting Labor Injunctions." *Yale Law Journal* 38, no. 7 (1929): 879–935.

Fried, Charles. *Right and Wrong*. Cambridge, MA: Harvard University Press, 1978.

Friedman, Lawrence Meir. *A History of American Law*. 3rd ed. New York: Simon & Schuster, 2005.

Fritz, Christian G. "The American Constitutional Tradition Revisited: Preliminary Observations on State Constitution-Making in the Nineteenth Century West." *Rutgers Law Journal* 25, no. 4 (1994): 945–98.

Gallagher, Carole. "The Movement to Create an Environmental Bill of Rights: From Earth Day, 1970 to the Present." *Fordham Environmental Law Journal* 9, no. 1 (1997): 107–54.

Gardner, James A. "The Failed Discourse of State Constitutionalism." *Michigan Law Review* 90, no. 4 (1992): 761–837.

Gewirth, Alan. "Are All Rights Positive?" *Philosophy and Public Affairs* 30, no. 3 (2001): 321–33.

Gillman, Howard. *The Constitution Besieged: The Rise and Demise of Lochner Era Police Powers Jurisprudence*. Durham: Duke University Press, 1993.

———. "How Political Parties Can Use the Courts to Advance Their Agendas: Federal Courts in the United States, 1875–1891." *American Political Science Review* 96, no. 3 (2002): 511–24.

———. "Party Politics in Constitutional Change: The Political Origins of Liberal Judicial Activism." In *The Supreme Court and American Political Development*, edited by Ronald Kahn and Kenneth Ira Kersch. Lawrence: University Press of Kansas, 2006.

Ginsburg, Tom. *Judicial Review in New Democracies: Constitutional Courts in Asian Cases*. Cambridge: Cambridge University Press, 2003.

Glendon, Mary Ann. *Rights Talk: The Impoverishment of Political Discourse*. New York: Free Press, 1991.

Gottlieb, Amy Zahl. "The Influence of British Trade Unionists on the Regulation of the Mining Industry in Illinois, 1872." *Labor History* 19, no. 3 (1978): 397–415.

Graham, Frank, and Ada Graham. *The Adirondack Park: A Political History.* 1st ed. New York: Knopf, distributed by Random House, 1978.

Graves, W. Brooke. "Fourth Edition of the Model State Constitution." *American Political Science Review* 35, no. 5 (1941): 916–19.

Green, Steven K. "The Blaine Amendment Reconsidered." *American Journal of Legal History* 36, no. 1 (1992): 38–69.

———. "Blaine Amendment." In *Encyclopedia of American Civil Liberties*, edited by Paul Finkelman. New York: Routledge, 2006.

Griffin, Stephen M. *American Constitutionalism: From Theory to Politics.* Princeton, NJ: Princeton University Press, 1996.

Grimm, Dieter. "The Protective Function of the State." In *European and US Constitutionalism*, edited by Georg Nolte. New York: Cambridge University Press, 2005.

Groat, George. "The Eight Hour and Prevailing Rate Movement in New York State." *Political Science Quarterly* 21, no. 3 (1906): 414–33.

Grodin, Joseph R., Calvin R. Massey, and Richard B. Cunningham. *The California State Constitution: A Reference Guide*, Reference Guides to the State Constitutions of the United States. Westport, CT: Greenwood Press, 1993.

Hall, Kermit L. "Mostly Anchor and Little Sail: The Evolution of American State Constitutions." In *Toward a Usable Past: Liberty under State Constitutions*, edited by Paul Finkelman and Stephen E. Gottlieb. Athens: University of Georgia Press, 1991.

Halper, Louise. "'A Rich Man's Paradise': Constitutional Preservation of New York State's Adirondack Forest, a Centenary Consideration." *Ecology Law Quarterly* 19, no. 2 (1992): 193–268.

Hardin, Russell. *Liberalism, Constitutionalism, and Democracy.* Oxford: Oxford University Press, 1999.

Hart, Vivien. *Bound by Our Constitution: Women, Workers, and the Minimum Wage.* Princeton, NJ: Princeton University Press, 1994.

Hartog, Hendrik. "The Constitution of Aspiration and 'the Rights That Belong to Us All'." *Journal of American History* 74 (1987): 1013–34.

Hartz, Louis. *The Liberal Tradition in America; an Interpretation of American Political Thought since the Revolution.* 1st ed. New York: Harcourt, 1955.

Hattam, Victoria Charlotte. *Labor Visions and State Power: The Origins of Business Unionism in the United States*, Princeton Studies in American Politics. Princeton, NJ: Princeton University Press, 1993.

Hellerich, Mahlon. "Public Education and the Pennsylvania Constitutional Convention of 1873." *History of Education Journal* 9, no. 1 (1957): 1–7.

Hershkoff, H. "Positive Rights and State Constitutions: The Limits of Federal Rationality Review." *Harvard Law Review* 112, no. 6 (1999): 1131–96.

———. "State Courts and the 'Passive Virtues' Rethinking the Judicial Function." *Harvard Law Review* 114, no. 7 (2001): 1833–1941.

Hershock, Martin. "To Shield a Bleeding Humanity: Conflict and Consensus in Mid-Nineteenth Century Michigan Political Culture." *Mid-America An Historical Review* 77, no. 1 (1995): 33–50.

Hinsdale, B. A. *Education in the State Constitutions*: n.p., 1889.

Hirschl, Ran. *Towards Juristocracy: The Origins and Consequences of the New Constitutionalism.* Cambridge, MA: Harvard University Press, 2004.

Hohfeld, Wesley Newcomb. "Some Fundamental Legal Conceptions as Applied in Judicial Reasoning." *Yale Law Journal* 23, no. 1 (1913): 16–59.

Holmes, Stephen, and Cass R. Sunstein. *The Cost of Rights: Why Liberty Depends on Taxes*. New York: Norton, 2000.

Howard, A. E. Dick. "Education in Virginia's New Constitution." *Compact* 5, no. 2 (1971): 17–18.

Hundley, Norris. "Katherine Philips Edson and the Fight for the California Minimum Wage, 1912–1923." *Pacific Historical Review* 29, no. 3 (1960): 271–85.

Hurst, James Willard. *The Growth of American Law: The Law Makers*. Boston: Little Brown, 1950.

Illinois Constitutional Convention. *Debates and Proceedings of the Constitutional Convention of the State of Illinois: Convened at the City of Springfield, Tuesday, December 13, 1869*. Springfield: E. L. Merritt & Bro., printers to the Convention, 1870.

———. *Record of Proceedings: Sixth Illinois Constitutional Convention. December 8, 1969–Sept. 3, 1970*. Springfield, IL: John W. Lewis, 1970.

Ishay, Micheline. *The History of Human Rights: From Ancient Times to the Globalization Era*. Berkeley: University of California Press, 2004.

Jacoby, Karl. "Class and Environmental History: Lessons from 'the War in the Adirondacks'." *Environmental History* 2, no. 3 (1997): 324–42.

Jacoway, Elizabeth. "Jim Johnson of Arkansas: Segregationist Prototype." In *The Role of Ideas in the Civil Rights South*, edited by Anthony J. Badger and Ted Ownby, xiii. Jackson: University Press of Mississippi, 2002.

Jenkins, Blanche Leora. "Public Education in Maryland, 1863–1875." Master's thesis, University of Maryland, 1940.

Jewell, Malcolm Edwin, and Samuel Charles Patterson. *The Legislative Process in the United States*. New York: Random House, 1966.

Johnson, Kimberley S. *Governing the American State: Congress and the New Federalism, 1877–1929*, Princeton Studies in American Politics. Princeton, NJ: Princeton University Press, 2007.

Kaestle, Carl F. *Pillars of the Republic: Common Schools and American Society, 1780–1860*, edited by Eric Foner. 1st ed. American Century Series. New York: Hill and Wang, 1983.

Karia, Anil. "A Right to a Clean and Healthy Environment: A Proposed Amendment to Oregon's Constitution." *University of Baltimore Journal of Environmental Law* 14, no. 1 (2006): 37–78.

Katz, Sherry. "Socialist Women and Progressive Reform." In *California Progressivism Revisited*, edited by William Francis Deverell and Tom Sitton, xii. Berkeley: University of California Press, 1994.

Keck, Thomas M. "Beyond Backlash: Assessing the Impact of Judicial Decisions on LGBT Rights." *Law & Society Review* 43, no. 1 (2009): 151–86.

Kelley, Florence. "The United States Supreme Court and Utah Eight-Hours' Law." *American Journal of Sociology* 4, no. 1 (1898): 21–34.

———. *Some Ethical Gains through Legislation*. New York: The Macmillan Company, 1905.

Kennedy, Duncan. *Sexy Dressing, Etc.* Cambridge, MA: Harvard University Press, 1993.

Kentucky Constitutional Convention. *Report of the Debates and Proceedings of the Convention for the Revision of the Constitution of the State of Kentucky*, edited by Richard Sutton. Frankfort, KY: A. G. Hodges & Co., 1849.

Kersch, Kenneth Ira. *Constructing Civil Liberties: Discontinuities in the Development of American Constitutional Law*. Cambridge: Cambridge University Press, 2004.

Kirsch, Matthew Thor. "Upholding the Public Trust in State Constitutions." *Duke Law Journal* 46, no. 5 (1997): 1169–1210.

Klarman, Michael J. *From Jim Crow to Civil Rights: The Supreme Court and the Struggle for Racial Equality*. Oxford: Oxford University Press, 2004.

Knapp, Lebbeus. "The Origin of the Constitution of the State of Washington." *Washington Historical Quarterly* 4, no. 4 (1913): 227–75.

Knight, George. *History and Management of Land Grants for Education in the Northwest Territory*. 3 vols. Vol. 1, Papers of the American Historical Association. New York: G. P. Putnam's Sons, 1885.

Kury, Franklin L. *Natural Resources and the Public Estate: A Biography of Article I, Section 27 of the Pennsylvania Constitution, Written by Franklin L. Kury for the Maurice K. Goddard Chair Program*. Reed Smith Shaw & McClay, 1985.

———. "Pennsylvania's Environmental Amendment." Pennsylvania Land Trust Association, accessed August 8, 2012, http://conserveland.org/policy/envirorights.

Lassiter, Matthew D., and Andrew B. Lewis. *The Moderates' Dilemma: Massive Resistance to School Desegregation in Virginia*. Charlottesville: University Press of Virginia, 1998.

Lauck, Jon. "'The Organic Law of the Great Commonwealth': The Framing of the South Dakota Constitution." *South Dakota Law Review* 53, no. 2 (2008): 204–59.

———. "'You Can't Mix Wheat and Potatoes in the Same Bin': Anti-Catholicism in Early Dakota." *South Dakota History* 38, no. 1 (2008): 1–46.

Lawrence, W. Mason. "Equipping State Government to Meet Resource Needs." In *Transactions of the Thirty-Eighth North American Wildlife and Natural Resources Conference*. Washington, DC: Wildlife Management Institute, 1973.

Lazarus, Richard J. *The Making of Environmental Law*. Chicago: University of Chicago Press, 2004.

Leloudis, James L. *Schooling the New South: Pedagogy, Self, and Society in North Carolina, 1880–1920*, The Fred W. Morrison Series in Southern Studies. Chapel Hill: University of North Carolina Press, 1996.

Lewis, William Draper. "A New Method of Constitutional Amendment by Popular Vote." *Annals of the American Academy of Political and Social Science* 43 (1912): 311–25.

Lippke, R. L. "The Elusive Distinction between Negative and Positive Rights." *Southern Journal of Philosophy* 33, no. 3 (1995): 335–46.

London, Lena. "Homestead Exemption in the Wisconsin Constitution." *Wisconsin Magazine of History* 32, no. 2 (1948): 176–84.

Lonsdale, David L. "Chicanery in Colorado." *Red River Valley Historical Review* 4, no. 3 (1979): 33–43.

Louisiana Constitutional Convention. *Debates in the Convention for the Revision and Amendment of the Constitution of the State of Louisiana: Assembled at Liberty Hall, New Orleans, April 6, 1864*. New Orleans: W. R. Fish, Printer to the Convention, 1864.

Lovell, George I. *Legislative Deferrals: Statutory Ambiguity, Judicial Power, and American Democracy*. Cambridge, UK; New York: Cambridge University Press, 2003.

Lukas, J. Anthony. *Big Trouble: A Murder in a Small Western Town Sets Off a Struggle for the Soul of America*. New York: Simon & Schuster, 1997.

Lutz, Donald. "The United States Constitution as an Incomplete Text." *Annals of the American Academy of Political and Social Science* 46 (1988): 23–32.

——. "The State Constitutional Pedigree of the U.S. Bill of Rights." *Publius: The Journal of Federalism* 22, no. 2 (1992): 19–45.

Lynch, Thomas, and Jan S. Stevens. "Environmental Law—the Uncertain Trumpet." *University of San Francisco Law Review* 5, no. 1 (1970): 10–24.

Maloney, Ryan. "Smoking Laws, High-Speed Trains, and Fishing Nets a State Constitution Does Not Make: Florida's Desperate Need for a Statutory Citizens Initiative." *University of Florida Journal of Law & Public Policy* 14, no. 1 (2002): 93–124.

Mandel, Paul. "Labor Politics, Hayden Style." In *American Labor in the Southwest: The First One Hundred Years*, edited by James C. Foster, xii. Tucson: University of Arizona Press, 1982.

Marmor, Andrei. *Interpretation and Legal Theory*. Rev. 2nd ed. Oxford: Hart, 2005.

Maryland Constitutional Convention. *The Debates of the Constitutional Convention of the State of Maryland: Assembled at the City of Annapolis, Wednesday, April 27, 1864*. Edited by Wm Blair Lord and Henry M. Parkhurst. Annapolis: R. P. Bayly, 1864.

Maryland Constitutional Convention of 1867. *Debates of the Maryland Constitutional Convention of 1867 (as Reprinted from Articles Reported in the* Baltimore Sun*)*. Edited by Francis A. Richardson and Philip B. Perlman. Baltimore: Hepbron & Haydon, 1923.

Maryland Constitutional Convention of 1967. *Proceedings and Debates of the 1967 Constitutional Convention*. Vol. 104, Archives of Maryland: Maryland State Archives, 2000.

Matzen, John Mathiason. *State Constitutional Provisions for Education; Fundamental Attitude of the American People Regarding Education as Revealed by State Constitutional Provisions, 1776–1929*. New York: Teachers College, Columbia University, 1931.

McCann, Michael W. *Rights at Work: Pay Equity Reform and the Politics of Legal Mobilization*, Language and Legal Discourse. Chicago: University of Chicago Press, 1994.

McGinnis, Anthony. "The Influence of Organized Labor on the Making of the Arizona Constitution." Master's thesis, University of Arizona, 1930.

McGregor, Gregor I. *Environmental Law and Enforcement*. Boston: CRC Press, 1994.

McLaren, Robert. "Environmental Protection Based on State Constitutional Law: A Call for Reinterpretation." *University of Hawaii Law Review* 12, no. 1 (1990): 123–52.

McMahon, Kevin J. *Reconsidering Roosevelt on Race: How the Presidency Paved the Road to Brown*. Chicago: University of Chicago Press, 2004.

Melnick, R. Shep. *Between the Lines: Interpreting Welfare Rights*. Washington, DC: Brookings Institution, 1994.

Meyers, Marvin. *The Jacksonian Persuasion Politics and Belief*. Stanford: Stanford University Press, 1957.

Michelman, Frank I. "The Supreme Court, 1968 Term." *Harvard Law Review* 83, no. 1 (1969): 7–282.

————. "Socioeconomic Rights in Constitutional Law: Explaining America Away." *International Journal of Constitutional Law* 6, no. 3–4 (2008): 663–86.

Mills, Jon, and Timothy McLendon. "Strengthening the Duty to Provide Public Education." *Florida Bar Journal* 72, no. 9 (1998): 28–39.

Mink, Gwendolyn. *The Wages of Motherhood: Inequality in the Welfare State, 1917–1942.* Ithaca, NY: Cornell University Press, 1995.

Montana Constitutional Convention of 1971–2. Helena: Montana Legislature in cooperation with the Montana Legislative Council and the Constitutional Convention Editing and Publishing Committee, 1982.

Moravcsik, Andrew. "The Paradox of U.S. Human Rights Policy." In *American Exceptionalism and Human Rights*, edited by Michael Ignatieff. Princeton, NJ: Princeton University Press, 2005.

Nebraska Constitutional Convention. *Journal of the Nebraska Constitutional Convention: Convened in Lincoln, December 2, 1919.* 2 vols. Lincoln: The Kline Publishing Co., 1921.

Nejaime, Douglas. "Winning through Losing." *Iowa Law Review* (2011): 941–1011.

Neuborne, Burt. "State Constitutions and the Evolution of Positive Rights." *Rutgers Law Journal* 20, no. 4 (1989): 881–902.

New York Constitutional Convention. *Journal of the Constitutional Convention of the State of New York, 1915, Begun and Held at the Capitol in the City of Albany on Tuesday the Sixth Day of April.* Albany: J. B. Lyon Co., 1915.

New York State Constitutional Convention. *Constitutional Convention Proceedings.* Albany 1967.

New York State Federation of Labor. "Document No. 17: Memorial of the New York State Federation of Labor." In *Documents of the Constitutional Convention of the State of New York 1915.* Albany: J. B. Lyon Company, 1915.

New York State Office of Legislative Research. *Constitutional Protection of the Forest Preserve.* Albany, 1967.

North, Douglass C., and Barry R. Weingast. "Constitutions and Commitment: The Evolution of Institutional Governing Public Choice in Seventeenth-Century England." *Journal of Economic History* 49, no. 4 (1989): 803–32.

Novak, William J. *The People's Welfare: Law and Regulation in Nineteenth-Century America,* Studies in Legal History. Chapel Hill: University of North Carolina Press, 1996.

O'Brien, Molly, and Amanda Woodrum. "The Constitutional Common School." *Cleveland State Law Review* 51, no. 3 & 4 (2004): 581–642.

O'Brien, Ruth. *Workers' Paradox: The Republican Origins of New Deal Labor Policy, 1886–1935.* Chapel Hill: University of North Carolina Press, 1998.

Ohio Constitutional Convention. *Report of the Debates and Proceedings of the Convention for the Revision of the Constitution of the State of Ohio.* Columbus: S. Medary, Printer to the Convention, 1851.

Oklahoma Constitutional Convention. *Proceedings of the Constitutional Convention of the Proposed State of Oklahoma: Held at Guthrie, Oklahoma, November 20, 1906 to November 16, 1907.* Muskogee: Muskogee Printing Co., 1907.

Orren, Karen. *Belated Feudalism: Labor, the Law, and Liberal Development in the United States.* Cambridge: Cambridge University Press, 1991.

Paris, Michael. *Framing Equal Opportunity: Law and the Politics of School Finance Reform.* Stanford, CA: Stanford Law Books, 2010.

Park, Joseph. "The History of Mexican Labor in Arizona During the Territorial Period." PhD Diss., University of Arizona, 1961.

Parkinson, Thomas I. "The Future of the Workmen's Compensation Amendment." *Proceedings of the Academy of Political Science in the City of New York 5*, no. 2 (1915): 98–117.

Pennsylvania Constitutional Convention. *Debates of the Convention to Amend the Constitution of Pennsylvania: Convened at Harrisburg, November 12, 1872, Adjourned, November 27, to Meet at Philadelphia, January 7, 1873*. Harrisburg: B. Singerly, 1873.

Pfaelzer, Jean. *Driven Out: The Forgotten War against Chinese Americans*. 1st ed. New York: Random House, 2007.

Phillips, Michael J. *The Lochner Court, Myth and Reality: Substantive Due Process from the 1890s to the 1930s*. Westport, CT: Praeger, 2001.

Pinguelo, Fernando. "Laboratory of Ideas: One State's Successful Attempt to Constitutionally Ensure a Healthier Environment." *Buffalo Environmental Law Journal* 4, no. 2 (1997): 269–90.

Platt, Rutherford H. "Toward Constitutional Recognition of the Environment." *American Bar Association Journal 56*, no. 11 (November 1970): 1061–4.

Pope, James Gray. "Labor's Constitution of Freedom." *Yale Law Journal* 106, no. 4 (1997): 941–1031.

Primus, Richard A. *The American Language of Rights, Ideas in Context*. Cambridge: Cambridge University Press, 1999.

Raz, Joseph. "Intension in Interpretation." In *The Autonomy of Law: Essays on Legal Positivism*, edited by Robert P. George, viii. Oxford: Oxford University Press, 1996.

Read, Daniel. *Address on the Means of Promoting Common School Education: Delivered in the Hall of the House of Representatives, at Indianapolis, on the Evening of Dec. 30, 1851*. Indianapolis: The House of Representatives. J. P. Chapman, State Printer, 1852.

Rebuffoni, Dean. "Voters Back Environmental Amendment by Huge Margin." *Star-Tribune Newspaper of the Twin Cities Mpls.—St. Paul*, November 8, 1990, 11A.

Reed, Douglas S. "Popular Constitutionalism: Toward a Theory of State Constitutional Meanings." *Rutgers Law Review* 30, no. 4 (1999): 871–932.

———. *On Equal Terms: The Constitutional Politics of Educational Opportunity*. Princeton, NJ: Princeton University Press, 2001.

Reisner, Edward. *The Evolution of the Common School*. New York: The MacMillan Company, 1930.

Ritter, Gretchen. *Goldbugs and Greenbacks: The Antimonopoly Tradition and the Politics of Finance, 1865–1896*. New York: Cambridge University Press, 1997.

Roberts, E. E. "The Right to a Decent Environment: Progress Along a Constitutional Avenue." In *Law and the Environment*, edited by Malcolm F. Baldwin and James K. Page, xviii. New York: Walker, 1970.

Rodgers, Daniel T. "American Exceptionalism Revisited." *Raritan* 24, no. 2 (2004): 21–47.

Ross, William G. *A Muted Fury: Populists, Progressives, and Labor Unions Confront the Courts, 1890–1937*. Princeton, NJ: Princeton University Press, 1994.

Rubenfeld, Jed. "Moment and the Millennium." *George Washington Law Review* 66, no. 5/6 (1998): 1085–1111.

Sax, Joseph L. *Defending the Environment; a Strategy for Citizen Action*. New York: Knopf, 1971.

Sax, Joseph L., and Joseph F. DiMento. "Environmental Citizen Suits: Three Years' Experience under the Michigan Environmental Protection Act." *Ecology Law Quarterly* 4, no. 1 (1974): 1–61.

Schapiro, Robert A. "Identity and Interpretation in State Constitutional Law." *Virginia Law Review* 84, no. 3 (1998): 389–457.

Schattschneider, E. E. *The Semisovereign People: A Realist's View of Democracy in America*. Hinsdale, IL: Dryden Press, 1975.

Schauer, Frederick. "The Exceptional First Amendment." In *American Exceptionalism and Human Rights*, edited by Michael Ignatieff. Princeton, NJ: Princeton University Press, 2005.

Scheingold, Stuart A. *The Politics of Rights: Lawyers, Public Policy, and Political Change*. New Haven: Yale University Press, 1974.

Scheppele, Kim Lane. "Aspirational and Aversive Constitutionalism: The Case for Studying Cross-Constitutional Influences through the Negative Model." *International Journal of Constitutional Law* 1, no. 2 (2003): 296–324.

Shannon, William Hunter. "Public Education in Maryland (1825–1968): With Special Emphasis Upon the 1860's." Ed.D. thesis, University of Maryland, 1964.

Sheridan, Thomas E. *Arizona: A History*. Tucson: University of Arizona Press, 1995.

Shon, James T. "Article X: Conservation and Development of Resources." In *Hawaii Constitutional Convention Studies*, edited by Legislative Reference Bureau. Honolulu, Hawaii, 1978.

Shue, Henry. *Basic Rights: Subsistence, Affluence, and U.S. Foreign Policy*. Princeton, NJ: Princeton University Press, 1980.

Shugerman, Jed Handelsman. *The People's Courts: Pursuing Judicial Independence in America*. Cambridge, MA: Harvard University Press, 2012.

Simpson, Charles R. "The Wilderness in American Capitalism: The Sacralization of Nature." *International Journal of Politics, Culture, and Society* 5, no. 4 (1992): 555–76.

Sklansky, David A. "Quasi-Affirmative Rights in Constitutional Criminal Procedure." *Virginia Law Review* 88, no. 6 (2002): 1229–1300.

Sklar, Kathryn Kish. *Florence Kelley and the Nation's Work: The Rise of Women's Political Culture, 1830–1900*. New Haven: Yale University Press, 1995.

Skocpol, Theda. *Protecting Soldiers and Mothers: The Political Origins of Social Policy in the United States*. Cambridge, MA: Belknap Press of Harvard University Press, 1992.

Smith, Rogers M. *Civic Ideals: Conflicting Visions of Citizenship in U.S. History*, The Yale ISPS Series. New Haven: Yale University Press, 1997.

State of Michigan Constitutional Convention. *Official Record: Proceedings*. Lansing, 1961.

Sunstein, Cass R. *The Second Bill of Rights: FDR's Unfinished Revolution and Why We Need It More Than Ever*. New York: Basic Books, 2004.

———. "Why Does the American Constitution Lack Social and Economic Guarantees?" *Syracuse Law Review* 56, no. 1 (2005): 1–26.

Swift, Fletcher Harper. *Federal and State Policies in Public School Finance in the United States*. Boston: Ginn and Company, 1931.

Tarr, G. Alan. *Understanding State Constitutions*. Princeton, NJ: Princeton University Press, 1998.

Terrie, Philip. "The Adirondack Forest Preserve: The Irony of Forever Wild." *New York History* 62, no. 3 (1981): 261–88.

———. "Forever Wild Forever: The Forest Preserve Debate at the New York State Constitutional Convention of 1915." *New York History* 70, no. 3 (1989): 251–74.

———. *Contested Terrain: A New History of Nature and People in the Adirondacks.* Syracuse: Syracuse University Press, 1997.

Texas Constitutional Convention of 1875. *Debates in the Texas Constitution of 1875.* Edited by Seth Shepard McKay. Austin: University of Texas, 1930.

Thompson, Barton H. "Constitutionalizing the Environment: The History and Future of Montana's Environmental Provisions." *Montana Law Review* 64, no. 1 (2003): 157–98.

Thorpe, Francis Newton. *The Federal and State Constitutions: Colonial Charters, and Other Organic Laws of the States, Territories, and Colonies Now or Heretofore Forming the United States of America.* 7 vols. Washington, DC: Government Printing Office, 1909.

Tobin, Richard J. "Some Observations on the Use of State Constitutions to Protect the Environment." *Environmental Affairs* 3, no. 3 (1974): 473–93.

Tucker, John. "Constitutional Codification of an Environmental Ethic." *Florida Law Review* 52 (2000): 299–327.

Tucker, William. "Environmentalism and the Leisure Class." *Harper's* December (1977): 49–62.

Tyack, David B., Thomas James, and Aaron Benavot. *Law and the Shaping of Public Education, 1785–1954.* Madison: University of Wisconsin Press, 1987.

Tyack, David B., and Robert Lowe. "The Constitutional Moment: Reconstruction and Black Education in the South." *American Journal of Education* 94, no. 2 (1986): 236–56.

Urofsky, Melvin. "State Courts and Protective Legislation During the Progressive Era: A Reevaluation." *Journal of American History* 72, no. 1 (1985): 63–91.

Waldron, Jeremy. *Law and Disagreement.* Oxford: Oxford University Press, 2001.

Wallis, John Joseph. "National Bureau of Economic Research / University of Maryland State Constitution Project." http://www.stateconstitutions.umd.edu.

Warren, Charles. "The Progressivenes of the United States Supreme Court." *Columbia Law Review* 13, no. 4 (1913): 294–313.

Weinrib, Laura. "From Public Interest to Private Rights: Free Speech, Liberal Individualism, and the Making of Modern Tort Law." *Law and Social Inquiry—Journal of the American Bar Foundation* 34, no. 1 (2009): 187–223.

Wellman, Carl. *Real Rights.* Oxford: Oxford University Press, 1995.

Whittington, Keith E. *Constitutional Construction: Divided Powers and Constitutional Meaning.* Cambridge: Harvard University Press, 1999.

———. *Constitutional Interpretation: Textual Meaning, Original Intent, and Judicial Review.* Lawrence: University Press of Kansas, 1999.

———. "Congress before the Lochner Court." *Boston University Law Review* 85, no. 3 (2005): 821–58.

———. *Political Foundations of Judicial Supremacy: The Presidency, the Supreme Court, and Constitutional Leadership in U.S. History,* Princeton Studies in American Politics. Princeton, NJ: Princeton University Press, 2007.

Wilcox, Delos F. *Government by All the People; or, the Initiative, the Referendum, and the Recall as Instruments of Democracy*. New York: The Macmillan Company, 1912.

Wilentz, Sean. *Chants Democratic: New York City & the Rise of the American Working Class, 1788–1850*. New York: Oxford University Press, 1984.

Williams, Robert F. *The Law of American State Constitutions*. Oxford; New York: Oxford University Press, 2009.

Winder, John S., Jr. "Citizen Groups, the Law and the Environment." *Utah Law Review* 1970, no. 3 (1970): 404–13.

———. "Environmental Rights for the Environmental Polity." *Suffolk University Law Review* 5, no. 3 (1971): 820–49.

Wood, Gordon. *The Creation of the American Republic, 1776–1787*. New York: Norton, 1969.

Yanaconne, Victor John, Jr. "The Environment and the Law." *Forum* 9, no. 5 (1974): 795–828.

Yoon, Lois. "Article VIII: Public Health and Welfare." In *Hawaii Constitutional Convention Studies*, edited by Legislative Reference Bureau. Honolulu, 1978.

Zackin, Emily. "Popular Constitutionalism's Hard When You're Not Very Popular: Why the ACLU Turned to Courts." *Law & Society Review* 42, no. 2 (2008): 367–95.

INDEX

❖

Note: Page numbers in *italics* indicate figures; those with a *t* indicate tables.